THE CHURCH IN THE 21ST CENTURY

Facing Today's Social Issues

INFORMATION MANUAL
FOR MINISTERS AND CHURCH WORKERS

PASTOR JOE HAYES

Foreword by Paul Weaver

SERENDIPITY

Copyright © Joe Hayes, 2002

First published in 2002 by
Serendipity
Suite 530
37 Store Street
Bloomsbury
London

All rights reserved.
Unauthorised duplication
contravenes existing laws

British Library Cataloguing-in-Publication data
A catalogue record for this book is available from the British Library

ISBN 1-84394-024-8

Printed and bound by Alden Digital, Oxford

*To my wife Lizzie for encouraging me to be
what God wants me to be*

*Also to the members of
Emmanuel Community Church, Barrow-in-Furness,
for allowing me to be all that God wants me to be*

Grateful thanks are given to Christine Walsh for her hours of support in proof reading.

Thanks also to the "Property Trust" for sponsoring this book as part of their social concern policy.

Property Trust
14 Bridgford Road
West Bridgford
Nottingham
NG2 5AF
Telephone: 0115 982 1199

For the latest information visit:
www.c21c.org

CONTENTS

Foreword ix
Introduction 1
The Family 5
The Family and Domestic Violence 9
The Family and Divorce 16
The Family and Child Abuse 24
Single Parent Families 34
Step-Parenting 41
Bullying 44
Teenage Pregnancy 51
Cohabitation 56
Euthanasia 61
Abortion 65
Debt 69
Poverty 72
Homelessness 76
Mental Illness 81
Eating Disorders 88
Alternative Sexuality 93
Work and Unemployment 98
Ageism 102
Racism 108
Sexism 116
Disabled Rights 122

ANIMAL RIGHTS	128
ENVIRONMENTALISM	132
DRUG ABUSE	135
ALCOHOL ABUSE	142
HIV & AIDS	151
BEREAVEMENT	158
SEXUAL EXPLOITATION	163
ADVICE ON LOBBYING	168
A RECOMMENDED QUALITY ASSURANCE POLICY	170
CLONING	178
ALTERNATIVE MEDICINE	193
GENETIC MODIFICATION	206
REFUGEES AND ASYLUM SEEKERS	211
SUICIDE	219
CRIMINALITY	233
SHORT INTRODUCTION TO FUNDRAISING	239
APPENDIX A	242
APPENDIX B	245
APPENDIX C	246
EXAMPLE OF A FAMILY CENTRE	248

FOREWORD

The twenty-first century presents the church with many challenges, none less than the challenge of twenty-first-century leadership. This leadership has to be able to distinguish not only the difference between twentieth-century issues and twenty-first-century issues within the church, but also how to help the church to become effective in the maze of social need and opportunity.

When I began my church leadership ministry back in the early sixties we did not face the problems that society is throwing up today. Most people becoming Christians brought very little baggage with them. Today the majority of new converts bring to the church a range of serious hang-ups, habits, and hurts with them. These areas require both the power of the Holy Spirit to set them free and an equipped and understanding church to provide a loving environment where they can grow and mature in safety. There are many support agencies that can sharpen the effectiveness of the local church in specialized areas such as physical, emotional and sexual abuse together with all aspects of addiction.

Joe Hayes is an Assemblies of God minister who has given himself to address through training and practice such issues. Joe has advised and represented the Fellowship of Assemblies of God on social issues. He has also lectured at conferences on many issues of concern within our society today. I am sure that this book will contribute to the massive learning curve that many leaders in the church today are having to scale, in order to lead their members to a new and relevant church for the twenty-first century. Hurt people need healing, healed people become the helpers of others.

PAUL WEAVER
(NATIONAL SUPERINTENDENT OF ASSEMBLIES OF GOD
CHURCHES IN THE UK & IRELAND)

x | THE CHURCH IN THE 21ST CENTURY

INTRODUCTION

Ministering in the Postmodern World

The commission to communicate the Gospel of Jesus Christ to every man, woman and child is an ever-increasing challenge. The population of the United Kingdom continues to increase; by 2026 it is estimated that there will be 64.3 million people alive in the UK.

	1991	1999	2021	2026
England	42,208	49,793	53,715	54,443
Wales	2,891	2,937	3,047	3,062
Scotland	5,107	5,119	5,058	5,016
N. Ireland	1,607	1,692	1,821	1,835
UK	57,814	59,501	63,642	64,355

Social Trends 31 © crown copyright 2001

The aim of this manual is fourfold:

1. To Provoke an increased awareness of contemporary social issues affecting the members of communities the Church has been commissioned to reach with the love of the Gospel of Jesus. The awareness section of each topic is in no way meant to be exhaustive, they are there to provide a basic understanding.

2. To Provide related and up-to-date statistical information at the time of going to print. Official statistics are updated every five and ten years.

3. To Provide Churches with a quick and easy method of finding organizations, individuals or churches ministering in the related topic.

4. To suggest Practical methods that will be principled and pastoral in their approach to ministering in a particular area.

Preamble

In 1 Chor. 12: 32, we read of some key people who were involved in making David King over Israel. The "Sons of Issachar" were renowned as men of understanding. The Sons of Issachar were people who understood their times and the people of their generation, they understood the values of their people, the expectations of their people, the needs of their people, what was influencing their people. Because the Sons of Issachar had this understanding they knew what the people should do, therefore, they were able to give advice and direction.

Church leaders of the twenty-first century can understand what is influencing the people of their community. Church leaders today can seek to comprehend the values, hopes and needs of those whom they seek to minister unto.

With an increased awareness churches will, I believe, be able to minister more effectively, taking action that will affect their neighbourhoods with the love of the Gospel.

The Apostle Paul faced the challenge of the Gnostics, Luther faced the challenge of Romanism, the church of the eighteenth century was mocked by modernism, and now the church of the twenty-first century faces the challenge of post-modernism. The Church's reaction to the postmodern world can be threefold:

Retreat: **by burying their heads in self-grafting doctrines.**

Reconcile: **by accommodating the new liberal spiritual values of the 21st century.**

Resist: **by actively applying biblical values and principles to the many contemporary social issues that are influenced by the spirit of post-modernism.**

J.D. Hunter in *Faith and Modernity* (published by © Regum) makes the following comments:

> ...the culture of modernity. It's structures of reality present themselves with such massive force that people who should know better, say evangelical historians and theologians often scratch their heads and wonder what all of this talk about modernity is anyway. But rather than pursue it, all too many lapse back into dissecting and fighting the doctrinal battles of the sixteenth and seventeenth centuries. The abiding assumption for them, as it is for many people of faith, is that culture is 'morally neutral.' If we can only get our doctrine straight and pray more, all will be well. That feeling of unease will disappear; all will be right again. Such an assumption is, to say the least, misplaced. The reason is that the challenge the Church now faces is nothing like it has ever before faced.
>
> The task of coming to terms with the context in which the Church finds itself is not a task for independent intellectuals but one for the Church itself. At stake is its faithfulness to its creeds and traditions; at stake is its integrity as the spiritual body of Christ on earth. It is a huge and on-going undertaking. Questions concerning what is going on and what should be done need to be asked again and again at every level of church life.

The two heroes of modernism, 'reason and science' were hailed as the saviours of the human race since the days of the enlightenment. Both reason and science have failed to bring an end to suffering and man's inhumanity to man.

Wars continue, cancer and Aids remain incurable, the Great Society promised by socialism failed in communism, science has polluted the environment and thus we now find ourselves in the postmodern area that laughs at modernism's promises and offering something to please everyone.

Perhaps the greatest threat to the church of the twenty-first century, postmodernism is some thing that is hard to pin down but yet so many people are able to embrace its value base. Postmodernism can be describe firstly as a 'Mood' that distrusts reason and disdains the absolutes of the Biblical message, and secondly as a 'Methodology' that provides theories and ideas to undermine any form of absolutes. Thirdly postmodernism is a 'Movement' although in many ways formless, academics and ethicists within institutions seek to advocate diversity and undermine absolutes. Finally postmodernism can be described as a 'Metamorphosis' in that it is bringing about one of the fastest and most far-reaching social and cultural changes that history has ever experienced.*

Post-modernism has made truth relative, in that 'one idea is as good as another.' The basis for determining reliability of a truth is no longer Scripture or even reason as modernism claimed but 'What feels good to you.'

Biblical revelation and reason are thus replaced by the 'personal-pleasure-principle.' Instead of people saying they agree or disagree with a proposition, we hear how much they 'like' or 'dislike' a particular idea.

People of the postmodern world pick and choose what they enjoy from a wide range of theories and religions, reliant solely on their individual preferences and choices.

Moral principles are replaced by personalised 'moral mottoes': 'You have to decide what's right for you'; 'What's right for one person might not be right for someone else'; 'Who are we to judge?'; 'Just be yourself.' What makes an action moral or immoral is whether or not the person made a choice and whether it was good for them or not.

People shy away from admitting to being 'for' abortion or euthanasia, instead they are 'pro-choice.' The only relevant question is whether or not the woman had a choice in the abortion or whether a person can choose when to die.

The pro-choice lobby seems to be at the bottom of many social controversies. Claiming that people should be allowed to 'please themselves' and 'tolerate everyone else.'

People are clamouring for 'the right to die,' justifying suicide and even euthanasia insofar as the person 'chooses' to die.

Sexual perversions become totally acceptable and even chic when they are thought of as 'lifestyle choices.'

Demands for illegal drugs to be made legal because of personal choice.

Family values and structure is a matter of personal preference and what a person does behind his front door is their business.

The popularity of the post modern, pro-choice stance is a 'moral anarchy' in that the moral absolutes of scripture are being forced to the side-lines of society as out dated and bigoted. The spin-off from postmodernisms moral anarchy is: families without values continue to break down, additions lead to debt, poverty

---

* See Appendix C, for a breakdown of the shift in popular belief from modernism to postmodernism and a biblical response.

and homelessness, toleration of sexual diversity opens the door to even greater sexual perversions and society increasingly becomes a supermarket of faiths and theories to whom we should express tolerance.

Yours In His Service
JOE HAYES BSc (HONS)

THE FAMILY

AWARENESS

The following information is included to raise the social awareness and understanding of ministers in relation to the contemporary issues facing the family.

- The picture of the modern family as we embark on the on the 21st century is that it comes in a variety of forms. The modern media image of the happy nuclear family is far from what many people experience of family life. In many congregations there are lone teenage parents, divorced and separated parents. In the last three decades lone parents have more than doubled in the UK to over 1.3 million.

- Ideologies and discourses that challenge the family aim their attack upon the concept of the nuclear family. The challenge upon the family concludes that the nuclear family is not a fact of nature but a particular cultural formation and construction for reproduction.

- This argument of course opens the door of acceptability to alternative living arrangements, such as co-habitation and same-sex relationships. Both of which Scripture does not condone.

- Some families that come into churches are termed by sociologists and politicians as being 'dysfunctional' because the parents lack motivation to improve on their situation, they rely heavily on the welfare state and their children lack parental discipline. The term 'Dysfunctional Family' is often used in political rhetoric when politicians are seeking to blame the Family as the cause of social problems. The Government's response to what they term 'Problem Families' rather than families with problems, has been to seek to mentor them in good parenting and relationship skills. This of course provides the Church in the 21st century with wonderful opportunities to teach biblical values relating to the family and relationships.

- The biblical family was a person's source of nurture, and support. The basic composition of the family changes from the Old Testament to the New Testament. Therefore, the search for the traditional biblical family is difficult. What perhaps is of crucial importance for the 21st century church in a different culture and generation is to understand the essential family structures, relationships, commitments, and functions or roles of the biblical family.

Assessment

The following are some of the most up-to-date statistics in relation to the family.*

	1961	1971	1981	1991	2000
ONE FAMILY HOUSEHOLDS					
Living alone	4	6	8	11	12
Couple with no children	18	19	20	23	25
Dependent children	52	52	47	41	39
Non-dependent children	12	10	10	11	9
Lone parent	3		6	10	11
Other households	12	9	9	4	6
People in private households (% in millions)	—	53.4	53	55.4	57
People not in private households (% in millions)	—	0.9	0.8	0.8	—
Total population (% in millions)	51.4	54.4	54.8	56.2	—

SOCIAL TRENDS 31 © CROWN COPYRIGHT 2001

The above table reveals that at the turn of the new century in Great Britain, about three-quarters of people living in private households were in a couple family household. More people lived in the so-called traditional family household than in any other type of family, while just over one in ten people lived alone and a similar proportion lived in a lone parent household.

Shift in Family Lifestyles

The General Household Survey, completed by the Office of National Statistics in 1995 found that there has been a fundamental shift in family lifestyles. The results were obtained from interviews with people aged 16 or over in a random sample of private households involving about 18,000 adults from around 10,000 homes. Owen Rowlands, who presented the results said:

> These facts are of current interest because of rising concerns over changing family patterns and whether or not cohabitation provided a stable basis for having children.

- **The proportion of couples cohabiting has continued to rise and reached a peak of one in four of all lone females aged between 18 to 49 in 1995. Between 1979 and 1991, the proportion of single, widowed, divorced and separated women in that aged group who were cohabiting doubled from 11% to 23%.**

* Please see appendix A

- The survey found that women in their late 20s and men in their late 20s and early 30s were most likely to be cohabiting.
- The mean household size has continued to decline and now stands at 2.4 persons, compared with the former 2.91. The most common type of household is one with a married couples with no dependent children.
- Fewer married or cohabiting couples are having children, with the figures dropping from around 30% in the early 1980s to 24% in 1995.
- In the last decade alone the number of full-time working mothers has trebled and the number working part-time has doubled. Last year, two-thirds of women were either working or unemployed and looking for work and those in part-time work amounted to nearly 50%.
- The proportion of lone parents bringing up children has increased by 8% to 22% between 1971 and 1995 – a three-fold increase.

© THE INDEPENDENT 29.11.1996

Addressing

The following is a list of practical suggestions that may enable churches and organizations to take action that will alleviate the problems facing families in their locality.

- The issue facing the church of the 21st century is not making known the moral decline of the Western World, nor is it how can we reach these families but how do we treat and teach these families as they will undoubtedly come through church doors.
- The family that is termed dysfunctional does not need strong heavy-handed discipline to teach their children how to behave when at church but gentle and loving guidance on parental authority that begins in their home.
- Teach on family roles, such as 'Being a good Mother,' 'Being a good Father,' 'Being a good Wife,' 'Being a good Husband' and 'Being good Children/Teenagers.'
- Run parenting classes for the Church and the community.
- Open the church building up to Government funded groups that support the Family.
- Encourage the mature and experienced to mentor the younger and un-experienced in being a parent or wife/husband.
- Discourage moral condescension towards single parent families. Reminding teenage parents of their moral mistake will only make them miserable, teaching them that God promises to be a Father to the fatherless will increase their dependence upon God.
- Taking the example of our Saviour the church can reach out to those of our

generation that are stigmatised as social problems, they are not a problem to God and He can touch and transform their lives. Action is always going to speak louder than words to many of these families and so the practical friendship and support of the people within our congregations will win them over to the Lord.

Affirmation

The following is a list of churches, organizations or individuals who are taking action to alleviate the problems facing the family. They will, we believe, be able to offer practical and professional advice to assist you in your efforts, to take action to support local families.*

FAMILIES FIRST
173 FRINTON ROAD
KIRKBY CROSS
FRINTON-ON-SEA
CO13 0PD
TEL: 01255 671616
FAX: 01255 671616

CHURCHES TOGETHER FOR FAMILIES
27 TAVISTOCK SQUARE
LONDON
WC1H 9HH
TEL: 0207 387 8413

Books that deal with the issue of the family:

0785274499, *Shaping of a Christian Family*, E. Elloit, Thomas Nelson
0854766413, *Spirit Filled Family*, T Lahaye, Kingsway £5.99
087123114X, *The Christian Family*, Christenson, BHP
0801021855, *Family*, Balswick, BAKER
028104824X, *Celebrating Families*, Osborn, SPCK
188127392X, *Five Signs of a Loving Family*, Chapman, NORTH
0340665149, *I Believe in the Family*, Collins, H&S
— *What is a Family*, Edith Schaeffer
Atkinson, David, *To Have and to Hold* (London, Collins, 1979)
Dominion, Jack, *Marriage: The Definitive Guide to What Makes a Marriage Work* (London, Heinemann, 1995)
Friday, Nancy, *My Mother My Self* (London, Fontana, 1977)
Fukuyama, F., *The Great Disruption: Human Nature and the Reconstitution of Social Order* (London, Profile Books,1999)
Hite, Shere, *The Hite Report on the Family: Growing Up Under Patriarchy* (London, Bloomsbury 1995)
Oakley, Ann, *From Here to Maternity* (Harmondsworth, Penguin, 1981)
Storkey, Alan, *Marriage and its Modern Crisis: Repairing Married Life* (London, Hodder & Stoughton, 1996)
Torrance, D.W., *God, Family and Sexuality* (Carberry, The Handsel Press, 1997)

* Please see appendix B

THE FAMILY AND DOMESTIC VIOLENCE

AWARENESS

The following information is included to raise the social awareness and understanding of ministers in relation to the contemporary issue of domestic violence.

- ❖ Domestic violence is a crime that largely goes unreported. Many victims of domestic violence find themselves trapped in an emotional prison. Self blame, financial dependence, responsibility for children and fear of reprisals keep countless sufferers of domestic violence bound within a marital hell.

- ❖ Domestic violence ranges from being kicked, pushed through windows, thrown downstairs, punched, thrown against walls, choked, hit with bottles and stabbed with knives. The most common forms of domestic violence involve punches to the face and the body often leading to bruising, bleeding and fractured or broken bones.

- ❖ The majority of reported domestic violence takes place within the poorer sections of society, however, this in no way suggests that domestic violence does not take place within wider society.

- ❖ Some families that come into churches are termed by sociologists and politicians as being 'dysfunctional' because the parents lack motivation to improve on their situation, they rely heavily on the welfare state and their children lack parental discipline.

- ❖ Debate as to the cause of domestic violence revolves around the following four major areas:

  ✳ Pathological: this argument is based upon an evolutionary model which suggests that men are basically brute beasts and aggression is an instinct built into their nature. One side of the argument even goes as far as to suggest that women are the cause of domestic violence because their basic instinct is masochistic, therefore, women are 'asking for it.'

  ✳ Psychological: this argument suggests that men who are violent towards their wives are basically getting their own back on their mothers who dominated them in childhood; 'the uncontrollable anger of a violent man emanates from unresolved conflicts with his parents resolving in a displacement of anger and aggression onto the most convenient targets in his life – his wife and girl friends... Such men are described as frightened victimized bullies who experience mood swings, pain and anger...unmet needs are created in childhood and express themselves as violence in later life'.

- **Private Problems:** this argument claims domestic violence is a result of the dysfunctional family. A volatile relationship is because the couple are basically incompatible; poor socialisation and bad communication skills means the couple simply rub each other up the wrong way, therefore, violence is inevitable.

- **Patriarchal:** this is a feminist argument that suggests the reason for domestic violence is not the result of one man's aggression towards another individual woman but is a manifestation of a historically and culturally male-dominated society.

◆ **A Biblical Response:** Violence of any form is a sin and its root is evil.

- **Psalm 140: 1–4.** Rescue me, O Lord, from evil men; protect me from men of violence, who devise evil plans in their hearts and stir up war every day. They make their tongues as sharp as a serpent's; the poison of vipers is on their lips. Selah

- Keep me, O Lord, from the hands of the wicked; protect me from men of violence who plan to trip my feet.

A typical victim's story

At first I used to think he was crazy – hitting me like that for no good reason but in the end I thought it was me – that I must be no good to anybody or anything. You know what I mean – no confidence in myself. And I just let myself go...and if I did get dressed up he would say – You don't look any different, you're nothing but a great big fat ugly cow – and nobody would want you except me. I got that for three and a half years solid. So I believed it in the end. Sometimes I used to think I was going round the bend – he used to go fishing all night sometimes and then sleep all day. And we had this great big carving knife downstairs and I used to go upstairs and stand with it and think 'If I stick it in him – will I get done for murder?' And sometimes after he threw me out I used to get three or four bottles of aspirins and go in a cafe and think 'Get myself a couple of cups of tea – take all these and the problem's solved – all this will be finished with'. But there was always Paul to consider I used to think if I leave him with him what's he going to grow up like – twisted – like his dad.

(© CRAWC, 1984, P.4)

ASSESSMENT

The following are some of the most up-to-date statistics in relation to the family and domestic violence. (Please see appendix A.)

Incidence of domestic assaults, by gender

England and Wales in Lifetime	Males	Females	All
No domestic assault	85%	77%	81%
Chronic levels of assault	5%	12%	9%
Intermittent levels of assault	10%	11%	10%
All	100%	100%	100%

In Lifetime	Males	Females	All
No domestic assault	96%	96%	96%
Chronic levels of assault	2%	2%	2%
Intermittent levels of assault	3%	3%	2%
All	100%	100%	100%

THE SURVEY WAS CARRIED OUT IN 1996, RESPONDENTS WERE AGED 16–59, VICTIMS OF CHRONIC ASSAULT WERE THOSE WHO REPORTED THREE OR MORE ASSAULTS. VICTIMS OF INTERMITTENT ASSAULT REPORTED ONE OR TWO INCIDENCES OF ASSAULT.

SOCIAL TRENDS 30, © CROWN COPYRIGHT 2000

The above table reveals that twenty-three per cent of women and fifteen per cent of men aged 16 to 59 in England and Wales said that a current or former partner had assaulted them at some time in their lives. Around four per cent of both women and men said that they had experienced domestic assault in the previous year. Women were twice as likely as men to say they had been injured by such an assault and were more likely to have experienced repeated assaults during the year. There were an estimated 6.6 million incidents of domestic assault in 1995 (that is, reported to the police). Although, on average, women were more likely to have experienced repeated assault, the total number of assaults in the year was evenly split between women and men as there are more men than women aged 16 to 69 in the population. Among women, it was the 20- to 24-year-olds who were the most likely to say they had experienced domestic assault while for men it was those aged 30 to 34.

UK Statistics on Domestic Violence

© TARA GODSON AT THE BODY SHOP UK

✝ 1 in 4 women may experience violence in their relationships with men (Women's Aid Federation [England] report, 1992)

✝ Severe, repeated and systematic violence occurs in at least five of every hundred marriages in Britain

✝ Between 40 and 45% of murdered women are killed by their male partners

✝ Between 1 and 2 women are murdered by their male partners every week; more than 25% of all violent crime reported to the police is domestic violence of men against women, making it the second most common violent crime (Domestic Violence – *Action for Change*, G. Hague & E. Malos, 1993)

- ✠ 100,000 women per year seek treatment in London for violent injuries received in the home (*Punching Judy*, BBC 1 TV program, 1989)
- ✠ 30,000 women and children stay in refuges in the UK every year
- ✠ In Wolverhampton, UK, 1 in 6 women had suffered some form of domestic abuse; one quarter of all assaults are in domestic circumstances (*Domestic Violence* – Report of an Inter-Agency Working Party, 1992)
- ✠ In Edinburgh, Scotland, out of 3,020 cases of violence reported to the police, three-quarters of those were wife assault; one of the main problems experienced by the refuge movement (in the UK) is both the inadequacy and uncertainty of funding (*Domestic Violence* – Home Office Research Study 107)
- ✠ Some women's refuges receive no grant aid at all; London Women's Aid could only find space in a women's refuge for 40% of the 5,000 women who came to them for help in 1990
- ✠ A refuge in the Southwest of England was only able to house 142 of the 490 women who were referred to them in desperate need of help; in a local authority with a population of over a million people, there are currently just 19 refuge spaces (*Domestic Violence – Action for Change*, G. Halos & E. Malos, 1993)

A fifth of refuges have no full time staff at all; approximately 35% of the refuge places deemed a minimum requirement (for England) in 1975 are in existence in 1994. And recent studies have calculated that the estimated required number of refuge places should be substantially increased: the demand is almost double that recommended in the mid-seventies; approximately 129 volunteer hours go into running a refuge every month (© *Funding Refuge Services*, Mog Ball, 1994)

Addressing

The following is a list of practical suggestions that may enable churches and organizations to take action that will alleviate the problem of domestic violence in their locality.

- → Domestic violence is a crime; therefore legal interventions can be called upon.
- → Many Local Councils run female refuges for women and their children. Church families could provide safe homes for victims to turn to in a crisis.
- → Provide them with a telephone number they can call in an emergency, such as yourself or trusted members of the church who could come to their aid quicker than the police. Be careful, however, not to get involved in the dispute.
- → Social workers are not responsible for dealing with issues of domestic violence; however, where children are involved their intervention can be called upon.

- → There are of course many forms of counselling available; it is recommended when possible to seek the support of Christian counsellors who will hopefully not be influenced by militant feminist groups.

- → Preachers could consistently challenge the macho male image, teaching upon the biblical principles of sacrificial love and what it means to be a good husband.

- → Listen to the victim; be prepared to believe the victim, even if their abuser is the last person in the world you think would beat their partner. Encourage the victim to take action – this may be to get out of the home for period or ask the victim to confront their abuser in your presence.

AFFIRMATION

The following is a list of churches, organisations or individuals who are taking action to alleviate the problem of domestic violence. They will, we believe, be able to offer practical and professional advice to assist you in your efforts to take action to support victims of domestic violence. (Please see appendix B.)

CHRISTIAN FAMILY CONCERN
42 SOUTH PARK HILL ROAD
CROYDEN
CR2 7YB
TEL: 0208 688 0251
FAX: 0208 686 7114
EMAIL: CHRISTFC@SURFAID.ORG

GROWING THROUGH
3 GRANGE ROAD
ERDINGTON
BIRMINGHAM
B24 0DG
TEL: 0121 681 6855
EMAIL: DALEERICKS@AOL.COM
WWW.GROWING-THROUGH.ORG

DOMESTIC VIOLENCE HELPLINE 0161 839 8574 (THIS LINE HAS A STRONG CHRISTIAN INFLUENCE)

The following information is provided by the Home Office to support victims of domestic violence.

WOMEN'S AID NATIONAL DOMESTIC VIOLENCE HELPLINE: 0345 023 468

This service can give you support, help and information. They will discuss the practical and legal options available, and if you wish refer you to a local Women's Aid refuge and advice service, or other sources of help. All calls are taken in strictest confidence. The helpline is open from 10 a.m. to 5 p.m. Monday to Thursday and from 10 a.m. to 3 p.m. on Fridays. Outside these hours you can contact your local Women's Aid service through the local phone book, or access the Women's Aid website (www.womensaid.org.uk). In Wales you can also call Welsh Women's Aid on 01222 390874.

LOCAL WOMEN'S AID REFUGE SERVICES

There are nearly 300 local refuge projects in England and Wales. Many local Women's Aid groups also run advice centers, drop-in centers or outreach services to more isolated areas, as well as local helplines. You can call in to see someone, or telephone for advice and support, without having to stay in a refuge.

REFUGE 24-HOUR NATIONAL CRISIS LINE: 0990 995 443

This service provides information, support and practical help, 24 hours a day, 7 days a week, to women experiencing domestic violence. It can refer women and their children to refuges throughout the UK.

MEN'S ADVICE LINE AND ENQUIRIES: 0181 644 9914

Information, support and advice to men experiencing domestic violence. Open from 9 a.m. to 10 p.m., Monday and Wednesday. Local projects for men are available in some areas.

VICTIM SUPPORT: 0845 3030 900

Victim Support offers information and support to victims of crime, whether or not they have reported the crime to the police. All help given is free and confidential. You can contact Victim Support direct, or ask the police to put you in touch with your local group. The national helpline is open from 9am to 9pm Monday to Friday and from 9 a.m. to 7 p.m. on Saturdays, Sundays and Bank Holidays.

SHELTERLINE: 0808 800 4444

Emergency access to refuge services.

THE POLICE

Many kinds of domestic abuse are criminal offences, and the police take all domestic violence very seriously. Most forces have specially trained, experienced officers who will listen and speak to you separately from your partner. Women can ask to be seen by a female officer. The police can, if you wish, arrange medical aid, transport and a safe place for you to go. Their first priorities are your safety and well-being and, if applicable the safety and well-being of your children. To contact the police in an emergency, dial 999. At other times, you can contact your local police station. You can find the number in your telephone directory.

THE SAMARITANS: 0345 909090

24-hour confidential emotional support for anyone in crisis. The number given above links up all their branches; or you can use the number of your local branch, which you will find in your phone book.

NATIONAL CHILD PROTECTION HELPLINE (NSPCC): 0800 800 500

This free, confidential service for anyone concerned about children at risk offers counselling, information and advice.

CARELINE: 0181 514 1177

A national confidential counselling line for children, young people and adults on any issue including family, marital and relationship problems, child abuse, rape and sexual assault, depression and anxiety.

RELATE

Relationship counselling, for non-emergency situations. There will be a local number in your phone book.

Books that deal with the issue of Domestic Violence

0853648174, *Domestic Violence and the Church*, Conway, PAT

0853648689, *Women, Abuse and the Bible*, Kroeger/Beck, PAT

0745937225, *Domestic Violence: Picking Up The Pieces*, Helen L. Conway, £7.99, Lion Publications

0859697320, *Women & Violence*, Mils & Topolski

Barron, J., *Not Worth the Paper...? The Effectiveness of Legal Protection for Women and Children Experiencing Domestic Violence* (Bristol, WAFE, 1990)

Bhavnaani, K.K., 'Is Violence Masculine?' in *Shabnam Grewal* et al (eds.)

Charting the Journey: Writings by Black and Third World Women (London, Sheba, 1990)

Hooper, Carol-Ann, *Mothers Surviving Child Sexual Abuse* (London, Routledge, 1992)

Newman, Rebecca, *Releasing the Scream* (London, Hodder & Stoughton, 1994)

Radford, J. and D. Russel (eds), *Femicide: The Politics of Woman Killing* (Buckingham, Open University Press, 1992)

THE FAMILY AND DIVORCE

AWARENESS

The following information is included to raise the social awareness and understanding of ministers in relation to the contemporary issues divorce.* A policeman recently "cautioned" a man for assaulting his wife's lover. He also gave him a copy of Rob Parson's book *Loving Against the Odds*. The man wrote later saying, "Thank you for saving my marriage. If it wasn't for your kindness I would have given up. I have forgiven my wife for her affair. I realize now why it happened."

We are living in times where church leaders continually face the pastoral problems of marital breakdown and the associated family trauma. Marriage is frequently undermined and undervalued by a society that promotes 'alternative lifestyles' as equally valid to marriage. The failure of traditional marriage has encouraged these alternative lifestyles and the cry for tolerance has often silenced the church's voice as irrelevant.

Marital breakdown is an accepted norm today. The notion of "till death us do part" is totally unrealistic in the thinking of secular Britain. Every year, in England and Wales, around 150,000 couples split up.

Marital heartache exists in probably one third of all adults and many carry feelings of failure and hurt because of marital breakdown.

Broken homes are common place in Britain, with many children growing up in unstable relationships and often without proper fathering/mentoring. A typical street could be described like this:

> Perhaps in the first house are a mother, father and their two children, a group which is often called an 'average family'. But there are all sorts of other households in the street as well, of various ages and ethnic origins: a married couple whose two children have grown up and moved away; a single mother with one child; a stepfamily with three children from previous relationships; two gay men who have lived together for many years; a cohabiting couple with two children; a couple who have not be able to have children of their own but take a keen interest in their several godchildren; a family with three children, an uncle and a widowed grandmother; some young people sharing a flat for a few years, who spend occasional weekends with their parents; a couple with two foster children; an elderly man living on his own, whose children live in other parts of the country; a woman in her forties who has never married, but who is in touch with her two sisters and their children…

* Thanks to Pastor Paul Finn for his contributions to this section.

The list could go on. Most streets in Britain today reflect at least some of this variety. Which of these households should be called families and on what grounds?

The debate as to the cause of marital breakdown continues without any definitive answer. However, major causes are:

- **Communication** – the inability to share honestly and openly, within marriage, the feelings, hopes, desires and needs of a couple.
- **Common misunderstandings** – over responsibility in marriage and differences between men and women and their roles.
- **Career plans** – and the change in the role of women. Men losing their significance in the workplace.
- **Children** – lack of parenting skills and loving, stable homes.
- **Community breakdown** – where couples no longer have the support of family and friends to help then through difficult times and the stress of human relationship.

The Biblical response is that the scriptures offer clear help and hope for successful marriage and that biblical principles, if applied, bring success. (Ephesians 5: 22–33)

A typical story:

> My husband is a real family man and totally dedicated to me and our three children. He has a lot of responsibility at our church and is so very busy there. I so much want us to do things together, but where is the time? I'd like us to go for a walk together – to have times when we hold hands and say 'I love you' – times without the kids there or even the need to make love. I love him dearly and I want no other – I know that I need to change too, but I'm so frightened that when the children have flown the nest, there will be nothing left. We so rarely go to bed at the same time – I'm half asleep when he comes up. Then, if he makes the effort to come up early, I know what he wants, rightly, and I can't. I feel used. I want him to spend time with me – not just for sex – a quick five minutes – but to walk and talk and not to watch TV. You see, I'm such a failure.

Many live with a sense of failure in a failing marriage, unaware of how they can change that which is tearing them apart.

ASSESSMENT

The following are some of the most up-to-date statistics in relation to the family and divorce. (Please see appendix A.)

Marriage facts in England and Wales

- There were 267,000 marriages in 1998, 1.9 per cent fewer than in 1997.
- Two out of five marriages were solemnised by a religious ceremony in 1998. This is a marked decline compared with 1991 where just over half of all marriages were solemnised by a religious ceremony.
- Civil marriage in approved premises (non-religious) continues to rise, with more than one in ten couples choosing to marry in them.
- 163,000 civil marriages took place in 1998, which is a drop by 1.5 per cent compared with 1997.
- Marriage rates continue to decline. In 1988 46 males per 1000 chose to marry. In 1998 29 males per 1000 chose to marry. In 1988 39 females per 1000 chose to marry, whereas in 1998 26 per 1000 chose to marry. In 1998 the mean average age at marriage was 34.1 years for men and 31.5 years for women.

SOURCE: POPULATION TRENDS 99, SPRING 2000

Divorce facts in England and Wales

- There were one per cent fewer divorces in 1998 compared with 1997.
- Nearly 145,000 decrees absolute were granted in 1998 of which 70 per cent were granted to the wife.
- In 1998 more divorces were granted on grounds of separation than adultery, whereas in 1991 there were more divorces granted on the grounds of adultery than separation.
- In 1998 165.6 thousand petitions were filed for divorce. This was one per cent more than in 1997.
- The divorce rate for men and women has fallen to 12.9 per 1000 married men and 12.8 per 1000 married women in 1998, the lowest rate since 1990.
- The mean age at divorce continues to rise; in 1998 it was 40.4 years for men and 37.9 years for women. This reflects the increase seen in recent years in the mean age at marriage.
- Over 40 per cent of men and women divorcing in 1998 were aged between 30 and 39 at divorce.
- Divorce rates are highest from men and women aged between 25 and 29 years.
- Nearly 71 per cent of all divorces in 1998 were between couples where the marriage had been the first for both parties.
- Nearly one out of every five men and women divorcing in 1998 were divorced prior to marriage, compared with only one in ten men and women in 1981.

✦ **Over 80,000 couples (55 per cent) divorcing in 1998 had at least one child aged under 16.**

SOURCE: POPULATION TRENDS 98, WINTER 1999

These latest government facts reveal something of the state of marriage in England and Wales and the consequent impact upon family life. It highlights disturbing trends which the Church needs to take seriously.

Marriages: by type of ceremony, in Great Britain

	Religious	Civil	All
	[Per cent (%)]		[Thousands]
First marriages			
1971	—	—	380
1981	69	31	255
1991	67	33	215
2001	54	46	173
Remarriages			
1971	—	—	67
1981	19	81	134
1991	25	75	126
2001	21	79	121
All marriages			
1971	60	40	447
1981	52	48	388
1991	51	49	341
2001	40	60	293

SOCIAL TRENDS 31 © CROWN COPYRIGHT 2001

The above table reveals that changes in household and family patterns reflect changes in the partnering and marital status of the population over time. Marriage is still the usual form of partnership between men and women. However, the total number of marriages in the United Kingdom has fallen from a peak in 1972. In 1997 there were 310,000 marriages, among the lowest figures recorded during the twentieth century.

The number of first marriages has decreased substantially since its peak in 1970. In 1997 there were 181,000 first marriages for both partners, less than half the number in 1970. Slightly over two-fifths of marriages in 1997 were remarriages for either or both partners. Early in the twentieth century remarriage was relatively uncommon, but since the 1960s the number of remarriages has increased. While most of the few remarriages at the turn of the century in England and Wales involved a widow or widower, more recently at least one partner remarrying has usually been divorced. These trends were notably accentuated following the implementation of the Divorce Reform Act 1969 in 1971.

Following falls in the **average age at first** marriage between 1919 and 1970, there has been a tendency for people to **marry for** the first time slightly later in life in recent years. Between 1971 and 1997 the mean age at first marriage in England and Wales rose from 24 years to 29 years for men, and from 22 years to 27 years for women. Rises in pre-marital cohabitation help to explain the recent trend towards later marriage, but other factors such as the increased and longer participation in further and higher education, particularly among women, have also contributed.

The types of marriage ceremonies people have been able to choose have changed over time. Civil wedding ceremonies were first permitted in England and Wales under the Marriage Act 1836 that was implemented the following year. This Act also allowed Catholics and Non-conformists to marry in their own place of worship. In 1995 the Marriage Act 1994 came into force in England and Wales. The first part of the act allowed couples to marry by civil ceremony outside their district of residence, and the second part introduced the ability to marry in 'approved premises'. For venues to be registered as approved premises, the local authority must be satisfied that they are readily identifiable wedding venues that will support the dignity of marriage, and have no recent or continuing connection with any religion. There were just over two thousand approved premises in May 1998, about half of which were hotels.

Since the introduction of civil wedding ceremonies in 1837 there has been a shift away from religious to civil marriages. In 1993 the number of civil ceremonies started to outnumber religious ones, and by 1997 three in five weddings in Great Britain were conducted with civil ceremonies. Differences exist between the types of ceremonies for first and subsequent marriages. In 1997 more first marriages had a religious than a civil ceremony but, for second and subsequent marriages, civil ceremonies outnumbered religious ones by four to one.

European Divorce Rates

According to results from the European Union's statistical office:

- **Almost one in three marriages in the EU ends in divorce. In a total population of 370 million this would equal 666,000 divorces.**
- **Belgium had the highest divorce rate in 1995 (3.5 per 1000 inhabitants). This was partly due to a change in the divorce laws in that year.**
- **Britain was next (2.9), Finland, (2.7), Sweden (2.6), Denmark (2.5) and Germany (2.1).**
- **The lowest divorce rates are found in the Catholic and Orthodox countries; Portugal (1.2), Greece (1.1), Spain (0.8) and Italy (0.5).**
- **European marriages are still more stable than in the US where every second marriage ends in divorce.**

> The figures show that in Europe, fewer and fewer couples want to marry. In the 1970s there were 8 marriages per 1,000 inhabitants. In 1995 this figure had decreased to 5.1. Though the number of marriages has declined in the USA it has not dropped as far and is still higher than the previous European figure, in 1995 the US figure was 8.9 per 1000 inhabitants.

© GERMAN IDEA, ENGLISH EDITION, JANUARY 20 1998

Divorce and Fatherhood

> 9 out of 10 fathers leave to become the non-resident parent.

> 50% of these fathers see their children just once a week, and divorced fathers have just a one-in-twenty chance of getting custody

> Around 50% of fathers lose contact with their children altogether after two years. 'Conventional wisdom' has long held that children want parents to stay together no matter what, but increasingly those dealing with children caught up in consistent parental conflict are suggesting we should stop saying divorce is always worse than anything and understand that living with warring parents may be yet more damaging. The important thing then is to have a well-managed divorce and for parents to do the best they can to give the children they still have a family, albeit not living under the same roof.

FIGURES FROM NATIONAL COUNCIL FOR ONE PARENT FAMILIES, THE DSS AND OTHER GOVERNMENT STATISTICS.
© THE GUARDIAN, 05/02/98

ADDRESSING

The following is a list of practical suggestions that may enable churches and organizations to take action that will alleviate the problem of divorce in their locality.

† Preparation for marriage should be given to all couples in the six months preceding their marriage.

† Marriage enrichment seminars/classes should be regularly offered to all couples associated with the church and be made available to the wider community.

† Counseling for marriage and family should be accessible through the local church and be offered by Christian/approved counsellors.

† The profile of marriage should be raised and maintained by the Church as a timeless model for the good of the whole family and community.

† Single parents should be affirmed, supported and cared for through the church having a system of support in place.

† Parenting courses could be offered to train and assist parents in the basic skills of raising their children, especially for the formative years.

- † Crisis pregnancy should be understood and loving care given to all who face this traumatic crisis.
- † At no time should the church condemn or reject those who face such family traumas.
- † Preachers should teach the principles of Christian marriage in a relevant and appropriate way, and speak out against today's popularism which increasingly devalues and demeans marriage.
- † Ensure that your marriage is a Godly role model and make sure you give time to getting it right in your own home first.

AFFIRMATION

The following is a list of churches, organizations or individuals who are taking action to alleviate the problems of divorce. They will, we believe, be able to offer practical and professional advice to assist you in your efforts to take action to support family. (Please see appendix B.)

DIVORCE CARE
57A WINDSOR ROAD,
FOREST GATE
LONDON
E7 0QY
TEL: (0208) 534 7339
WWW.DIVORCECARE.COM
A CHRISTIAN MINISTRY TO THE SEPARATED & DIVORCED, PROVIDING BOOKS, VIDEOS, TAPES AND COURSES

NATIONAL COUNCIL FOR ONE PARENT FAMILIES
255 KENTISH TOWN ROAD
LONDON
NW5 2LX
TEL: (0800) 018-5086
WWW.ONEPARENTFAMILIES.ORG.UK
THEY HAVE A WIDE RANGE OF INFORMATION ON BENEFITS AND TAX, LEGAL RIGHTS, HOLIDAYS, MAINTENANCE, CHILD SUPPORT, RETURNING TO WORK, ETC

PARENTLINE PLUS
(INCORPORATING STEPFAMILIES ASSOCIATION)
3RD FLOOR CHAPEL HOUSE
18 HATTON PLACE
LONDON
EC1N 8RU
TEL: (0207) 209-2460
FREE PHONE HELP LINE (0808) 800-2222
WWW.PARENTLINEPLUS.ORG.UK
THEY HAVE A TELEPHONE HELP LINE FOR PARENTS & STEP-PARENTS UNDER STRESS

GROWING THROUGH
3 GRANGE ROAD
ERDINGTON
BIRMINGHAM
B24 0DG
TEL: 0121 681 6855
EMAIL DALEERICKS@AOL.COM
WWW.GROWING-THROUGH.ORG

Books that deal with the issue of divorce

0310573912, *Complete Divorce Recovery Handbook*, Splinter, Zond
0859696847, *Divorce and Separation*, Willans, Sheldon
0745938043, *Divorce: Living Through the Agony*, Kirk, Lion
0715148885, *Children and Divorce*, Smith/Bradford, CHP
1857924215, *Divorce*, Retief, CFP
0854766456, *Suddenly Single*, Stanton, Kingsway
0830816437, *Moving On After He Moves Out*, Conway, IVP
0862018544, *How to Stay Sane When Families Crack Up*, Piper, SU

Remarriage

0800786483, *Step-family Problems*, Frydenger, Spire
0715138332, *Marriage in Church After Divorce*, CHP
0830812830, *Divorce and Re-Marriage*, House, IVP
080242564X, *Divorce and Re-Marriage*, Evans, Moody
0225668203, *Divorce and Second Marriage*, Kelly, Cass

THE FAMILY AND CHILD ABUSE

Awareness

The following information is included to raise the social awareness and understanding of ministers/church leaders in relation to the contemporary issues surrounding child abuse.

- **When child abuse is uncovered it often becomes an issue of 'who's to blame.' Politicians sometimes blame 'problem families,' the media blame 'public bodies' such as social workers. Often the abused and the abuser are forgotten amidst arguments over 'Why?' and 'Who?'.**

- **The reasons why some people abuse children and others don't are varied; abusers are suggested to be 'perverted', 'some girls are sexually delinquent', 'family breakdown', 'psychological fixations' or 'intuitional problems'.**

- **Attempts have been made to produce sociological and psychological profile of child abusers without any real success. One researcher working with sexual abusers commented that he 'couldn't stop being amazed that they were all regular guys, ordinary working men and average pillars of the community.' (© Snowdon, R. (1980)** *Working with incest offenders: excuses, excuses, excuses*, **Aegis, 29. pp. 88–102.)**

- **The definitions of abuse are dependent upon what we consider normal child care and abuse, the boundaries between good childcare and abuse can vary. For example 'smacking', 'withdrawing privileges' or 'not giving a child what s/he want' can be considered 'good discipline' or 'abuse/neglect.' The Government offer the following definitions of what constitutes child abuse.**

Definitions of Abuse

The definitions of child abuse recommended as criteria for registration by the Department of Health, for England and Wales, 1999.

- **Abuse and Neglect**
  Somebody may abuse or neglect a child by inflicting harm, or by failing to act to prevent harm. Children may be abused in a family or in an institutional or community setting; by those known to them or, more rarely, by a stranger.

- **Physical Abuse**
  Physical abuse may involve hitting, shaking, throwing, poisoning, burning or scalding, drowning, suffocating, or otherwise causing physical harm to a child. Physical harm may also be caused when a parent or career feigns the

symptoms of, or deliberately causes ill health to a child whom they are looking after. This situation is commonly described using terms such as factitious illness by proxy or Munchausen syndrome by proxy.

❖ **Emotional Abuse**
Emotional abuse is the persistent emotional ill-treatment of a child such as to cause severe and persistent adverse effects on the child's emotional development. It may involve conveying to children that they are worthless or unloved, inadequate, or valued insofar as they meet the needs of another person. It may feature age or developmentally inappropriate expectations being imposed on children. It may involve causing children to frequently feel frightened or in danger, or the exploitation or corruption of children. Some level of emotional abuse is involved in all types of ill-treatment of a child, though it may occur alone.

❖ **Sexual Abuse**
Sexual abuse involves forcing or enticing a child or young person to take part in sexual activities, whether or not the child is aware of what is happening. The activities may involve physical contact, including penetrative (e.g. rape or buggery) or non-penetrative acts. They may include non-contact activities, such as involving children in looking at, or in the production of pornographic material or watching sexual activities, or encouraging children to behave in sexually inappropriate ways.

❖ **Neglect**
Neglect is the persistent failure to meet a child's basic physical and/or psychological needs, likely to result in the serious impairment of the child's health or development. It may involve a parent or career failing to provide adequate food, shelter of clothing, failing to protect a child from physical harm or danger, or the failure to ensure access to appropriate medical care of treatment. It may also include neglect of, or unresponsiveness to, a child's basic emotional needs.

❖ **Organized Abuse**
Organized or multiple abuse may be defined as abuse involving one or more abuser and a number of related or non-related abused children and young people. The abusers concerned may be acting in concert to abuse children, sometimes acting in isolation, or may be using an institutional framework or position of authority to recruit children for abuse.

Organized and multiple abuse occur both as part of a network of abuse across a family or community, and within institutions such as residential homes or Schools. (A child may suffer more than one category of abuse).

Recognizing and Responding to Abuse

(Used with permission from *Guidance to Churches Manual*, a comprehensive child *protection manual produced by the Churches* Child Protection Advisory Service. PO Box 133 Swanley Kent BR8 7UQ). The following signs may or may not be indicators that abuse has taken place, but the possibility should be considered.

✝ **PHYSICAL SIGNS OF ABUSE**
Any injuries not consistent with the explanation given for them
Injuries which occur to the body in places which are not normally exposed to falls, rough games, etc.
Injuries which have not received medical attention
Neglect – under nourishment, failure to grow, constant hunger, stealing or gorging food, untreated illnesses, inadequate care, etc.
Reluctance to change for, or participate in, games or swimming
Repeated urinary infections or unexplained tummy pains
Bruises, bites, burns, fractures etc which do not have an accidental explanation
Cuts/scratches/substance abuse

✝ **INDICATORS OF POSSIBLE SEXUAL ABUSE**
Any allegations made by a child concerning sexual abuse
Child with excessive preoccupation with sexual matters and detailed knowledge of adult sexual behaviour, or who regularly engages in age – inappropriate sexual play
Sexual activity through words, play or drawing
Child who is sexually provocative or seductive with adults
Inappropriate bed-sharing arrangements at home
Severe sleep disturbances with fears, phobias, vivid dreams or nightmares, sometimes with overt or veiled sexual connotations
Eating disorders – anorexia, bulimia

✝ **EMOTIONAL SIGNS OF ABUSE**
Changes or regression in mood or behaviour, particularly where a child withdraws or becomes clinging. Also depression/aggression, extreme anxiety.
Nervousness, frozen watchfulness, Obsessions or phobias, Sudden under-achievement or lack of concentration
Inappropriate relationships with peers and/or adults
Attention-seeking behaviour
Persistent tiredness
Running away/stealing/lying

ASSESSMENT

The following are some of the most up-to-date statistics in relation to child abuse. (Please see appendix A.)

Children on the child protection registers: by age

	England, Wales & N. Ireland (in thousands)					
	Under 1	1–4 yr	5–9 yr	10–15 yr	16+ yr	All
1988	2.9	14.4	3.9	10.5	1.7	43.3
1989	2.9	15	14.8	11.5	1.7	45.9
1991	3.1	15.9	15.7	12.6	1.8	49.3
1992	2.7	13	13.3	11.3	1.6	42.2
1993	2.5	10.9	11	9.9	1.2	35.6
1994	2.9	11.5	11.7	10.6	1.1	38
1995	3.2	11.8	11.6	10.5	1	38.2
1996	2.9	11	10.9	9.6	1.1	35.6
1997	3.1	10.9	11.2	9.5	0.9	35.8
1998	3.1	10.8	11.2	9.4	0.8	35.5

SOCIAL TRENDS 30 © CROWN COPYRIGHT 2000

The above table reveals that there has not been much change in the age distribution of children on the child protection register in the last ten years, with the exception of a slight increase in the proportion of children aged under 1 year.

In 1999 the number of children on the Child Protection Registers for England, Wales and N. Ireland saw an increase over 2,000, bringing the total to over 37,000.

In 1998–99, the NSPCC received around 82,000 thousand requests for assistance of which 5 per cent were sexual abuse cases, 3 per cent were physical abuse cases and 3 per cent were neglect cause.

SOCIAL TRENDS 31 © CROWN COPYRIGHT 2000

Children's experiences of domestic violence

(The following is a summary of *The Hidden Victims*, a report published by NCH Action for Children. © NCH Action for Children)

- Of violent men studied, 83% were fathers to one or more children in the family.
- The violence experienced by mothers and children. 73% of mothers in the survey said their children had witnessed violent incidents, and 67% had seen their mothers beaten.
- 27% said their violent partners had also physical assaulted their children. Several said their partners had sexually abused their children.
- 10% of the mothers were sexually abused in front of their children.
- 99% of the mothers said their children had seen them crying and upset because of the violence.

The short-term effects of domestic violence on children

Living in a violent home can impact on every aspect of a child's life and behaviour. In the short term, children may be fearful, withdrawn, anxious, aggressive, and confused, and suffer from disturbed sleep, difficulties at school and problems in making friends.

- 91% of mothers surveyed believed their children were affected in the short term.
- 25% said their children had become aggressive towards them and towards other children.
- 31% developed problems at school.
- 72% said their children had been frightened, 48% that they had become withdrawn and 34% said they had developed bed-wetting problems.
- 13% of mothers said their children had run away from home because of the violence.
- 31% said their children had intervened to protect them. 27% said their children had tried to protect siblings.
- 84% had found their children harder to look after in a violent situation because they were depressed; more than half thought this was because they were frightened or exhausted.

The longer-term effects of domestic violence on children

Many young people have vivid recollections of domestic violence. Longer-term effects include lack of self-confidence and social skills, violent behaviour, depression and difficulties in forming relationships. Disrupted schooling means children fail to reach their potential while others leave home early to escape the violence.

- 86% of mothers believed their children were affected in the longer term.
- 33% thought their children had become violent and aggressive and harder to control, 29% that they were resentful and embittered, and 21% that their children lacked respect for them.
- 31% said their children had low self-esteem and 24% thought their children had problems trusting people and forming relationships.

Addressing

The following is a list of practical suggestions that may enable churches and organizations to take action that will alleviate the problems of child abuse in their locality.

- **Churches should have child protection policies in place**
  according to Government recommendations in *Safe from Harm* (1991) and

Working together to Safeguard Children (2000), child protection policies in place. Churches may also find that insurance companies expect churches to follow Government recommendations. The *Guidance to Churches Manual*, a comprehensive child protection manual produced by the Churches' Child Protection Advisory Service. PO Box 133 Swanley Kent BR8 7UQ provides a model child protection policy for the local church to adopt.

✞ **Churches should remember that child abuse is a crime and the minister is not authorized to investigate allegations.**

How to Respond to a Child Wanting to Talk About Abuse

(Used with permission from *Guidance to Churches Manual*, a comprehensive child protection manual produced by the Churches' Child Protection Advisory Service. PO Box 133 Swanley Kent BR8 7UQ.)

It is not easy to give precise guidance, but the following may help:

✞ **GENERAL POINTS**

Show acceptance of what the child says (however unlikely the story may sound)
Keep calm
Look at the child directly
Be honest
Tell the child you will need to let someone else know – don't promise confidentiality
Even when a child has broken a rule, they are not to blame for the abuse
Be aware that the child may have been threatened or bribed not to tell
Never push for information. If the child decides not to tell you after all, then accept that and let them know that you are always ready to listen.

✞ **HELPFUL THINGS YOU MAY SAY OR SHOW**

"I believe you" (or showing acceptance of what the child says)
"Thank you for telling me"
"It's not your fault"
"I will help you"

✞ **DON'T SAY**

"Why didn't you tell anyone before?"
"I can't believe it!"
"Are you sure this is true?"
"Why?" "How?" "When?" "Who?" "Where?"
Never make false promises
Never make statements such as "I am shocked, don't tell anyone else"

✞ **CONCLUDING**

Again reassure the child that they were right to talk and show acceptance
Let the child know what you are going to do next and that you will let

them know what happens (you might have to consider referring to Social Services or the Police to prevent a child or young person returning home if you consider them to be seriously at risk of further abuse)

Contact the person in your church/organization responsible for co-ordinating child protection concerns or contact an agency such as CCPAS for advice or go directly to Social Services/Police/NSPCC

Consider your own feelings and seek pastoral support if needed

AFFIRMATION

The following is a list of churches, organizations or individuals who are taking action to alleviate the problems of child abuse. They will, we believe, be able to offer practical and professional advice to assist you in your efforts to take action against child abuse. (Please see appendix B.)

CHILDLINE
FREEPOST 1111
LONDON
N1 0BR
0800 1111
HEAD OFFICE, TEL 0207 2391000

CHURCHES CHILD PROTECTION ADVISORY SERVICE (PCCA)
PO BOX 133
SWANLEY
BR8 7UQ
TEL 0845 120 4554
WEB SITE: WWW.CCPAS.CO.UK
EMAIL: INFO@CCPAS.CO.UK

CHILD LINK
CHALLENGE HOUSE
29 CANAL ST
GLASGOW
G4 0AD
TEL 0845 60111 34

BARNARDO'S
TANNERS LANE
BARINGSIDE
ILFORD
IG6 1QG
TEL 020 8550 8822
EMAIL: MEDIA.TEAM@BARNARDOS.ORG.UK
WWW.BARNARDOS.ORG.UK

CALOUSTE GULBENKIAN FOUNDATION
98 PORTLAND PLACE
LONDON
W1N 4ET
TEL 020 7636 5313
EMAIL: INFO@GULBENKIAN.ORG.UK
WWW.GULBENKIAN.ORG.UK

CHILDREN 1ST
41 POLWARTH TERRACE
EDINBURGH
EH11 1NU
TEL 0131 337 8539
EMAIL: INFO@CHILDREN1ST.ORG.UK
WWW.CHILDREN1ST.ORG.UK

CHILDREN ARE UNBEATABLE
77 HOLLOWAY RD
LONDON
N7 8JZ
TEL 020 7700 0627
EMAIL: INFO@CHILDRENAREUNBEATABLE.ORG.UK
WWW.CHILDRENAREUNBEATABLE.ORG.UK

ECPAT
THOMAS CLARKSON HOUSE
THE STABLEYARD
BROOMGROVE RD
LONDON, SW9 9TL
TEL 020 7501 8927
EMAIL: ECPAT@ANTISLAVERY.ORG
WWW.ECPAT.ORG.UK

EPOCH (END ALL PHYSICAL PUNISHMENT OF CHILDREN)
77 HOLLOWAY RD
LONDON
N7 8JZ
TEL 020 7700 0627
EMAIL: EPOCH-WORLDWIDE@MCRL.POPTEL.ORG.UK

INTERNET WATCH FOUNDATION
5 COLES LANE
OAKINGTON
CB4 5BA
TEL 01223 237700
EMAIL: ADMIN@IWF.ORG.UK
WWW.INTERNETWATCH.ORG.UK

KIDSCAPE
2 GROSVENOR GARDENS
LONDON
SW1W 0DH
TEL 020 7730 3300
EMAIL: CONTACT@KIDSCAPE.ORG.UK
WWW.KIDSCAPE.ORG.UK

NATIONAL CRIMINAL INTELLIGENCE SERVICE
PO BOX 8000
LONDON
SE11 5EN
TEL 020 7238 8000
WWW.NCIS.GOV.UK

NCH
85 HIGHBURY PARK
LONDON
N5 1UD
TEL 020 7704 7000
WWW.NCHAFC.ORG.UK

NSPCC
NATIONAL CENTRE
42 CURTAIN RD
LONDON
EC2A 3NH
TEL 020 7825 2500
EMAIL: INFO@NSPCC.ORG.UK
WWW.NSPCC.ORG.UK

Books that deal with the issue of child abuse

1856072797, *The Church and child sexual abuse*, ed. Conway/Duffy/Shields, Columba Press
0340694645, *Fingernail Moon*, Webster, H&S
1854243985, *Surviving Sexual Abuse*, Brown, MON
0946616418, *Child Sexual Abuse*, Hancock/Mains, HB
0281046476, *Christianity and Child Sexual Abuse*, Cashman, SPCK

PCCA Child Care Resource List

Tel. 01322 667207

Title and description	Price
Adoption and Fostering – For Christians thinking about adopting or fostering children	FREE
Caring Magazine – For foster parents, adopters and those working with children.	FREE
The Best of Caring Volume 3 – See advert on back page	£3.00
Binding The Broken, Releasing The Captive – Poems by Pauline Pearson, including "Why Didn't I Say No?"	£5.00
Child Abuse – Guidance For Teachers, as sold to over 1000 schools. Special offer price	£2.50
Day Care and The Children Act – Deals with all aspects of the Act (apart from child-minding) including race, culture and religion. Revised Jan 2000 edit. With latest DfEE regs.	£3.00
Evangelical Alliance Guidelines – Allegations Of Abuse – The Church's Responsibilities – Prepared with the PCCA's help	£0.75
Guidance To Churches – Dealing With Child Abuse & Appointing Children's Workers – Practical guidelines now with specimen policies	£7.00
Guidance To Churches – Dealing With Child Abuse & Appointing Children's Workers, Bulk order for five or more copies. (Min 5)	£5.00

Guidance To Churches Plus Policy Documents Disk – Model policy documents & application forms on disk for you to load and adapt for your church. (Available in Word 97 format only)	£21.50
Workers child protection pocket guide. (six panels, folds into credit card size)	10p

PCCA Tapes

Building Positive Esteem In Children – Some helpful suggestions on how to work with young people to establish a good self image. Tackles an often ignored issue.	£3.00
The Children Act – Basic concepts of the Act and how it applies to churches and carers	£3.00
The Church And Child Abuse – (2 tapes and detailed notes) A live recording of the popular 3 hour PCCA seminar. (State if you require N Ireland or Scottish versions.)	£7.85
The Church As A Family – A practical approach to caring for individuals within the church. Challenges the church to live and operate as a family, encouraging people to get involved.	£3.00
Counselling Children – Guidelines and advice for those involved in these specialised, delicate and important situations. A useful resource for counsellors and ministers.	£3.00
Dealing With Kids In Crisis – A first aid kit for children's workers. How to deal with the emotional fallout for you and the children and young people you work with.	£3.00
Help! I'm A Parent – Some practical parenting advice with the help of a drama group.	£3.00
Risks And Rewards – This tape outlines the risks and dangers to youth workers and the rewards of this seemingly endless and thankless task.	£3.00

Videos

Facing the Unthinkable Video Workpack – Designed for in-house training over three sessions or a day. (See advert on page 3) Suggested donation	£100.00
A Duty to Care – 1/2 hour video designed to highlight the need for an effective child protection policy – for management committees, church councils etc. Special Offer	£17.50
PCCA Today – 20 minute video introducing the work of PCCA.	Donation

Other Suggested General Reading

Adopting A Child – Prue Chennells & Chris Hammond (BAAF) A guide for people interested in adoption	£7.40
Adopting Or Fostering A Sexually Abused Child – Catherine Macaskill (Batsford). If you're fostering or adopting a child with such problems, this book is definitely for you!	£15.99
Caring For The Whole Child – John Bradford (The Children's Society) A holistic approach to spirituality.	£8.95
Child Sexual Abuse – A Hope For Healing – Hancock & Mains (Highland Books) One of the best books around on the subject	£5.99
Child Sexual Abuse And The Churches – Patrick Parkinson (Hodder & Stoughton) A well-balanced book that uses research as well as accounts from survivors of abuse. Reduced	£6.99
Children & Bereavement – Wendy Duffy (NS/CHP) How to help children deal with death.	£4.95
Christian Counselling Resource on Personal Esteem – (Grace Ministries) A booklet for counsellors and for those they help.	£1.20
Creative Methods in Counselling – Althea Pearson (Marshal Pickering) Useful book for those in pastoral ministry/counsellors	£8.99
Eating Disorders – (Family Reading Centre) Guidance for teachers and youth workers on the cause and symptoms of eating disorders. A useful resource for schools, youth clubs etc	£3.50
Free to Love – Dr Margaret Gill (Eagle) Sexuality and pastoral care.	£8.99
Growing Through Grief And Loss – Dealing with life's tough times – Althea Pearson (Marshall Pickering).	£7.99
Helping Children in a Changing Family – (Children's Society) All about divorce and children	£1.25

Helping Victims Of Sexual Abuse – Heitritter & Voight – (Bethany House) A sensitive, biblical guide for counsellors, victims and families.	£8.99
I Believe In The Family – Gary Collins (Hodder & Stoughton) Looks at the importance of families and ways to strengthen them.	£9.99
Keep Them Safe – (Kidscape) Helping children to protect themselves	30p
Living with Grief in Schools – (Family Reading Centre) Advice for teachers and others working with children	£3.50
Pastoral Care For Young People – Edited by Mark Vernon (Marshall Pickering) Eleven articles on issues facing young people today. Well written by a variety of writers.	£7.99
Preventing Bullying – (Kidscape) A parent's guide to help children and young people	30p
Seven for a Secret – Tracey Hansen (Triangle) One woman's secret and her road to hope	£4.99
Talking About Adoption To Your Adopted Child – Prue Chennells & Marjoria Morrison (BAAF) How do you tell your child they are adopted? Some useful points.	£7.40
The Courage To Tell – Margaret Kennedy (CTBI) Christian survivors of sexual abuse tell their stories of pain and hope. Also suggestions for services in churches	£12.95
The Lost Art of Forgiving – Johann C. Arnold (Plough Publishing) Stories showing the healing power of forgiveness in all situations	£7.99
What's So Amazing About Grace – Philip Yancey (Zondervan) All about grace and forgiveness – a really good read.	£7.99
When Someone You Know Is Sexually Abused – Susie Shellenberger (Focus on the Family) Useful resource book for youth workers.	£3.50
Who Cares? – (CPAS) Effective pastoral care of under 11's in church based groups. Tackles a wide number of issues.	£7.50
When the Unthinkable Happens – a booklet to raise awareness of abuse and abusers.	£1.50
Why My Child? – Michelle Elliott (Kidscape) This is a guide for parents of children who have been sexually abused. It answers common questions and tackles many issues.	£0.20

Books For Use With Children

Alice's Dad – a book for children who grieve – Bill Merrington (Kevin Mayhew)	£4.99
Beat The Bullies – The Willow Street Kids – Michele Elliott (Kidscape) Teaches children how to deal with bullies in and out of school.	£4.50
Be Smart Stay Safe – The Willow Street Kids – Michele Elliott (Kidscape) For Junior school aged children teaching them how to protect themselves in difficult situations.	£4.50
My Book, My Body – Colouring Book (Children's Society) To help young children protect themselves	£3.99
Secret Never To Be Told – Cathie Bartlam (SU) A useful book for teenage girls who may be dealing with abuse	£3.25
The Hideaway – a book for children who grieve – Bill Merrington (Kevin Mayhew)	£4.99
When Your Parents Split Up – (Children's Society) Divorce and children	£1.25
You Can Beat Bullying – (Kidscape) A guide for young people	30p

SINGLE PARENT FAMILIES

Awareness

The following information is included to raise the social awareness and understanding of ministers/church leaders in relation to the contemporary issue of single parent families.

- Many politicians fighting for the moral high ground in family policy have supported the ideal media image of the family and thus stigmatized lone parents by suggesting that 'lone parenthood leads to under achievement in children, juvenile delinquency, crime and a general social disintegration.' Generally politicians are more interested in social harmony than the heart ache that many lonely single parent families are experiencing.

- Of course we want to see children brought up in the marital home; however, the reality of the world today is that families are breaking down and those parents and children need the compassion and comfort of the Church reaching out and ministering to them.

- As a result of bereavement, domestic violence, desertion, and even promiscuity many people sadly find themselves in the position of being single parents. The function of the biblical family was to teach and nurture children in the ways of the Lord. This function of course is not beyond the single parent family.

- Whether a family home is made up of mother, father and child/ren or just one parent and child/ren they can both be encouraged to operate as biblical families, teaching and nurturing children according to biblical values and principles for the family.

- Take into consideration some of the difficulties that single parents may face when seeking to set up home for the first time.

- Social and family stigma attached to having an illegitimate child.

- Family breakdown, feeling they have let their family down.

- Future plans, hopes and dreams may have to be set aside.

- Finding a place to live, most young parents want to be close to family, the local council or housing agency may not be able to provide accommodation in the desired locality. Some single parents end up living far away from the support of family and friends or crowded into the extended family home creating more pressure.

- → Finding furniture for the home, such as bed (self) bed/cot (child) sofa/chairs, table, cooker, fridge, washing machine, dryer, television, phone, carpets (bedrooms), carpet (living rooms), vacuum cleaner.
- → Finding items for the coming baby.
- → Learning to cook.
- → Trying to understand the Social Security system.

ASSESSMENT

The following are some of the most up-to-date statistics in relation to single parent families. (Please see appendix A.)

Families headed by lone parents as a percentage of all families with dependent children, by marital status in Great Britain.

Lone Mother	1971	1976	1981	1986	1991–2	1996–7	1998–9
Single	1%	2%	2%	3%	6%	7%	9%
Widowed	2%	2%	2%	1%	1%	1%	1%
Divorced	2%	3%	4%	6%	6%	6%	8%
Seperated	2%	2%	2%	3%	4%	5%	5%
All Lone Mothers	7%	9%	11%	13%	18%	20%	22%
Lone Fathers	1%	2%	2%	1%	1%	2%	2%
Married/Cohabiting couple	92%	89%	87%	86%	81%	79%	75%
All families with dependents	100%	100%	100%	100%	100%	100%	100%

SOCIAL TRENDS 30 © CROWN COPYRIGHT 2000

This table reveals that in 1971, 7 per cent of families with dependent children were lone mother families; by 1998-99 this had trebled to 22 per cent. Before the mid-1980s much of the rise in lone parenthood was due to divorce, while since then single lone motherhood (never-married, non-cohabiting women with children) grew at a faster rate. Lone parenthood is not just a recent phenomenon. There is some evidence that lone parent families were just as frequent in the sixteenth and seventeenth centuries as they are now although they declined in the nineteenth and early twentieth century. However, widowhood was usually the cause for these families then, whereas today there are relatively few widowed lone parents.

Single Parents Double

- ❖ The number of British one parent families with dependent children has almost doubled in 13 years to nearly one in four.
- ❖ This is by far the highest proportion in Europe, with only Ireland seeing a faster growth rate from less than 7% in 1983 to 13% last year.
- ❖ Currently some 23% of families with dependent children are headed by a lone

❖ parent (the figures exclude cohabiting couples and those who married after the birth of their children). In 1971 the figure was 8%.

❖ Most lone parents are women and nearly 30% of those in Britain have a child under five.

❖ No figures were available for Sweden and Denmark, but figures for other European countries were as follows; Finland 17%, Belgium and France 15%, most other countries were between 11–14%, with the lowest two being Greece on 7% and Spain on 8%.

❖ The high figure in Britain is thought to be a combination of a high divorce rate and the growing tendency of women to have children outside marriage.

© The Daily Telegraph, 30/9/98.

Children and Divorce in 1998

❖ There are 1.7 million single parent families in Britain.
❖ Almost 3 million children are living in one parent families.
❖ 21% of all families are lone parents.
❖ 90% of all lone parents are women.
❖ Of lone parents, 9% are men, 4% are widowed mothers, 32% are divorced mothers, 23% are married but separated, 36% have never been married.
❖ Less than 4% of lone mothers are under 20.
❖ 41% of lone parents live on less than £100 per week.
❖ 1.1 million parents are on Income Support.

Figures from National Council for One Parent Families, the DSS and other government statistics.

© The Guardian, 05/02/98

Addressing

The following is a list of practical suggestions that may enable churches and organizations to take action that will alleviate the problems faced by single parent families.

The following list of suggestions were made by the © Family Policy Studies Center to deal with and alleviate poverty when seeking to support the family. Churches could take note of the pressures that single families face and seek to lessen them in their local community.

† Understanding the reality of poverty
  Ensure policies based on real understanding of present-day family structures.
  Enable people living in poverty to effect policy changes themselves by their participation in anti-poverty campaigns.

Explain rights clearly, and honor them.
Prioritize preventative family work rather than only giving help at a time of crisis.

† **Benefit and taxation system**
Increase benefits to realistic levels to allow for real costs of bringing up children.
Make benefits available to all 16–19-year-olds.
Make the claiming of benefits, e.g. family credit, simpler for those moving in and out of work.

† **Day and child care**
Invest in good quality, affordable child care and nursery care.
Provide day care for under-threes.
Provide affordable day care in colleges and training institutes to enable adults to improve their futures.

† **Young people**
Develop better understanding of why young people are at particular risk of poverty.
Ensure policies based on realistic assessment of families' ability/inability to support young people (lack of benefits for 16- and 17-year-olds and low rates for older young people put enormous pressure on families).

† **Family life and parenting skills**
Prepare young people, in schools, for parenthood, the responsibilities of family life and the complexity of family relationships.
Encourage young people and adults to acknowledge lifetime family commitments for elderly people as well as children.
Set up family support services which recognize all parents need confidential support and which make asking for help a sign of responsible parenthood.

† **Single parents**
Becoming a lone parent[1] whatever the reason, rapidly heralds poverty. There should be comprehensive government policies, which do not discriminate against single parents, for all families.
Lone parents increasingly have the dual responsibility of child care and that of their elderly family. Carers policies should recognize that many carers will be single parents.

† **Jobs and work**
TECs and employers should create opportunities for teenagers leaving school.
There should be greater equality in the work place with better working conditions for women.

FACING TODAY'S SOCIAL ISSUES

Greater flexibility in working hours would enable careers and single parents to go out to work.

† **Education and training**
Help adults to return to education and training by introducing a comprehensive system of educational and training grants that make allowance for family responsibilities.

† **The departmentalization of poverty**
Like family policy, poverty policies suffer because there is no co-ordination of government responses to it.
Promote a government and interdepartmental commitment to invest in child care.
Keep families together to deal with their problems, don't split them up because finding the funding is easier that way.
Programs to end discrimination in work and in access to education and training should be implemented.

† **Community support**
Give greater support to outreach work in the community through churches, youth clubs, voluntary organizations.
Consider policies to enhance the quality of life for those whose lives are impoverished and isolated.

On the basis of the Family Policy centre's recommendations churches could seek to take the following action.

† **Single parents are more likely to face the problems of poverty than other families. Therefore offer cheap and affordable childcare, play groups or parent and toddler groups.**

† **Encourage mature parents to mentor younger parents.**

† **Run parenting classes.**

AFFIRMATION

The following is a list of churches, organizations or individuals who are taking action to alleviate the problems faced by single parent families. They will, we believe, be able to offer practical and professional advice to assist you in your efforts to take action to support single parent families. (Please see appendix B.)

CARE FOR THE FAMILY
PO BOX 488
CARDIFF CF1 1RE (02920) 810800
WWW.CARE-FOR-THE-FAMILY.ORG.UK

CHEER
23 CALBOURNE ROAD
LONDON SW12 8LW (0208) 673 1493

EMAIL: CHEER@TALK21.COM
SUPPORTS THOSE PARENTING ALONE.

CHILD LINK
CHALLENGE HOUSE
29 CANAL STREET
GLASGOW
G40 AD
(LOCAL CALL RATE 0845 601 1134)

CHRISTIAN LINK ASSOCIATION OF SINGLE
PARENTS (CLASP)
'LINDEN,' SHORTER AVENUE
SHENFIELD, ESSEX
CM15 8RE
(01277) 233848
EMAIL:
OFFICE@CLASPCHARITY.FREESERVE.CO.UK

CREDIT ACTION
6 REGENT TERRACE
CAMBRIDGE CB2 1AA
TEL 01223 324034
FREEPHONE HELPLINE (0800) 591084
WWW.CREDITACTION.COM

CRUSE BEREAVEMENT CARE
126 SHEEN ROAD, RICHMOND
SURREY TW9 1UR

BEREAVEMENT COUNSELLING
TEL: HELPLINE 0870 167 1677
OFFICE: 020 8940 4818

DIVORCE CARE
57A WINDSOR ROAD
FOREST GATE
LONDON
E7 0QY
(0208) 534 7339
WWW.DIVORCECARE.COM
A CHRISTIAN MINISTRY TO THE SEPARATED &
DIVORCED, PROVIDING BOOKS, VIDEOS, TAPES
AND COURSES

GINGERBREAD ASSOCIATION FOR LONE PARENT
FAMILIES
16-17 CLERKENWELL CLOSE
LONDON
EC1R 0AA
(0207) 488 9300

LISTENING EAR
44 GAYVILLE ROAD
LONDON
SW11 6JP
(0207) 223-5054

NATIONAL ASSOCIATON OF CHILD CONTACT
CENTERS
MINERVA HOUSE
SPANIEL ROW
NOTTINGHAM
NG1 6EP
(0115) 948-4557
EMAIL: INFOR@NACCC.ORG.UK
WWW.NACCC.ORG.UK

NATIONAL COUNCIL FOR ONE PARENT FAMILIES
255 KENTISH TOWN ROAD
LONDON
NW5 2LX
(0800) 018-5026

PARENTLINE PLUS
(INCORPORATING STEPFAMILIES ASSOCIATION)
3RD FLOOR CHAPEL HOUSE
18 HATTON PLACE
LONDON
EC1N 8RU
(0207) 209-2460
FREEPHONE HELPLINE (0808) 800-2222
WWW.PARENTLINEPLUS.ORG.UK

PCCA CHRISTIAN CHILD CARE
PO BOX 133
SWANLEY
KENT
BR8 7UQ
(01322) 667207
EMAIL: INFO@PCCA.CO.UK
WWW.PCCA.CO.UK

POSITIVE PARENTING PUBLICATIONS
2A SOUTH STREET
GOSPORT
HANTS
PO12 1ES
TEL 02392 528787

WWW.PARENTING.ORG.UK
E-MAIL: INFO@PARENTING.ORG.UK
CANAAN CHRISTIAN CENTRE
21 HOLT ROAD
SHERINGHAM
NORFOLK
NR26 8NB
TEL: 01263 824300
EMAIL: MENDEK@TALK21.COM

Books that deal with the issues faced by single people and single families

0851111947, *Single Issue*, Hsu, IVP

0830816909, *Playing the Tuba at Midnight*, Rand, IVP

0854767150, *No Sex Please, We're Single*, Gregory, Kingsway

0860654680, *God is a Matchmaker*, Prince, Kingsway

STEP-PARENTING

Awareness

The following information is included to raise the social awareness and understanding of ministers in relation to the contemporary issue of stepfamilies.

- Psychologists suggest that the fairy stories 'Cinderella' and 'Snow White' are unhelpful for children because they can separate in their minds a 'good' mother from the 'bad' mother. The stepmother in both these fairy stories are presented as wicked, jealous and unreasonable and so many new stepmothers have an uphill struggle to win the trust and love of their new children.

- Stepping into a stepfamily is all about losses and gains. For child/ren and their parent stepping into a stepfamily is about losing from the family home a biological parent and partner through divorce or bereavement and gaining a step-parent and at times step brothers and sisters.

- Blending two families is no easy task and brings with it a mixture of stresses and strains upon the family home that a biological family do not face.

- Stepchildren may continue to see their biological parent and may create divided loyalties and the pressure to please both sets of parents. There is pressure to be the 'perfect family' so as to make things work this time round. Getting to know a new step father or mother, getting to know step children and getting to know step brothers and sisters all takes time. For some step parents it may be becoming instant parents. Different family rules and rewards can cause confusion and upset. Different choice of food and drink can result in conflict at meal times. For some children moving into a stepfamily may mean having to move away from family and friends and thus losing contact. Combining families inevitably means for some a loss of privacy for children having to share a bedroom and a loss of focused attention from their biological parent.

- Julie Andrews in *The Sound of Music* seems to have things relatively easy with her seven stepchildren. Many children react to a new step parent coming into their family with feelings of anger, hurt, guilt, they feel confused, hurt and betrayed. Some stepchildren respond to the change with behaviour problems at home and school, some become depressed and turn to drugs and alcohol.

Assessment

The following are some of the most up-to-date statistics in relation to the issue of step families. (Please see appendix A.)

* 8% of all families in Great Britain were classed as stepfamilies.
* 54% of women brought children from a previous relationship into a new stepfamily.
* 12% of men brought children from a previous relationship into a new step family.
* 4% of men and women both brought children from a previous relationship into a new stepfamily.

SOURCE GENERAL HOUSE HOLD SURVEY 1996–97,
COHABITING COUPLES ARE CLASSED AS STEP FAMILIES.

Child Line make the following comment and prediction about step families in the UK.

* Only 40% of the population consist of a married couple with dependent children, compared to 52% in 1961, although this situation is still the most common experience for seven in ten young people.
* Divorce now ends one in two new marriages, with two out of every three remarriages failing. 25% of children will now see their parents divorce.
* Forecasts suggest that the number of step families will continue to grow, with increasing numbers of children spending some of their childhood in a one parent household. Currently, about one in ten children currently live with one natural parent and one step-parent.

ADDRESSING

The following is a list of practical suggestions that may enable churches and organizations to minister effectively to step families.

> Stepfamilies have needs that are different to first time marriage families and therefore churches and their leaders need to take time to understand the stresses and strains of blending two families.
> Often because stepfamilies do not fit neatly into churches theological frame works leaders have not known how to minister to their growing numbers coming into churches.
> Be sensitive to the feelings of step families, the last thing a family under stress needs to hear when they come to church is a sermon that is ranting and raving about the breakdown of the traditional family being responsible for all social evils.
> In parenting classes address the issues facing stepfamilies. Encourage church, youth and children workers to understand and be sensitive to issues and needs of stepchildren.
> Despite the difference between first and second time families, both can with the support of God and His people be successful.

"It seems that the successful formation of a stepfamily depends on a number of factors. First, how the end of the earlier relationship was handled. Secondly, how and when the prospective parent was introduced to the children, and lastly whether there can be a fairly relaxed attitude about the time it takes for a new family to settle down. There will have to be a transition period lasting several years, and it is as well not to expect too much too soon. Different needs have to be balanced and if that includes children or partners from an earlier relationship the situation becomes more complex.

It takes time to build up family memories made up of events and shared experiences, but with a lot of hard work stepfamilies can, and do, move on to mobilize the family strength."

© Jill Curtis, 2000

Affirmation

The following is a list of churches, organizations or individuals who deal with multi-cultural issues. They will, we believe, be able to offer practical and professional advice to assist. (Please see appendix B.)

DIVORCE CARE
57A WINDSOR ROAD
FOREST GATE
LONDON E7 0QY
(0208) 534 7339
WWW.DIVORCECARE.COM
A CHRISTIAN MINISTRY TO THE SEPARATED & DIVORCED, PROVIDING BOOKS, VIDEOS, TAPES AND COURSES

NATIONAL COUNCIL FOR ONE PARENT FAMILIES
255 KENTISH TOWN ROAD
LONDON
NW5 2LX
(0800) 018-5026

THEY HAVE A WIDE RANGE OF INFORMATION ON BENEFITS AND TAX, LEGAL RIGHTS, HOLIDAYS, MAINTENANCE, CHILD SUPPORT, RETURNING TO WORK, ETC

PARENTLINE PLUS
(INCORPORATING STEPFAMILIES ASSOCIATION)
3RD FLOOR CHAPEL HOUSE
18 HATTON PLACE

GINGERBREAD ASSOCIATION FOR LONE PARENT FAMILIES
16–17 CLERKENWELL CLOSE
LONDON EC1R 0AA
(0207) 336-8183

Books that deal with the issue of step families

0800786483, *Step-family Problems*, Frydenger, Spire
0715138332, *Marriage in Church After Divorce*, CHP
0830812830, *Divorce and Re-Marriage*, House, IVP
080242564X, *Divorce and Re-Marriage*, Evans, Moody
0225668203, *Divorce and Second Marriage*, Kelly, Cass

BULLYING

AWARENESS

The following information is included to raise the social awareness and understanding of ministers in relation to the contemporary issue of bullying.*

- Bullying is not always easy to define. However, Dan Olweua, an expert in the field of the prevention of bullying, says that bullying includes:
  - Physical. **Pushing, kicking, hitting, pinching and other forms of violence or threats.**
  - Verbal. **Name-calling, sarcasm, spreading rumours, persistent teasing.**
  - Emotional. **Excluding (sending to Coventry), tormenting, ridicule, humiliation.**
  - Racist. **Racial taunts, graffiti, gestures.**
  - Sexual. **Unwanted physical contact or abusive comments.**
- Persistent bullying can result in
  - Depression
  - Low self-esteem
  - Shyness
  - Poor academic achievement
  - Isolation
  - Threatened or attempted suicide
- Bullying of course is not limited to school; children are bullied at home (see section on The Family and Child Abuse). Adults in all walks of life are bullied in the workplace and in the home (see section dealing with The Family and Domestic Violence and also the section on Ageism).

ASSESSMENT

The following are some of the most up-to-date statistics in relation to the issue of bullying. (Please see appendix A.)

Fear of Being Bullied

Students were asked: 'Do you ever feel afraid of going to school because of bullying?' The females are more fearful than the males, and the Year 6s are more concerned than the year 10s.

* Thanks to Kidscape for their input on this section.

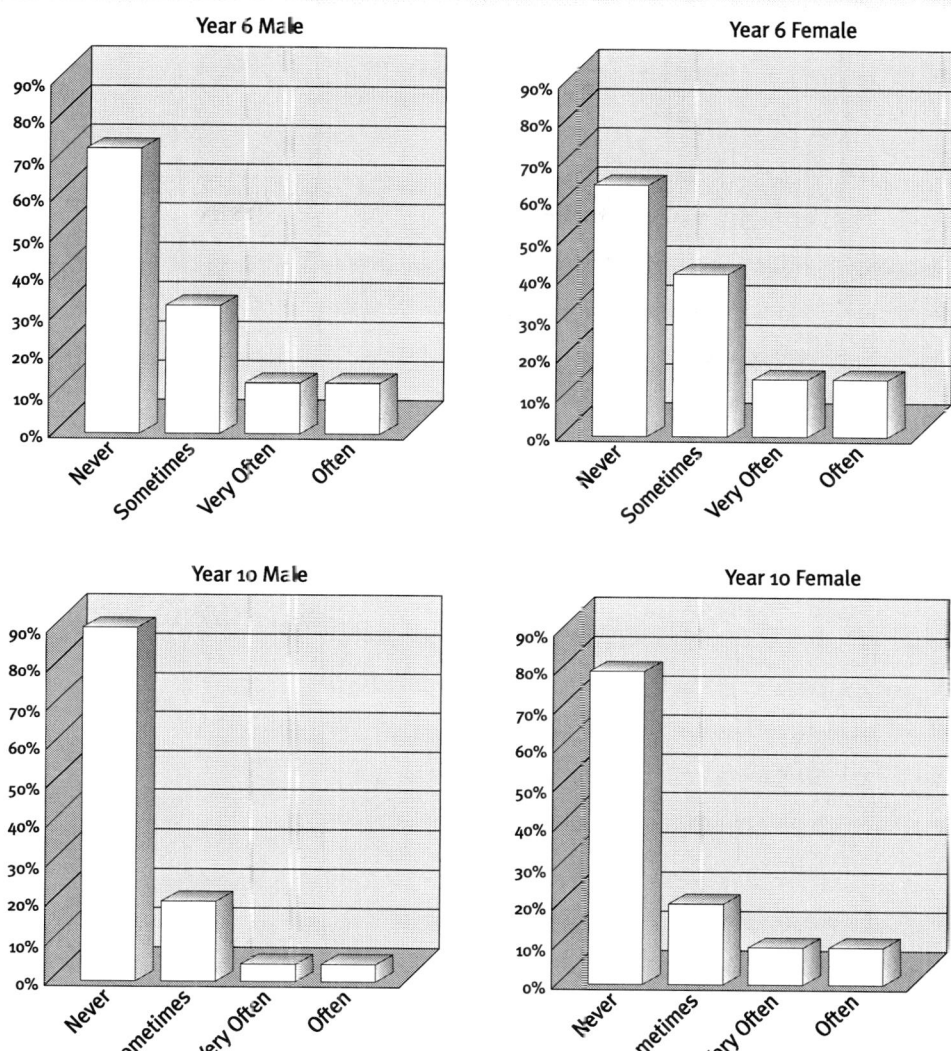

SOURCE. SCHOOLS HEALTH EDUCATION UNIT

WORKPLACE BULLYING

Approximately one in ten people (10.5% of employees surveyed) reported themselves as having been bullied at work over the past six months.

ADDRESSING

The following is a list of practical suggestions that may enable churches and organizations to minister effectively to those who bully and those being bullied.

> A child may indicate by their behaviour that he or she is being bullied. If a child shows some of the following signs, bullying may be responsible and you might want to ask if someone is bullying or threatening them.

Children may:

- be frightened of walking to and from school
- change their usual route
- not want you to go on the school bus
- beg you to drive them to school
- be unwilling to go to school (or be 'school phobic')
- feel ill in the mornings
- begin truanting
- begin doing poorly in their school work
- come home regularly with clothes or books destroyed
- come home starving (bully taking dinner money)
- become withdrawn, start stammering, lack confidence
- become distressed and anxious, stop eating
- attempt or threaten suicide
- cry themselves to sleep, have nightmares
- have their possessions go missing
- ask for money or start stealing (to pay the bully)
- continually 'lose' their pocket money
- refuse to talk about what's wrong
- have unexplained bruises, cuts, scratches
- begin to bully other children, siblings
- become aggressive and unreasonable
- give improbable excuses for any of the above

➢ Helping children who are being bullied.

- If you or a parent are concerned that a child is being bullied, ask him or her directly. Children who are being bullied are often frightened to tell what is happening so be prepared for the child to deny at first that there is anything wrong.
- Encourage the child by saying that you want to help and support them, whatever the problem.
- Take the child seriously and find out what exactly what has been going on.
- Don't promise to keep the bullying a secret but reassure the child that you will help them sort out the problem.

- ❖ If you find that the child is a perpetual victim and they are bullied wherever they go, try to find out how the child reacts to other people. Perhaps they don't know how to talk or play with other children? Help them develop social skills by role playing with them pretend you are another child and help the child work out acceptable responses.

- ❖ If you discover the child is being bullied because they have a socially unacceptable habit (picking their nose for example) help them change this behaviour.

Affirmation

The following is a list of churches, organisations or individuals who deal with the issue of bullying. They will, we believe, be able to offer practical and professional advice to assist. (Please see appendix B.)

ANDREA ADAMS TRUST
SHALAMAR HOUSE
24 DEREK AVENUE
HOVE
EAST SUSSEX BN3 4PF
A TRUST SET UP IN MEMORY OF THE LATE EXPERT ON WORKPLACE BULLYING. FOR A FACT SHEET AND BROCHURE, AND TO ASK ABOUT TRAINING AND ADVICE WORKSHOPS, SEND AN A4 STAMPED ADDRESSED ENVELOPE TO THE ABOVE ADDRESS.

KIDSCAPE
2 GROSVENOR GARDENS
LONDON, SW1W 0DH
TEL: 020 7730 3300
FAX: 020 7730 7081
WEBSITE: WWW.KIDSCAPE.ORG.UK
EMAIL: CONTACT@KIDSCAPE.ORG.UK
PROVIDES FREE LEAFLETS AND BOOKLETS FOR PARENTS, CHILDREN AND TEENAGERS ABOUT BULLYING, HOW TO DEAL WITH CHILD ABUSE, KEEPING CHILDREN SAFE AND COPING WITH 'NORMAL' TEENAGE BEHAVIOUR.

ADVISORY CENTRE FOR EDUCATION (ACE)
1B ABERDEEN STUDIOS
22 HIGHBURY GROVE
LONDON N5 2EA
ADVICE LINE FOR PARENTS, TEACHERS AND GOVERNORS: TEL 0207 354 8321 (2–5 P.M. MON–FRI)
EMAIL: ACE-ED@EASYNET.CO.UK
WWW.ACE-ED.ORG.UK
PRODUCES A WIDE RANGE OF EXCELLENT MATERIAL, DESCRIBING YOUR RIGHTS, HOW TO COMPLAIN UNDER THE VARIOUS ACTS.

CARELINE
ARDINAL HEENAN CENTRE
326 HIGH ROAD
ILFORD IG1 1QP
TEL 0208 514 1177
TELEPHONE COUNSELLING FOR ANYONE EXPERIENCING BULLYING OR OTHER PROBLEMS.

CHILDREN'S LEGAL CENTRE
TEL 01206 873820 (10 A.M.–12.30 P.M., 2–4.30 P.M. MON–FRI)

NATIONAL CHILD PROTECTION HELPLINE (NSPCC)
FREEPHONE 0800 800500
A 24-HOUR HELPLINE FOR ANYONE CONCERNED ABOUT A CHILD AT RISK OF ABUSE (INCLUDING BULLYING), INCLUDING CHILDREN THEMSELVES.

PARENTLINE
ENDWAY HOUSE
THE ENDWAY
BENFLEET
ESSEX SS7 2AN
TEL 0808 3002222 (MON–FRI 9 A.M.–9 P.M.; SAT 9.30 A.M.–5 P.M.)
WWW.PARENTLINE.ORG.UK
HELPLINE FOR PARENTS AND CAREERS OF CHILDREN. LISTENING, INFORMATION AND COUNSELLING. DEALS WITH MANY ISSUES INCLUDING SCHOOL BULLYING, ABUSE, HARD-TO-HANDLE BEHAVIOUR, RACISM. REFERRALS TO LOCAL PARENTLINE GROUPS.

PARENTS' ADVICE CENTER
FRANKLIN HOUSE
12 BRUNSWICK STREET
BELFAST BT2 7GE
24-HOUR HELPLINE 02890 310891
FOR PARENTS AND YOUNG PEOPLE IN NORTHERN IRELAND. OFFERS LISTENING, SUPPORT, GUIDANCE AND COUNSELLING RELATING TO ANY FAMILY PROBLEM.

THE SCOTTISH COUNCIL FOR RESEARCH IN EDUCATION
15 ST JOHN STREET
EDINBURGH
EH8 8JR
TEL: 0131 557 2944
A FULLY COMPREHENSIVE RESOURCE ONLINE WITH LINKS AND FURTHER ADVICE:
HTTP://WWW.SCRE.AC.UK/BULLY/

LUCKY DUCK PUBLISHING
34 WELLINGTON PARK
CLIFTON
BRISTOL
BS8 2UW
TEL/FAX: 0117 973 2881
INFORMATION, LEAFLETS, VIDEOS AND BOOKS ON MANAGING BEHAVIOUR IN SCHOOLS AND TRAINING. EMPHASIS ON PREVENTING AND REACTING TO BULLYING, INCLUDING THE 'NO BLAME' APPROACH. SEND YOUR NAME AND ADDRESS FOR A LEAFLET OF MATERIAL AVAILABLE TO LUCKY-DUCK@DIAL.PIPEX.COM

NATIONAL WORKPLACE BULLYING ADVICE LINE
DEPT C5
PO BOX 67
DIDCOT
OXON OX11 0YH
ADVICE LINE: 01235 212 286
FAX: 01235 861721
HTTP://WWW.SUCCESSUNLIMITED.CO.UK/

OFSTED
ALEXANDRA HOUSE
33 KINGSWAY
LONDON
WC2B 6SE
TEL: 0207 4216800/ 0207 4216744
WEBSITE: WWW.OFSTED.GOV.UK/INDEXA.HTM

SCHOOL REPORTS ARE AVAILABLE ON THE OFSTED WEBSITE
DAVID HART GENERAL SECRETARY
NAHT
1 HEATH SQUARE
BOLTRO ROAD
HAYWARDS HEATH
WEST SUSSEX
RH16 1BL
TEL: 01444 472472/472404
EMAIL: INFO@NAHT.ORG.UK
FOR PARENTS CONSIDERING EDUCATING CHILDREN AT HOME

SCHOOLHOUSE HOME EDUCATION ASSOCIATION
311 PERTH ROAD
DUNDEE
DD2 1LG
TEL: 01382 646964
FAX: 01382 640472
EMAIL: INFO@SCHOOLHOUSE.ORG.UK

HOME EDUCATION ADVISORY SERVICE
PO BOX 98
WELWYN GARDEN CITY
HERTS
AL8 6AN
TEL: 01707 371854
WWW.HEAS.ORG.UK

EDUCATION NOW
113 ARUNDEL DRIVE
NOTTINGHAM
NG9 3FQ

EDUCATION OTHERWISE
PO BOX 7420
LONDON
N9 9SG.

Below are just some of the many websites available on the internet if you know of any others or you run one yourself please drop us an email websites@bullying.co.uk Education Otherwise A great many families who withdraw their children from school in order to home-educate do so as a result of bullying. It's very important that families who are having bullying problems are aware that home-education is an option.

For bullied teachers and their spouses:
Gill Hetherington is the wife of a former deputy head, bullied out of his job. Her website is Bully Dissolver at www.bullydissolver.com Contact Gill on gillh@bullydissolver.com

For parents needing information on private/public schools:
ISIS, the Independent Schools Information Service: 020-7798-1500. Email national@isis.org.uk

For Leeds parents interested in the stories behind the headlines:
Children's Support Network Union. So controversial Leeds City Council wanted to close it down. Website: www.members.tripod.com/truthline/

For parents seeking the official DFEE line on legal issues and statues:
The DFEE website: www.dfee.gov.uk. Email: info@dfee.gov.uk or to email a minister dfee.ministers@dfee.gov.uk

For info specifically for parents: website: www.parents.dfee.gov.uk.

For parents and teachers interested in education issues:
The Guardian has an education website: www.educationunlimited.co.uk. The *Times Educational Supplement* is at www.tes.co.uk

For workplace bullying:
Tim Field has a fantastic site called Bully Online at www.successunlimited.co.uk and he can be emailed for advice on timfield@successunlimited.co.uk. Tim has found that teachers make up a very high proportion of those contacting him. A useful resource and invaluable support for anyone whose job is making them ill

For parents thinking of a legal remedy:
Barrister Neil Addison runs www.harassment-law.co.uk and you can find out about up-to-date legal issues regarding injunctions.

For bullied children in the West Country: Exeter Parents Against Bullying. A site run by Nick Bolt epab@eurobell.co.uk

For youngsters in West and North Yorkshire: Sport of all types, and details of training courses and clubs is on the Leeds-based Young Sport at www.youngsport.co.uk.

For parents seeking information on home educating: www.choiceineducation.co.uk, www.home-education.org.uk, www.silencingthe-bell.btinternet.co.uk

Books that deal with the issue of bullying. Most of the following books can be obtained from "Kidscape," see above address

Feeling Happy, Feeling Safe. Colour picture book for children under 6 – stories about getting lost, strangers, bullying and more. £5.99

TEENSCAPE. Manual for teaching 12–16-year-olds about personal safety. Covers bullying, saying no, abuse etc. £8.95

How to Stop Bullying, Kidscape Training Guide New! 90 practical anti-bullying exercises to use with students aged 5–16. Include staff training and anti-bullying policies £15.00

Protecting Children. Bargain! Training manual for those working with abused children in a non-therapeutic way (teachers, foster carers, health visitors etc). Includes video about child sex abusers. Now only £10.00

The Willow Street Kids. Be Smart, Stay Safe. Follow these friends as they deal with strangers, bullies and others who try to bother them, including a known adult. £4.50

The Willow Street Kids. Beat the Bullies. The friends move to secondary school and run into bullies – one they knew from Primary school. Find out how they beat the bullies. Ages 7–11. £4.50 Primary Programme. Revised manual plus FREE VIDEO. Practical, low-key lessons for 5–11 year-olds about keeping safe from bullies, strangers and known adults who may try to harm them. £35.00

Primary Activity Book. This is included in the 'Primary Programme' listed above. Available on its own. £6.00

Under Fives Programme. Manual for teaching young children about bullies, strangers, what to do if lost, and saying no. £8.00

Keeping Safe. Classic guide for parents giving common-sense advice about keeping children safe. £6.99

Bullying. A Practical Guide to Coping for Schools. Tried and tested ideas for teaching about bullying. £17.00

Sticks and Stones Video. Realistic bullying incidents and roleplays about bully courts. Ages for 11–66. Great for discussion and drama. £25.85

Cosmo And Dibs Video. Five short, fun stories for ages 3–6. Teaching notes. £14.60.

Now I Can Tell You My Secret Video. Class taught about safe touching. Boy tells about abuse. Teaching notes. £28.70.101

Ways To Deal With Bullying. A Guide For Parents. NEW! Common sense ideas to overcome problems, build self-esteem, make friends. £8.00

TEENAGE PREGNANCY

AWARENESS

The following information is included to raise the social awareness and understanding of ministers/church leaders in relation to the contemporary issue of teenage pregnancy.*

Government responses to the increasing teenage pregnancy rate in the UK (see statistics below)

1. Reducing the rate of teenage conceptions, with the specific aim of halving the rate of conceptions among under-18s by 2010.

2. Getting more teenage parents into education, training or employment, to reduce their risk of long- term social exclusion.

The action plan for achieving these goals falls into four categories: a national campaign (involving Government, media and voluntary sector) to improve understanding and change behaviour; joined-up action so that strategy is coordinated at both local and national levels; better prevention of the causes of teenage pregnancy (including better education in and out of school, access to contraception, targeting at-risk groups and a new focus on reaching young men): and better support for pregnant teenagers and teenage parents (with a focus on returning to education, child-care help and intensive support for parents and child, with the prospect that no under-18 lone parent be put in a lone tenancy).

As Christians we acknowledge the scale of the problem and would certainly like to be part of the answer. Government proposals when looked at closely contain some mixed messages. In 1992, in the *Health of the Nation* document, the previous Government proposed to reduce the rate of conceptions in women under the age of 16 by at least 50 per cent by the year 2000. This led to a rise in services for teenagers that would make contraception more readily available. As we have seen through the 90s, this policy has failed.

It is no surprise that early sexual activity damages young people. God's boundaries, especially marriage, were given by God for our protection as well as our provision. If sex outside marriage carries with it risks and consequences, teenage sex even more so. Teenage girls seem to be particularly at risk since their cervical lining produces mucus that nourishes sexually transmitted infections (STIs) (as women reach their 20s or have a baby, that lining is replaced by a tougher lining of the vagina) and teenagers in general have lower levels of antibodies (including to STIs). Whilst the sheath can provide some protection against STIs, it is by no means total, and use of the pill can actually make

---

* Thanks to Image for their contributions to this section

teenagers more susceptible to certain STIs because it alters the acid/alkaline balance of the vagina. Added to this, teenagers are notoriously bad users of contraception. Since one in three pregnancies in the UK is unplanned, according to Brook, it is little wonder that the present campaign has on the agenda a more intensive marketing of the morning-after pill.

Not only, though, are there physical risks from early sexual activity but emotional, psychological and spiritual risks and consequences which have taken a back seat in the debate. Guilt, shame and possibly even suicide (now the third most common cause of death in the under-25s) are possible consequences. Sexual activity is taking place before young people are mentally and emotionally mature, and this is likely not only to affect their own emotional and psychological development but it may affect future relationships too. There is certainly no condom that can protect the heart.

Both in and out of the pregnancy centers it is possible to see the emotional scarring and low self-esteem that can result when a teenage relationship ends after sexual involvement.

The guilt felt by these experiences can lead to a distancing from God and religion. For Christian young people there is a waning of involvement with and enthusiasm and love for Jesus as sin intrudes. 'Praise God that there is always forgiveness for those who are willing to ask for it and admit failure.' 1 John 1: 9.

Interestingly, the Social Exclusion Unit's report acknowledged the effectiveness of several abstinence-based education programs in the US in delaying sexual activity, but that is not a route they have chosen.

Surely the time has come to look at primary prevention and raise the expectation for our young people. We believe that early sexual activity with or without pregnancy is damaging young people. If the church will not make a stand and be a voice in this area, then who will?

Statistically Britain has the highest teenage pregnancy rate in the EU. Abortion in Britain among teenagers is also the highest within the European Union. Holland has the lowest abortion and teenage pregnancy rate in Europe, yet Holland is renowned for it's openness towards sexual topics. This statistical comparison between Britain and Holland suggests that greater communication about sexual topics is a way forward in reduce unplanned teenage pregnancies in the UK. An opportunity therefore, for Christians in schools to communicate the morals and values of Scripture to teenagers. 'The thief comes only to steal and kill and destroy; I have come that they might have life, and have it to the full.' John 10: 10

Assessment

The following are some of the most up-to-date statistics in relation to teenage pregnancy. (Please see appendix A.)

- ➢ **In this country at the start of the new Millennium there were nearly 90,400 conceptions a year to teenagers; around 7,700 to girls under 16 and 2,200 to girls 14 or under. Sixty per cent of teenage conceptions resulted in live births.**

The UK has teenage birth rates which are twice as high as Germany, three times as high as France and six times as high as the Netherlands – in fact, higher than any other country within Western Europe.

- Ninety per cent of teenage mothers had babies outside marriage, and relationships started in the teenage years have at least a 50 per cent chance of breaking down. Teenage parents are more likely than their peers to live in poverty and unemployment and be trapped in it through lack of education, childcare and encouragement. In the longer term their daughters have a higher chance of becoming teenage mothers themselves.

- Around 50 per cent of teenage pregnancies end in abortion each year – about 45,000 abortions.

- STIs. Since 1995 there have been significant increases in the numbers of diagnoses of genital chlamydeous infection, genital warts and gonorrhoea. The rises were steepest for the 16 to 19-year-olds, particularly for chlamydeous (over 20 per cent a year). STIs are a major source of ill health which can have long-term physical and psychological health consequences. A recent Health Education Authority study found that one in four young people believed that the pill would protect them from

- In a single act of unprotected sex with an infected partner, teenage women have a one per cent chance of acquiring HIV, a 30 per cent risk of getting genital herpes and a 50 per cent chance of contracting gonorrhoea.

- The incidence of HIV/Aids infection remains unacceptably high, particularly in young men. Thirty-nine per cent of those with Aids in the UK are in their 20s, most of whom will have contracted HIV in their teens.

Live birth to teenage women, EU comparison, 1995

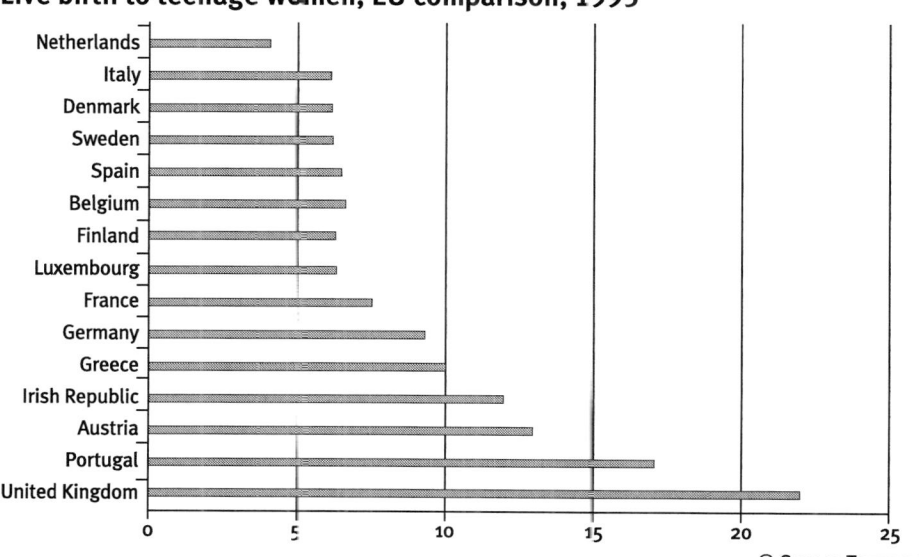

© Social Trends 2000

Addressing

The following is a list of practical suggestions that may enable churches and organizations to take action that will alleviate the problems of teenage pregnancy in their locality.

- "Open Pregnancy Crisis Centers" offering free pregnancy tests, counselling and practical support after the birth of a child.
- Teach teenagers openly about sex and sexual temptation. (With parental permission of course.)
- Teach the biblical principle of virginity before marriage in our congregations.
- Ask those who have regretted sex before marriage to bear testimony to their regrets.
- Seek training opportunities to prepare to talk in schools.
- Lobby the Government about the increasing rates of teenage pregnancy and abortion.
- Where possible promote adoption rather than abortion to pregnant teenagers.

Affirmation

The following is a list of churches, organizations or individuals who are taking action to alleviate the problems of teenage pregnancy. They will, we believe, be able to offer practical and professional advice to assist you in your efforts to take action to support family. (Please see appendix B.)

TEEN CHALLENGE UK
52 PENYGROES ROAD
GORSLAS
LLANELLI
SA14 7LA
TEL: 01269 842 718 FAX 01269 845 313
EMAIL: TCUK@GLOBALNET.CO.UK

CARE FOR LIFE
1 WINTON SQUARE
BASINGSTOKE
RG2 8EN
TEL: 01256 477300
FAX: 01256 477301
EMAIL: CFL@CARE.ORG.UK
WEBSITE: WWW.CARE.ORG.UK/CARELINE

IMAGE
COVERDALE CENTRE
COVERDALE CRESCENT
MANCHESTER
M12 4FG
TEL: 0161 273 8090
HELPLINE 0161 273 8400
EMAIL: IMAGE@MCR1.POPTEL.ORG.UK
WWW.IMAGENET.ORG.UK

Books that deal with the issue of teenage pregnancy.
1898938695, *Preparing to Parent Teenagers*, Scott-Evans
0880702044, *Daddy I'm Pregnant*, £7.50, Putman, Multinomah
0281050090, *God, Sex & Generation*, £5.99, Mike Starkey, SPCK

0745931227, *Children & Crime*, £7.99, Bob Holman, Lion
The Seduction Paul Francis, Marshall Pickering, 1995

Recommended reading and bibliography
The safe sex hoax, Dr Margaret White, OCU, 1998
Sex Appreciation, Patricia Driscoll, Womanity Press, 1988
Challenging thinking, OCU, 1999

The following documents can be found at the web site http://www.open.gov.uk
Sex and Relationship Education Guidance, Draft, March 16, 2000
Social Exclusion Unit Report on Teenage Pregnancies, June 1999
Department of Health Guidance on Tackling Teenage Pregnancy, January 2000
Sure Start, A Guide for Second-wave Programmes, March 2000

Leaflets
Teenagers: the facts about safe sex, Image
Why wait until marriage?, Image
How to be a better lover, Image
You didn't get pregnant, Image
If you think saying "No" is tough, Image
How to say no without losing his love, Womanity
Gone all the way. Now where?, Womanity
Secondary virginity: a new beginning, Womanity
On the verge of virginity, Womanity
Did you know you're special!, Positive Parenting Publications
New parents! Start here..., Positive Parenting Publications
Positive points for parents, Positive Parenting Publications
Adolescent sexuality, Trevor Stammers, CMF, 1998

Videos
Sex, lies and... the truth, Focus on the Family, 1993

COHABITATION

AWARENESS

The following information is included to raise the social awareness and understanding of ministers in relation to the contemporary issue of cohabitation.

- Cohabitation can simply mean any two people 'living together' under the same roof. A common understanding of cohabitation relates to an unmarried couple who live together, either at the same dwelling or under some other form of living relationship such as travelling or communal accommodation and regularly engage in sexual intercourse, sometimes called a "common law marriage."

- In England all marriage is regulated by statute: common law marriage as such ceased to exist with Lord Hardwick's Act of 1753. In Scotland the position is different, a cohabiting couple can be regarded as married by the law.

- Cohabitation is by far the most common living arrangement prior to marriage in the Western World. See table below.

Type of cohabitation can be categorized in the following way, (Taken from © Newcomb, M.D., in *Heterosexual Cohabitation Relationships*)

- **TEMPORARY OR CASUAL:** Research has found that many cohabiting relationships start in a casual way. A high proportion of couples have no thought-out reason for beginning the relationship: it just happens. In other cases the relationship is purely a temporary one: for example, research among cohabiting students in American colleges, has suggested that their relationships are more like 'steady dating' than anything else.

- **PREPARATION OR TRIAL FOR MARRIAGE:** Here there is already either a definite commitment to marry or some form of conditional commitment. Examples of the former would be where an engaged couple live together before the wedding for reasons of convenience; or where a couple are awaiting the dissolution of their existing marriages to other people. In other cases living together is seen as a trial for marriage: the couple will marry if the trial works out.

- **ALTERNATIVE OR SUBSTITUTE FOR MARRIAGE:** this includes couples who have rejected marriage and opted for cohabitation on ideological grounds. In certain cultures cohabitation has become so well-established that it is accepted as a social institution in its own right. Where cohabitation is the 'done thing' those who decide to live together have often not even considered marriage and therefore can not really be said to have consciously rejected it.

Perhaps many young British couples, especially in inner urban areas, are in this category.

➢ Reasons why people cohabit vary from a relationship which can be enjoyed outside marriage; a marriage would go the way so many others go and end in disaster; people feel that a time of cohabitation is the best preparation for marriage to know whether or not two people are right for each other; marriage is too much of a commitment; every one else does it; one or both members of the cohabiting relationship are already married.

➢ The reasons for the increase in cohabitation in the West are perhaps threefold:

a) The popular concept that "Sleeping together prepares the way for living together."

b) Contraception has made pre-marriage sexual intercourse less risky.

c) An unbiblical attitude to love and marriage.

Ephes. 5: 21-25: 'Submit to one another out of reverence for Christ. Wives, submit to your husbands as to the Lord. For the husband is the head of the wife as Christ is the head of the church, his body, of which he is the Saviour. Now as the church submits to Christ, so also wives should submit to their husbands in everything. Husbands, love your wives, just as Christ loved the church and gave himself up for her.'

ASSESSMENT

The following are some of the most up-to-date statistics in relation to the issue of cohabitation. (Please see appendix A.)

Percentage of non-married people cohabiting: by age and gender 1998-99

Great Britain	Percentages	
	Males	Females
16–19	1%	8%
20–24	18%	27%
25–29	39%	39%
30–34	44%	35%
40–44	36%	29%
45–49	31%	26%
50–54	28%	16%
55–59	17%	16%
60+	18%	12%
Total	26%	25%

SOCIAL TRENDS 30 © CROWN COPYRIGHT

What the above table reveals while the social stigma associated with people living together without marrying has diminished in recent years, finding from the British household Panel Survey in 1996 suggest that older people were more likely than younger people to think that living together is always wrong. These attitudes reflect people's experiences as young people are more likely to cohabit at younger ages than older people.

Women tend to cohabit at younger ages than men. The peak age group for cohabitation among unmarried women in Great Britain in 1998–99 was 25 and 29, with 39% of women cohabiting, while for men it was the 30 to 34 year age group, with 44% of men cohabiting.

Addressing

The following is a list of practical suggestions that may enable churches and organizations to minister effectively to those cohabiting.

- **Sexual relationships must be understood in the light of Biblical revelation concerning marriage, since the marriage relationship between a man and a woman is the only sexual relationship that God has created and blessed. Cohabitation therefore, is wrong. It is important when dealing with couples who are cohabiting to distinguish between, for example, a long-standing. loving, stable, monogamous cohabitation relationship and a casual relationship characterized by sexual intercourse. It would be silly to ignore such differences if the church is to help two people move from cohabiting to a marriage relationship as God ordained.**
- **Cohabiting couples should of course be advised to marry. Be patient when perhaps only one person in the cohabiting relationship has become a Christian and wants to please God.**
- **Should they live apart until the ceremony? If there are children in a cohabiting relationship, consider, is it wise to deprive children of their father/mother while waiting for the marriage ceremony?**
- **Communication on the wrongs of cohabitation can be done in the light of teaching positively on marriage. Many people in the congregation will either relate directly or indirectly to the subject.**
- **Take the opportunity at weddings to teach the positives of marriage and the negatives of cohabitation, e.g. "Cohabitation is a man-made relationship, Marriage is a God-ordained relationship."**

Affirmation

The following is a list of churches, organizations or individuals who are ministering to couples cohabiting. They will, we believe, be able to offer practical and professional advice to assist you in your efforts to minister to those cohabiting. (Please see appendix B.)

CANAAN CHRISTIAN CENTER
21 HOLT ROAD
SHERINGHAM
NORFOLK
NR26 8NB
TEL: 01263 824300
EMAIL: MENDEK@TALK21.COM
PROVIDING A SHORT TERM SECURE ENVIRONMENT FOR SINGLE PARENTS, THE HOMELESS AND THOSE IN GENERAL NEED.

CARE FOR THE FAMILY
PO BOX 488
CARDIFF
CF1 1RE
TEL: 029 2081 1733
FAX: 029 2081 4089
EMAIL: CARE.FOR.THE.FAMILY@DIAL.PIPEX.COM
WEBSITE: WWW.CARE.FOR.THE.FAMILY@DIAL.PIPEX.CO

CARE FOR LIFE
1 WINTON SQUARE
BASINGSTOKE
RG2 8EN
TEL: 01256 477300
FAX: 01256 477301
EMAIL: CFL@CARE.ORG.UK
WEBSITE: WWW.PREGNANCY.ORG.UK

CARING SERVICES
CHALLENGE HOUSE
29 CANAL STREET
GLASGOW
G4 0AD
TEL: 0141 332 7212
FAX: 0141 332 8500
EMAIL: CFS@CARE.ORG.UK
WEBSITE: WWW.CARE.ORG.UK

CHRISTIAN GUIDELINES
7 QUEEN STREET
BELFAST
BT1 6EA
TEL: 028 9023 0005
FAX: 028 9031 2098

CHURCH PASTORAL AID SOCIETY
ATHENA DRIVE
TACHBROOK PARK
WARWICK

CV34 6NG
TEL: 01926 458458
FAX: 01926 458459
EMAIL: MAIL@CPAS.ORG.UK
WEB SITE: WWW.CPAS.ORG.UK

THE COG WHEEL TRUST
THE MALTINGS
41 HIGH STREET
CAMBRIDGE
CB41 NQ3
TEL & FAX: 01223 464385
EMAIL: CWT@BTCLICK.COM

FEGANS
160 ST JAMES ROAD
TUNBRIDGE WELLS
KENT
TN1 2HE
TEL & FAX: 01892 538288

MARRIAGE RESOURCE
24 WEST STREET
WIMBORNE
BH21 1EW
TEL: 01202 849000
FAX: 01202 849934
EMAIL: MARRIAGE@NETCOMUK.CO.U
WEBSITE: WWW.MARRIAGERESOURCE.ORG.UK

MILL GROVE
10 CRESCENT ROAD
SOUTH WOODFORD
LONDON
E18 1JB
TEL: 020 8504 2702
FAX: 020 8506 0442.
EMAIL: MILLGROVE@BTINTERNET.COM

THE MÜLLER HOMES FOR CHILDREN
MÜLLER HOUSE
7 COTHAM PARK
BRISTOL, BS6 6DA
TEL: 0117 924 5001
FAX: 0117 924 4855
EMAIL: ADMIN@MULLERS.ORG
WEBSITE: WWW.MULLERS.ORG

PCCA CHRISTIAN CHILDCARE
PO BOX 133
SWANLEY
KENT
BR8 7UQ
TEL: 01322 667207
FAX: 01322 614788
EMAIL: INFO@PCCA.CO.UK
WEBSITE: WWW.PCCA.CO.UK

SPURGEON'S CHILD CARE
74 WELLINGBOROUGH ROAD
RUSHDEN
NORTHANTS
NN10 9TY
TEL: 01933 412412
FAX: 01933 412010
EMAIL: SCC@SPURGEONS.ORG

CHILDREN'S FAMILY TRUST
MKA HOUSE
4–6 ST ANDREWS ROAD
DROITWICH
WORCESTER
WR9 8DN
TEL: 01905 798229
FAX: 01905 798230
EMAIL: CAROLYNGUMBLEY@BTINTERNET.CO

CHRISTIAN FAMILY CONCERN
42 SOUTH PARK HILL ROAD
CROYDON
SURREY
CR2 7YB
TEL: 020 8688 0251
FAX: 020 686 7114
EMAIL: CHRISTFC@SURFAID.COM

NCH ACTION FOR CHILDREN
85 HIGHBURY PARK
LONDON
N5 1UD
TEL: 020 7704 7000
FAX: 020 7226 2537
WEBSITE: WWW.NCH.ORG.UK

PARENTTALK
PO BOX 23142
LONDON
SE1 0ZT
TEL: 0700 2000 500
WEBSITE: WWW.PARENTALK.CO.UK
EMAIL: INFO@PARENTALK.CO.UK

Books that deal with the issue of cohabitation

Cohabitation And Marriage, Forster, 0551028440, £8.99
Cohabitation: Biblical Perspective, Grove, 1851742298, £2.25
Cohabitation Or Marriage, Declan Flanagan, 0952993902, £2.99

EUTHANASIA

AWARENESS

The following information is included to raise the social awareness and understanding of ministers/church leaders in relation to the contemporary issue of euthanasia.*

Euthanasia is an issue of ethical debate in the UK which for many elderly people is becoming an increasing concern.

Euthanasia is the intentional killing of a patient either by act or omission, supposedly in the person's own interest. Voluntary euthanasia is killing the person at the person's request. Involuntary euthanasia is killing the person without his request, and possibly against his will. Non-voluntary euthanasia is killing a person unable to make such a request, such as a young child or sufferer from dementia.

Euthanasia is illegal (as is aiding someone to commit suicide). No British Government has been willing to legalize euthanasia – but taking innocent lives is happening under another name.

In 1993 British courts ruled for the first time that feeding a patient by tube was medical treatment, which could therefore be withheld from the patient if it were decided that it was in the patient's best interests to do so. Tony Bland, a young man left with brain damage after the Hillsborough football stadium disaster but not in pain and not dying, had food and water withheld from him, with the approval of the High Court, the Appeal Court and the House of Lords, until he died. Courts later gave permission for food and water to be withdrawn from some other patients in "persistent vegetative state."

In 1997 the Government published a green paper describing euthanasia as "a deliberate intervention with the express aim of ending life" (making no mention of killing by omission), and suggested legalizing the withdrawal of food and water from patients who were mentally incapacitated.

In 1999 the British Medical Association (BMA) issued new guidelines to doctors saying doctors could now withdraw medical treatment, including food and water, from seriously ill patients, like those having had a severe stroke or suffering from Alzheimer's disease or from seriously handicapped babies, if they considered it in the patient's best interests. The guidelines said they should not need to seek court permission. The BMA said this was not euthanasia, but withdrawing treatment in the patient's best interest. Throughout 1999 there were reports in the media of hospital patients having food and water withdrawn and being left to die. Police were investigating alleged cases of euthanasia at a number of hospitals.

* Thanks to Image for their contributions to this section

Much of the funds of an already stretched health service is spent on the elderly. The number of elderly is increasing, and is expected to continue to increase considerably.

Advocates of euthanasia say a person (particularly if he is terminally ill and in pain) should be allowed to decide how he wants his life to be ended. (In the past 30 years there have been tremendous advances in palliative care, and doctors now say it is no longer necessary for a patient to die in pain.) Christians believe God alone created human life, and He is sovereign over it. He alone has the right to take an innocent life, whether one's own or someone else's.

The Bible teaches that man, unlike the rest of the animal kingdom, is made in God's image and likeness (Gen 1: 26, 27). The Bible forbids the taking of innocent human life (Gen 9: 6; Ex 20: 13). For the Christian, the most important consideration will be 'You shall not murder' (Ex 20: 13).

There are arguments against allowing euthanasia apart from the Bible. It would be virtually impossible to ensure adequate safeguards. Once it were decided that life did not have absolute value and some people's lives were not worth living, where would it stop? The "slippery slope" argument is a valid one. Permitting abortion for a few women has led to abortion on demand. In Holland, voluntary euthanasia has led to involuntary euthanasia. What effect would euthanasia have on the medical profession? What would be the effect on the rest of society? How would euthanasia affect respect for life in the community? What would be the effect on relationships between the medical profession and patients?

Assessment

The following are some of the most up-to-date statistics in relation to euthanasia. (Please see appendix A.)

- As euthanasia is not legal in the UK, there are no official statistics; however, many individual cases are increasingly being reported

- Some European nations do allow legal euthanasia and their acceptance is used to challenge the UK's legal system to allow legal euthanasia

- A substantial majority of the British public support legalization of euthanasia

- Surveys of public opinion are notoriously fickle, but in this area they have been remarkably consistent, both over time and as between themselves. Although the precise numbers have varied somewhat, nationwide polls have been unanimous in showing a majority to be in favor of legalized voluntary euthanasia, with highly respected sources showing support as high as 82%

© British Social Attitudes Report, 1996.

The strongest support (86%) was in the case of the individual who has an incurable illness leaving him dependent upon a life support machine, unable to make a decision about his own future – as in the case of a permanent coma. This outweighed even the support in cases of persons suffering from a terminal, painful and incurable illness (80%).

© British Social Attitudes Report, 1996

⇨ **No nationwide poll has never shown a majority against voluntary euthanasia**

Those who know something of public opinion surveys will be aware that results can to some extent depend upon how the question is phrased. It is therefore worth noting that opponents of v.e. have found similar results upon commissioning their own research. A MORI poll commissioned by the anti-voluntary euthanasia group Doctors Who Respect Human Life in 1987 found 72% of respondents in favor of legalized euthanasia! Indeed, anti-v.e. groups have been unable to produce a single survey of UK opinion which did not show a majority in favour of legalization.

> Although 46% of Britain's doctors want to see euthanasia legalized, 44% do not. Almost 4 in 10 UK doctors would be prepared to help end the life of a terminally ill patient who wanted to die.
>
> Despite the fact that euthanasia in the Netherlands has been declared "beyond effective control" – a recent report estimated that one in five "assisted suicides" was without explicit consent – the Dutch government plans to bow to pressure from doctors and decriminalize euthanasia and assisted suicides.
>
> Michael Hewitt Wilson of the Alert campaign against euthanasia said; "A lot of people in Holland are frightened to go into hospital because of this situation."
>
> © THE TIMES 16.2.99 & 13.7.99

ADDRESSING

The following is a list of practical suggestions that may enable churches and organizations to take action that will alleviate the problem of euthanasia.

✧ **Lobby the Government on the issue**

✧ **Offer financial support to those in the ministry of preserving life**

✧ **Value the elderly members of your congregation and community and at the same time condemn euthanasia**

✧ **Increase awareness of the issue of euthanasia**

AFFIRMATION

The following is a list of churches, organisations or individuals who are taking action to alleviate the problem of euthanasia. They will, we believe, be able to offer practical and professional advice to assist you in your efforts to take action. (Please see appendix B.)

HELP THE AGED
ST JAMES' WALK
CLERKENWELL GREEN
LONDON
EC1R 0BE
TEL: 0207 278 1114
WEB SITE: WWW.HELPTHEAGED.ORG.UK
OR WWW.TRINITYCARE.CO.UK
EMAIL: HTA@PIPEX.DIAL.COM.UK

KEY CHANGE
5 ST GEORGE'S MEWS
43 WESTMINSTER BRIDGE ROAD
LONDON
SE1 7JB
TEL: 0207 633 0533
EMAIL: KEYCHANGE@KEYCHANGE.ORG.UK

PILGRIM HOMES
NASMITH HOUSE
175 TOWER BRIDGE ROAD
LONDON
ME1 2AL
TEL: 0207 407 5466
FAX: 0207 403 5433
EMAIL: PILGRIMHOMES@COMPUSERVE.COM

CHRISTIAN COUNSEL ON AGEING
EPWORTH HOUSE
STUART STREET
DERBY
DE1 2EQ
TEL: 01335 390 484
FAX: 01335 390 484
EMAIL: 106232.1524@COMPUSERVE.COM

HUMAN RIGHTS SOCIETY
MARINERS HARD
CLEY
HOLT
NR25 7RX
TEL: 01263 740 990

IMAGE
COVERDALE CENTRE
COVERDALE CRESCENT
MANCHESTER
M12 4FG
TEL: 0161 273 8090
HELPLINE 0161 273 8400
MAIL IMAGE@MCR1.POPTEL.ORG.UK
WWW.IMAGENET.ORG.UK

Books that deal with the issue of euthanasia

0340703524, *Euthanasia and the Churches*, Gill, CASS
086153204X, *Euthanasia: A Christian Perspective*, C. of Scot, SAP
0340694866, *Euthanasia: The Heart of the Matter*, Dunnett, H&S
Life and Death Decisions, Orr, Baker
Politically Correct Death, Beckwith, Baker

ABORTION

AWARENESS

The following information is included to raise the social awareness and understanding of ministers/church leaders in relation to the contemporary issue of abortion.

The arguments for and against abortion

The arguments against abortion

- State that human life begins at conception and believe that abortion destroys respect for human life.
- Abortion is violent for the mother and child and is uncivilized and unjust.
- Abortion is unnecessary and alternatives can be found.
- Women suffer from Post-Abortion Trauma which results in depression, guilt, broken relationships and emotional difficulties.
- Medical knowledge and science have advanced in recent years to such a degree that abortion is rarely necessary to save the life of the mother
- Many women use abortion as a contraceptive method.
- Tests can show if a child in the womb is disabled – anti-abortion organizations often believe that the child needs help with the difficulties or disabilities it may be born with.
- Whenever and however abortions are performed, they always end up in the loss of at least one life, possibly two (not very often).

The arguments for abortion

- The fertilized egg is potential life, based on scientific evidence the foetus is not viable (capable of independent life) in the early stage of pregnancy and is still part of the mother.
- Abortion has existed throughout history and making it legally or socially unacceptable does not drive it away.
- If women are to lead healthy, happy lives and offer the same to any children they may have, they need to be able to exercise control over their reproductive lives.
- Making abortion illegal in the nineteenth century in the UK led women with unwanted pregnancies to try dangerous methods to induce abortion.
- Legal abortion is safe, particularly when it is carried out in the first 12 weeks of pregnancy.
- The lack of a 100% reliable form of contraceptive means that unplanned pregnancy is a reality even in countries where contraception is available.

© BPAS BRITISH PREGNANCY ADVISORY SERVICE*

☆ **Human life begins at fertilization. Every cell in the human body contains 46 chromosomes. A male sperm, containing 23 chromosomes, and a female ovum, containing 23 chromosomes, come together to form a single cell with 46 chromosomes – 23 from the father and 23 from the mother. The sex of the new human being, his or her height, hair and eye colour are already determined by the contents of that single cell. Nothing is added to that single cell except food and water until that single cell becomes a mature adult.**

* Thanks to Image for their contributions to this section

☆ Shortly after fertilization, the cell begins to divide and multiply. Three weeks after fertilization, the baby's heart begins to beat. After six weeks, the baby has eyes, ears and internal organs. At two months, the baby can swim vigorously in the fluid which surrounds it. It has fingers and toes. Most abortions are carried out at between nine and twelve weeks. Since the *Human Embryology Act* in 1990, it is possible to have an abortion up to birth.

☆ A report in 1994 by the Commission of Inquiry into the operation and consequences of the Abortion Act said physical effects of abortion can include perforation of the uterus, increased risk of miscarriage, and tubal infection, which is the most common cause of infertility. Women who have had abortions can suffer from what has come to be known as post-abortion syndrome. Symptoms can include sleeplessness, anxiety, guilt, grief, anger, depression, drugs and alcohol abuse, self-destructive behaviour, difficulties with relationships and severe emotional pain.

☆ The Bible teaches that life begins at fertilization (Gen 25: 22,23; Psa 139: 13–16; Luke 1: 41, 44; Man 1: 18–20. If Jesus was divine from His conception, He must have been human from His conception too). Every human being is made in God's image, and man is forbidden to take innocent human life (Gen 1: 26, 27, 9: 5, 6). God has a plan and purpose for every human life (Jer 1: 5; Eph 1: 4, 2: 10; 2 Tim 1: 9). See Psa 82: 3, 4: Pro 24: 11, 12, 31: 8, 9.

ASSESSMENT

The following are some of the most up-to-date statistics in relation to the problem. (Please see appendix A.)

* **A 1995 MORI poll found that 66% of people questioned agreed that abortion should be "available on request" while only 15% strongly disagreed with this.**

* **Since the 1967 Abortion Act decriminalized abortion, there have been some five million abortions performed in NHS hospitals and private clinics in Britain. Abortions in England and Wales during 1998, the last year for which figures were available at the time of writing, were the highest ever at 187,402, with a further 12,424 in Scotland. That's over 15,000 abortions a month; 3,500 every week; 500 every day. These figures do not include countless thousands of early abortions caused by the morning-after pill and some so-called contraceptives which work not by preventing conception but by preventing the fertilized embryo from implanting in the uterus.**

1 in 3 pregnancies outside marriage are currently aborted compared with fewer than one in 10 pregnancies for women who are married.

In inner London 50% of pregnancies outside marriage are aborted.

Around 4,000 girls under 16 have abortions each year, in fact Britain has the highest teenage pregnancy rate in Europe.

Half of all pregnancies now occur outside marriage and the proportion is reaching two-thirds in some inner-city areas.

More than 170,000 pregnancies in England and Wales ended in abortion last year.

Unless there has been a startling reversal of recent trends, the proportion occurring outside marriage will have passed 50% last year.

Of all conceptions outside marriage 34.3% were terminated by abortion.

The figures were published in *Population Trends 95* along with an estimate that the number of cohabiting couples will reach almost 3 million by 2021.

A Gallup survey commissioned by Action Research revealed that a third of unborn babies found to be disabled are likely to be aborted.

Dr Peggy Norris, secretary of the World Federation of Doctors who Respect Human Life felt the figures highlighted the widespread attitude that disabled people 'have no value'. She said: "If a condition is detected during pregnancy, we still don't know the degree of disability. It is terrible to discard the fetus for being a lesser person. Disabled people have equal rights after they are born and they should have them before."

© DAILY MAIL 29.3.99

ADDRESSING

The following is a list of practical suggestions that may enable churches and organizations to take action that will alleviate the problem of abortion in their locality.

- ★ Take a pro-life stance where possible, making people aware of the issue and the scale of the problem.
- ★ Seek to offer post-abortion counselling.
- ★ Lobby the Government on the issue and the scale of the problem.
- ★ Joint in the pro-life national day of prayer, October 27th every year which is the day that abortion was decriminalized in the UK.
- ★ Offer financial support to those in the ministry of preserving life from conception.
- ★ Seek to understand the arguments, see above.

AFFIRMATION

The following is a list of churches, organizations or individuals who are taking action to alleviate abortion. They will, we believe, be able to offer practical and professional advice to assist you in your efforts to take action against abortion. (Please see appendix B.)

CARE FOR LIFE
PO BOX 389
SHERBORNE ST JOHN
BASINGSTOKE
RG24 9QF
TEL: 01256 477300
EMAIL: CFL@CARE.ORG.UK
WWW.PREGANCY.ORG.UK

IMAGE
COVERDALE CENTRE
COVERDALE CRESCENT
MANCHESTER
M12 4FG
TEL: 0161 273 8090
HELPLINE: 0161 273 8400
EMAIL: IMAGE@MCR1.POPTEL.ORG.UK
WWW.IMAGENET.ORG.UK

SOCIETY FOR THE PROTECTION OF UNBORN CHILDREN (SPUC)
PHYLLIS BOWMAN HOUSE
5 ST MATTHEW STREET
WESTMINSTER
LONDON
EW1P 2JT
TEL: 0207 222 5845
FAX: 0171 222 0630
EMAIL: ENQUIRY@SPUC.ORG.UK

Books that deal with the issue of abortion

071516578X, *Abortion and the Church*, No Definitive Author, CHP
0891076875, *Abortion Rites*, Olasky, CBUSA
0891098801, *In Defence of Life*, Fournier/Watkins, CBUSA
0232523088, *Practice of Abortion: A Critique*, Banner, DLT
0946680620, *Love Your Unborn Neighbour*, 7.99, SPUC
0880704721, *Prolife Answers to Prochoice Arguments*, Randy C. Alcorn, 7.50, MULTN

DEBT

Awareness

The following information is included to raise the social awareness and understanding of ministers/church leaders in relation to the contemporary issue of personal debt.

It is perhaps a paradox that the existence of the credit/loan industry is an indispensable contributor to national economic prosperity. By increasing the spending power of consumers, commercial sales will increase, the production consumer durables increase on demand and thus employment increases.

The increase in the credit/loan industry has also resulted in a social change. Frugality and thrift were once hallmarks of a responsible attitude to life. Save before you spend was the motto many people lived by. However, in contemporary society what was once considered "debt" is now called "credit" with advertisers convincing the masses that 'credit-worthiness' is prestigious. Buy now pay later has become today's motto. The pay later scenario is often at a high cost in interest or stress.

The sad reality for many people is prestigious credit-worthiness has become their prison and they have become a slave to debt. (See 2 Kig 4: 1) The heartlessness of the creditors system and the powerlessness of the debtor results in many individuals being "eternally bound to their creditors."

The growth of personal debt is an ever-increasing problem that is caused by the ease at which people can enter into an agreement for credit with financial institutions. When individuals fail to meet the repayment schedule these agreements are broken, the financial institutions then have a legal right to the money outstanding.

There are many reasons why people get into financial difficulty. These could be divorce, sickness, birth of a child, business failure, retirement, maternity leave, loss of overtime etc... or just plain bad financial management.

Many people will ignore their creditors' letters or telephone calls in the hope that their situation might improve, or something might turn up, or that their creditors will go away! But of course they never do.

Relationships can become strained due to the pressure and stress of juggling finances or 'robbing Peter to pay Paul'. The consequences of being in debt can lead to personal distress especially when there is the threat of harassment or little possibility of getting out of the debt. The distress can of course spill over into family life causing in many cases family break-up. Social isolation is inevitable when there is no money to socialize. Poverty in many cases is inevitable. In extreme cases even suicide may result.

Assessment

The following are some of the most up-to-date statistics in relation to the problem of debt. (Please see appendix A.)

Plastic Card Transactions: United Kingdom				
	1991	1994	1996	1998
Number of Transactions in Millions				
Debit Card	720	1,432	2,248	2,918
Credit Card	659	772	976	1,184
ATM	536	593	564	568
Charge Card	96	116	149	177
All Cards	2,011	2,609	3,938	4,847
Value of Transactions in Billions				
Debit Card	25	53	85	119
Credit Card	27	35	46	60
ATM	26	31	32	33
Charge Card	6	9	12	15
All Cards	85	128	175	228

Social Trends 30 © Crown Copyright 2000

The above table reveals that in the past 20 years plastic cards have become an increasingly popular means of acquiring cash and making purchases. Debit cards are used more than twice as often as credit cards. In 1998 there were 2.9 billion debit card transactions compared with 1.2 billion by credit card. The value of plastic card transactions has increased at a similar rate to the number of transactions, rising from £85 billion in 1991 to £228 billion in 1998.

The average value of a plastic card transaction in 1998 was £47.

Addressing

The following is a list of practical suggestions that may enable churches and organizations to take action that will alleviate the problem of debt in their locality.

> The key to preventing debt has to be education. Particularly for the younger generation, who are being taught to accept "credit-worthiness" as a rite of passage into social status.

> Run 'Financial Fitness' classes based upon the materials provided by the organizations listed below.

> Be prepared to offer interest-free loans. (Deu. 15: 7–8, Lev. 25: 35–37, Luke 6: 34–35)

> Provide free food parcels.

> Build a sharing "Koinonia" where material things, tools and skills can be used by all the members of a congregation. (See Acts 2: 42–27, 4: 32–35)

AFFIRMATION

The following is a list of churches, organizations or individuals who are taking action to alleviate debt. They will, we believe, be able to offer practical and professional advice to assist you in your efforts to take action against debt. (Please see appendix B.)

DEBT SOLUTIONS
HAVERING GRANGE CENTRE
HAVERING ROAD
ROMFORD
RM1 4HR
TEL: 01708 750 093
FAX: 01708 736 292
WEBSITE: WWW.DEBT-SOLUTIONS.CO.UK

CREDIT ACTION
6 REGENTS TERRACE
CAMBRIDGE
CB2 1AA
TEL: 01223 324034
FREEPHONE HELPLINE: 0800 591084

Books that deal with the issue of debt

1854243675, *Debt Free Living*, Burkett/Tondeur, MON
0842310045, *Getting Out of Debt*, Payton, TYN
0281050775, *Life After*, Northcott, SPCK
0551032162, *Making Life Rich Without Any Money*, Callaway, MPH

POVERTY

Awareness

The following information is included to raise the social awareness and understanding of ministers/church leaders in relation to contemporary issues.

The Bible has a lot to say about poverty: Deuteronomy 15.11 recognizes that, 'There will always be poor people in the land' but continues, 'Therefore I command you to be open-handed towards your brothers and towards the poor and needy in your land.' Many of Old Testament passages take up the plight of the poor and oppressed, the vulnerable of society (see Isaiah 3.13–15; Amos 2.6–7). Isaiah's prophecy (chapter 61) clearly describes Jesus' ministry: 'The Spirit of the Lord is on me, because he has anointed me to preach good news to the poor' (Lk 4.18). Jesus' compassion for the materially poor is expressed in many practical ways and is evident in his teachings (Lk 6.20–22). Ministering to the needy is recognized as a way of serving God (Mt 25.34–40). Paul encouraged Christians to contribute to the needs of the poor in the church (2 Cor 8.1–15), and such concern has been a cornerstone of the church's ministry to the world throughout its history

The feelings of a parent: "I hate being poor. I hate having to sit in the same room, having to save up for weeks on end to be able to go out for a night. I hate having to say no to the children. They're too young, they don't understand. I hate feeling inferior... It's depressing."

The early morning queue of people outside the Post Office waiting to collect their state benefit is a familiar scene on many of our high streets. Living for the next Giro has become a way of life for many people Fifty years of a welfare state has undoubtedly 'backfired' and left us with a 'dependency culture.' The theoretical debates over a definition of what it means to be living in poverty in the western world have simply served to distract from the central issue, which is the misery, that real people in Britain experience every day of the week.

Poverty has long been associated with the starving millions of Third World countries to whom the West sent their missionaries. Yet has always been and will continue in the twenty-first century to be a real problem for the West.

The unequal distribution of wealth from the industrial revolution resulted in the masses turning to the poorhouse for support. Beveridge's post-war promises of a Welfare State that would provide an acceptable standard of living for all its citizens continues to create confusion and debate over the issue of poverty. Just what is "an acceptable standard of living"? This statement can be defined in absolute terms or in relative terms.

Successive Governments have failed to offer any statistics on poverty in the UK. Preferring to refer to those living below the level of Income Support as being in poverty. This absolute definition of poverty, i.e. 'those living below the level of Income Support' basically eradicates the existence of poverty and exonerates the Government of any responsibility for those who choose to exclude themselves from receiving State benefits.

A relative definition of poverty compares the standard of living across society as is done when social scientists do when comparing the 'West and the Rest.' A relative definition prefers to view not as a lack of income but as a lack of access to resources without which the poor are excluded from normal society.

"Individuals, families and groups in the population can be said to be in poverty when they lack the resources to obtain the types of diet, participate in the activities and have the living conditions and amenities which are customary, or are at least widely encouraged or approved, in the societies to which they belong. Their resources are so seriously below those commanded by the average individual or family that they are in effect, excluded from ordinary living patterns, customs and activities."

TOWNSEND. P. (1979) © POVERTY IN THE UK, HARMONDSWORTH, PENGUIN

ASSESSMENT

The following are some of the most up-to-date statistics in relation to the problem of poverty. (Please see appendix A.)

People in poverty by personal, economic and family status in the UK: 1996–97

	Total number	Proportion poor	Number in poverty
Adult women	22.2m	24%	5.3m
Children	13.0m	35%	4.5m
Adult men	21.1m	20%	4.2m
Elderly	9.8m	31%	3.0m
Lone parent family	4.3m	63%	2.9m
Unemployed	4.6m	78%	2.3m
All	75.0m	25%	14.1m

SOURCE: DEPARTMENT OF SOCIAL SECURITY, 1998

Monitoring Poverty and Social Exclusion

In a different study to the one above, for 1997/8, the latest data available, the number of people on very low incomes (below 40% of average income) had risen by over a million to 8 million (after housing costs) in the two years to 1997/8. This represents an historic high. More than 2 million children still live in households where there is no adult in paid work.

In 1998/9 over two-thirds of heads of households in social housing did not have paid work, compared with one-third in other housing. More than a third of those in social housing live on weekly incomes of less than £100.

SOURCE: CATHERINE HOWARTH ET AL. *MONITORING POVERTY AND SOCIAL EXCLUSION*,
JOSEPH ROWNTREE FOUNDATION, 1999.

The Government has committed itself to annually assessing its progress in reducing poverty and social exclusion. In autumn 1999 the Government produced Opportunities for all: Tackling poverty and social exclusion. For the first time the Government has stated the statistical indicators by which its progress is to be judged.

ADDRESSING

The following is a list of practical suggestions that may enable churches and organizations to take action that will alleviate the problem of poverty in their locality.

- **The issue of poverty and the material divide that grows in Britain exists not only at Christmas time, but all year round. As poverty increases so does the 'door of opportunity' for the Church to reach out to despairing people in their communities.**

- **The Church cannot reduce the queue outside the Post Office and nor can we give money to every beggar however, we can reach out in social action to alleviate in some degree the despair of millions of people within our communities ensnared in poverty.**

"Dave and Julie were a young couple who lived for their next Giro. When the Lord brought them across our path, they sometimes lived on porridge for the few days before their social benefits were due. Our practical ministry of food provision opened a door of opportunity that led them both to the Lord and gave us the opening to teach them essential biblical skills for living. The Church has all the power of heaven on its side to impact the poor of its local communities. Churches are filled with an army of people who could teach from personal experience, parenting and household management skills. The doors of church buildings that are shut five or six days a week could be opened to offer cheap and affordable child care provision for the many despondent people in our communities whom God has called us to reach with His love."

© JOY DEC 1998 JOE HAYES

- **In many respects our social security system has robbed millions of people of their dignity, locking them into dependency upon the welfare system and thus demoralizing them by inferring they "sponge off society." The people of this age of independence find it so hard to ask but they need our help.**

- **Being caught in poverty, whatever definition is used is not a pleasant place for anyone to be. Local churches cannot alleviate the emotional and physical pain of the many millions caught in poverty. They can however, make a difference in their locality.**

- ✦ A key to alleviating individual or family poverty has to be education.
- ✦ Run "Financial Fitness" classes based upon the materials provided by the organizations listed below.
- ✦ Be prepared to offer interest free loans. (Deu 15: 7–8, Lev 25: 35–37, Lk 6: 34–35)
- ✦ Provide free food parcels.
- ✦ Offer practical help in the home, with cooking, cleaning and decorating. This ministry will help restore personal dignity.
- ✦ Build a sharing "Koinonia" where material things, tools and skills can be used by all the members of a congregation. (See Acts 2: 42–27, 4: 32–35)

Affirmation

The following is a list of churches, organizations or individuals who are taking action to alleviate poverty. They will, we believe, be able to offer practical and professional advice to assist you in your efforts to take action against poverty. (Please see appendix B.)

TURNABOUT TRUST
WINTERS
SHOPLAND ROAD
ROCHFORD
SS4 1LH
TEL: 01702 542 564
EMAIL: TURNTYER@TTTT.EVESHAM.NET

CHRISTIAN CONCERN
ST PAUL'S COMMUNITY RESOURCE CENTRE
HIGHTOWN
CREWE
CW1 3BY
TEL: 01270 586 186
FAX: 01270 250 683

CHURCH ACTION ON POVERTY
CENTRAL BUILDINGS
OLDHAM STREET
MANCHESTER
M1 1JT
TEL: 0161 236 9321
FAX: 0161 237 5459
WEBSITE: WWW.CHURCH-POVERTY.ORG.UK

CHILD POVERTY ACTION GROUP
94 WHITE LION STREET
LONDON
N1 9PF
TEL: 0207 837 797979
WEBSITE: WWW.CPAD.ORG.UK

Books that deal with the issue of poverty

0340694467, *Rich Christians in an age of hunger*, R. Sider, Hodder & Stoughton
1880240283, *Street Children*, Butcher, Word
1854244357, *Mustard Seed vs McWorld*, Sine, MON
Poor Have Faces, Ronsvalle, Baker

HOMELESSNESS

Awareness

The following information is included to raise the social awareness and understanding of ministers in relation to contemporary issues.

Beyond the major cities and the media attention at Christmas time, the homeless can be found all year round almost everywhere. Beyond the solitary beggar on many high streets thousands of young people can be found under bridges or cardboard boxes up and down the country. Most of the homeless are hidden from our sight and only come into view when politicians attempt to deal with the problem.

Most homeless people are not drunks or drug abusers or former mental patients. Most are able or willing to work. They are not the perpetual social problem many people believe they are. So who are the homeless?

© G. Bamley (1988) suggests several categories of homeless people in Britain;

1. People literally without a roof over their head, including those regularly sleeping rough, newly arrived migrants, victims of fire, flood, severe harassment or violence, and others.
2. People in accommodation specifically provided on a temporary basis to the homeless (hostels, bed and breakfast accommodation etc.).
3. People with insecure or impermanent tenures: this includes other ('self-referred') hotel or bed and breakfast residents, licensees and those in holiday lets, those in tied occupations who change job, tenants under notice to quit, squatters and licensed occupiers of short-life housing, and owner-occupiers experiencing mortgage foreclosure.
4. People shortly to be released from institutionalized accommodation, including prisons, detention centers, psychiatric hospitals, community or foster homes, and other hostels, who have no existing alternative accommodation or household to join.
5. Households which are sharing accommodation involuntarily.
6. Individuals or groups living within existing households where either (i) relationships with the rest of the household, or (ii) living conditions, are highly unsatisfactory and intolerable for any extended period.
7. Individuals or groups living within existing households whose relationships and conditions are tolerable but where the individual groups concerned have a clear preference to live separately, including cases where the 'potential' household is currently split but would like to live together.

© BAMLEY G. (1988) *THE DEFINITION AND MEASUREMENT OF HOMELESSNESS*

Why do people become homeless?

The following are some of the reasons given to local councils for homelessness:

- ☆ **My house was attached to my job.**
- ☆ **My partner was violent.**
- ☆ **We got behind with the mortgage when interest rates went up.**
- ☆ **I got ill and couldn't keep up the payments.**
- ☆ **The landlord wanted us out, he had other tenants who could pay more.**

☆ **I have been released from an institution (hospital or prison).**

☆ **I am a refugee.**

☆ **My parent's don't have any room.**

☆ **I was staying with a friend and they asked me to go.**

THE ABOVE IS TAKEN FROM THE © HOUSING AND INFORMATION PACK PROVIDED BY THE CATHOLIC HOUSING AID SOCIETY)

The following is an insight into the mind of a homeless person.

Homelessness

"You passed me by on your way to the theatre the other day; head up, shoulders stiff, eyes looking straight ahead at some imaginary destination deep in the distance. What did you think I was going to do? Mug you with my cardboard begging box?

You pretended not to see me on your way to the play, though your friend cast me a coin to scrub my unwanted image from his eyes. What was the play about I wonder? Did it give you good conversation on your way home past my bed?

Don't get me wrong. I wouldn't dream to trespass on your time, or deny your pleasure in your hard-earned recreation. All I ask is that your eyes acknowledge my existence next time you pass this way,

So if you step on my toes again beneath my grubby blanket you'll realize that you've done it, instead of simply passing by."

LAVERIC JOHN (A HOMELESS MAN) (© NEW STATESMAN AND SOCIETY, NOVEMBER, 1989, P.21)

ASSESSMENT

The following are some of the most up-to-date statistics in relation to the problem of homelessness. (Please see appendix A.)

To fix a definite figure on the number of people is perhaps impossible, because not all case are reported, however the follow statistics should give a rough estimate of the continuing size of the problem of homelessness. Although there is a clear reduction in the past five years the problem is still very real for many people.

Year	Total Decisions	Unintentionally homeless and in Priority need	Intentionally homeless and in Priority need	Homeless but not in Priority need
1994	269,630	118,490	5,080	65,990
1995	271,500	117,490	4,920	65,430
1996	263,900	113,590	5,070	60,950
1997	242,750	102,410	4,970	58,010
1998	246,600	105,840	6,120	54,470
1999	62,870	27,720	1,870	13,850

SOURCE: © DETR HOMELESSNESS STATISTICS

In the third quarter of 1999 (ending September 1999) local authorities made a total of 62,870 decisions on applications for housing from households eligible under the homeless provisions of the 1985 and 1996 Housing Acts. This is roughly 6% more than in the second quarter of 1999. The DETR state it is usual for the number of decisions to increase between the second and third quarter of the same year.

Estimate of the number of rough sleepers in a single night street count for 30 towns with the highest number of rough sleepers in England – June 1998 & 1999

Local Authority District	June 1998	June 1999
Westminster	237	234
Camden	59	66
Oxford	39	52
Lambeth	20	46
Manchester	31	44
Birmingham	56	43
Brighton and Hove	44	43
City of London	41	36
Bristol	42	32
Nottingham City	14	31
Stoke-on-Trent	20	31
Liverpool	17	30
Kensington and Chelsea	23	28
Southwark	31*	26
Chester	21*	26
Croydon	25	25
Cambridge	30	21
Waltham Forest	0*	20
Slough	12	20
Gloucester	16	20
Brent	29	19
Exeter	27	19
Bournemouth	44	18
York	12	18
Ealing	24	18
Leeds	8	17
Penwith	17	17
Richmond upon Thames	12	16
Hammersmith and Fulham	11	16
Watford	0*	15

SOURCE: © ROUGH SLEEPER'S UNIT PRESS RELEASE 15.12.99

*All figures are from single night street counts except those that are local authority estimates prior to undertaking a count.

Homelessness is one of the most acute signs of housing shortages. In 1998, a total of 166,430 households were officially recognized as homeless by local authorities in England. Shelter estimates that this represents about 400,000 people.

This figure is only the tip of the iceberg. It does not include most of the 41,000 people who are living in hostels and squats, or the 78,000 couples or lone parents sharing accommodation who cannot afford to set up a home on their own (England and Wales).

People from minority ethnic groups are over-represented among homeless households. In 1997, 56% of households accepted as homeless by local authorities in inner London were from ethnic minorities.

Furthermore, Shelter housing advice centres around the country are reporting instances where local authorities are re-housing homeless households directly through the housing register rather than recording them as homeless applicants. This means that homelessness figures are understated and are not reflecting the real problem of homelessness and housing need.

A new Shelter report found that two thirds of young people who sought assistance in the three areas covered in the research* had either slept out the night before, had nowhere to go that night or were threatened with imminent homelessness.

During 1997/98, 25% of Shelter's clients were young people under 25. Of these 80% had experienced homelessness.

Shelter estimates that around 2,000 people are sleeping on the street on any one night.

Addressing

The following is a list of practical suggestions that may enable churches and organizations to take action that will alleviate the problem of homelessness in their locality.

* Seek to change attitudes toward them. If people think that they are human debris, if people assume that they will always be living in the street and in shelters, people will probably also believe that any help you might give would be a wasted effort. Homeless people are individuals and families who Jesus reached out to with his love often stopping and talking to the beggar.

* On a practical level, the church could run or get involved in "Soup & Sandwich Runs."

* Empty church buildings could be opened for Job Clubs, Health Check-ups, free haircuts or the provision of lunches and clothes.

* Church members could be encouraged to lobby the Government on housing policy, as there are almost 750,000 council dwellings vacant in England alone.

* Year-long monitoring via agencies in three areas – Lincolnshire, Crawley, Sheffield.

Affirmation

The following is a list of churches, organizations or individuals who are taking action to alleviate homelessness. They will, we believe, be able to offer practical and professional advice to assist you in your efforts to take action against homelessness. (Please see appendix B.)

SHAFTESBURY HOMELESS PROJECT
LENA FOX HOUSE
41 CRIMSCOTT STREET
BERMONDSEY
LONDON
SE1 5TE
TEL: 0207 237 1286
EMAIL:
LENAFOXHOUSE@SHAFTESBURYSOC.CO.UK

BARNABUS PROJECT
102 IRLAM ROAD
FLIXTON
MANCHESTER
M41 6JT
TEL: 0161 748 4858/0161 950 6936
FAX: 0161 747 7379

ADULLAM HOMES HOUSING ASSOCIATION
GORDANA HOUSE
THE MOUNT
SHELTON
SHREWSBURY
SY3 8BH
TEL: 01743 365 050
FAX: 01743 365 070

OASIS TRUST
87 BLACKFRIARS ROAD
LONDON
SE1 8HA
TEL: 0207 928 9422
FAX: 0171 928 6770
EMAIL: OASISTRUST@COMPUSERVE.COM
WWW.OASISTRUST.ORG

NIGHTSTOP
ROOM 5
NORTHAM COMMUNITY CENTRE
KENT STREET
NORTHAM
SOUTHAMPTON
SO14 5SP
TEL: 02380 234188
THEY OFFER TRAINING FOR HOST FAMILIES WILLING TO TAKEN IN YOUNG VULNERABLE HOMELESS PEOPLE

Books that deal with the issue of homelessness:

1561791326, *As You Leave Home*, Jerry Jenkins, £10.50

080105897X, *Prodigals And those Who Love Them*, Graham, £7.99

0745940544, *Far From Home*, C. Nonhebel, £9.99

MENTAL ILLNESS

AWARENESS

The following information is included to raise the social awareness and understanding of ministers in relation to the contemporary issue of mental illness.*

Mental health problems are a leading course of illness, distress and disability. Mental illness accounted for 18,286 recorded deaths in 1991, with suicide being a significant cause of premature death. Mental illness is hard to define as an entity, as there are many varied forms of mental illness. The Department of Health has provided a guide to the symptoms associated with mental illness, such that according to the Mental Health Act mental illness means an illness having one of the following symptoms or characteristics:

1. More than a temporary impairment in intellectual functions shown by a failure of memory, orientation, comprehension and learning capacity.
2. More than a temporary alteration of mood of such degree as to give rise to the patient having a delusional appraisal of his situation, his past or his future, or that of others or to the lack of any appraisal.
3. Delusional beliefs, persecutory, jealous or grandiose.
4. Abnormal perceptions associated with delusional misinterpretations of events. This would include hearing voices or seeing things that are not there.
5. Thinking so disordered as to prevent the patient making a reasonable appraisal of his situation or having a reasonable communication with others.

There are various broad categories of mental illness, very broadly speaking there are psychiatric disorders of childhood and adolescence, then there are general adulthood mental illnesses and lastly there are the mental illnesses of the elderly. Mental health problems of general adulthood could occur in childhood and could also occur in the elderly. For the purposes of this paper I will restrict myself to mental illnesses of general adulthood. This can be divided under very broad headings of:

1. Psychotic disorders
2. Mood disorders
3. Anxiety disorders
4. Personality disorders
5. Substance-related disorders

The most constant feature of mental illness is that the symptoms cause severe distress either to the individual, himself or herself and/or to others and the second constant feature is that the functioning of an individual i.e. personal self care, social functioning, occupational functioning or academic functioning is disturbed.

Psychotic disorders are characterized by impaired reality testing, basically an inability to differentiate reality from fantasy. A patient who is psychotic is not able to distinguish between what is real and what is not. The three most common

* Thanks to Dr M. Kolisang, Consultant Psychiatrist for his contributions to this section

features of the psychotic disorder would be:

1. Hallucinations i.e. hearing voices or seeing things, basically perceiving a stimulus that is not there and that is not shared by others.
2. Delusions, which are firm fixed false beliefs, which are held to, even in the presence of the evidence to the contrary, which do not form part of a person's culture or sub-culture. There are various types of delusions.
3. Disturbed or disorganized speech, so that the person does not make sense in what they say.

The most common psychotic disorder is schizophrenia, which impairs the most basic functions that give people a feeling of individuality, uniqueness and self-direction (creating the reality boundary). It can present with the above mentioned psychotic symptoms, in addition it can present with negative symptoms i.e. lack of drive, lack of motivation and poverty of speech and disturbed behaviour. There are other psychotic disorders which are not schizophrenia.

Mood disorder

These disorders are characterized by profound changes in mood, either severe depression with a reduction in levels of activity or elation in mood with over activity or hyperactivity. These changes in mood are outside the normal variations of mood, which occur in everybody and they are associated with clinical distress and impairment of functioning. Clinical depression is a severe illness which is very costly in terms of poor quality of life, lost working hours, severely affected interpersonal relationships and other inconveniences to life. People who are clinically depressed cannot just 'snap' out of it or get their act together, they need professional and spiritual help.

Anxiety disorders

Everyone experiences some form of anxiety at some stage in their life (a diffuse unpleasant vague sense of apprehension) often accompanied by autonomic symptoms, such as headache, perspiration, palpitations, tightness in the chest, mild stomach discomfort and restlessness, as indicated by an inability to sit or stand still for along time. The particular constellation of symptoms present during anxiety tends to vary among people. Anxiety is an alerting signal; it warns of impending danger and enables the person to take measures to deal with the threat. Fear is a similar alerting signal, but should be differentiated from anxiety. Fear is a response to a known external definite or non-conflictual threat. Anxiety is a response to a threat that is unknown, internal vague or conflictual. Anxiety disorders make up one of the most common groups of psychiatric disorders. One national study in America showed that one in four people has met the diagnostic criteria for at least one anxiety disorder. Women are more likely to have an anxiety disorder than men. Examples of anxiety disorders include: generalized anxiety disorder, panic disorder with or without agoraphobia, post traumatic stress disorder, obsessive compulsive disorder, specific disorder with social phobia as one of its sub groups. One may also experience anxiety disorder due to a general medical illness e.g. asthma. Alcohol and other illicit drugs can induce severe anxiety in the long term.

Personality disorders

These are defined as enduring subjective experiences and behaviour that deviate from the cultural standards which are rigidly pervasive, have an onset in adolescence or in adulthood, are stable through time and lead to unhappiness and impairment. These disorders lead to severe inflexible and often distressing patterns of behaviour. People with personality disorders are more likely to refuse help and to deny that they have problems, than are people with other psychiatric disorders.

Mental illnesses have been stigmatized for a long time. They have been attributed to various causes including demon possession, personal weakness, faulty parenting and upbringing and a host of other causes. As a result one often finds people who are mentally ill, but who will not go for help because once it is known that they are mentally ill or they receive psychiatric treatment they may feel stigmatized. In Britain and Europe mental illness is more accepted as an illness that needs treatment, but in the Christian community one still finds people who have serious problems, who will not go for help and even if they do, they often resist taking treatment, stating that prayer alone would do. Mental illness although different in its manifestation from physical illnesses like hypertension is still an illness that needs assessment and treatment; as it is not wise for a person suffering from diabetes not to take their insulin it is similarly not wise for someone who is suffering from schizophrenia to refuse medication as their symptoms will get worse and their ability to function will deteriorate.

It is important to mention at this stage that there are no known causes for most major mental illnesses. A lot of effort has gone into research to identify the causes of mental illness. Through research some changes that occur in the brain e.g. chemical imbalances have been associated with some illnesses. It is highly possible that some illnesses may have their root in a spiritual problem like any other physical illness (e.g. unresolved hurts or unforgiveness).

It is very important that one exercises great caution when suspecting a spiritual problem. Because of the many developments in the field of psychiatry many effective drugs (medication) have been developed which have radically changed the course of mental illnesses. The prognosis of many disorders is much better and the quality of life of many patients has improved significantly.

Assessment

The following are some of the most up-to-date statistics in relation to the problem of mental illness. (Please see appendix A.)
NHS out-patient, community and day care contacts for people with mental illness.

England and Wales	Thousands			
Consultant Outpatient	1987–88	1992–93	1996–97	1997–98
New Attendances	219	238	304	312
Total Attendances	1712	1928	2225	2262
Day case finished consultant episodes	—	1	2	1
First patient contacts with clinical psychology and community nurse				
Community learning disability nursing	—	43	56	59
Clinical psychology service	—	191	244	257
Community psychiatric nursing	—	430	600	618
First attendance at NHS day care facilities				
Mental illness	—	60	71	68
Old age psychiatry	—	28	41	43
Child and adolescent psychiatry	—	3	2	2

SOCIAL TRENDS 30 © CROWN COPYRIGHT 2000

The above table reveals that in England and Wales over 300,000 new out-patient attendances for psychiatric specialties in 1997–98, an increase of over 40% since 1987–88. The increase is of course as a result of government policy that mental illness is cared for in the community.

Summary of key findings by MIND in a survey of the stigma, taboos and discrimination experienced by people with mental health problems:

- **A third of people (34%) said they had been dismissed or forced to resign from jobs**
- **69% of people had been put off applying for jobs for fear of unfair treatment**
- **Almost half (47%) the people had been abused or harassed in public, and 14% had been physically attacked**
- **A quarter (25%) of people felt at risk of attack inside their own homes**
- **26% of people were forced to move home because of harassment**
- **Almost a quarter (24%) of parents said their children had been teased or bullied, or that they were afraid it would happen**
- **25% of people had been turned down by insurance or finance companies**
- **Half (50%) of people felt unfairly treated by general health care services**
- **A third (33%) complained that their OP had treated them unfairly**
- **45% of people thought that discrimination had increased in the last five years compared with 18% who thought it had decreased**

THE ABOVE IS AN EXTRACT FROM *NOT JUST STICKS & STONES* BY JIM READ AND SUE BAKER, NOVEMBER 1996, PUBLISHED BY MIND. ©

Suicide is often a result of mental illness, statistical in the UK deaths by suicide is as common as deaths from road traffic accidents. Which means over 5,000 people a year in England alone take their own life an average of one every two hours. 10% of people with schizophrenia eventually die from suicide, 15% of suicides are a result of depression, a similar number commit suicide as a result of dependence upon alcohol or other drugs. The suicide rate for young men between 15 and 24 years old rose by 75% at the beginning of the 90s.

Addressing

The following is a list of practical suggestions that may enable churches and organizations to take action that will alleviate the problem of mental illness in their locality.

Mental health services are well distributed all over the country, every hospital has a psychiatric department and every community has a community psychiatric department (community mental health teams). Most general practitioners have had some form of training in psychiatry and should be able to pick some of the symptoms and either treat them themselves or refer them to psychiatric services.

However some people do get missed or overlooked. For those people who have been diagnosed as suffering from a psychiatric disorder they need to feel accepted and supported in their communities and churches. People should not fear that they will be told that they have a spiritual problem if they are mentally ill. Similarly people should not be discouraged from taking their treatment on the basis that they are Christians.

There are various things churches could do to help people with mental disorders. Firstly, recognize the resources that are already available in the community and use them appropriately. Such resources include community mental health centers, community mental health day centers, non-governmental organizations like MIND, National Schizophrenic Fellowship and other supportive organizations.

Some churches have established a support group for people with specific mental illnesses within their congregations. An example which comes to mind is the eating disorder support group at the Rhema church in South Africa. The aim of such support groups would be to provide an ongoing support, allowing people who are ill to discuss and share their problems in a supportive environment. Such groups could meet practical needs like giving advice or referring people to agencies that can provide advice and help with benefits and other needs.

If the mentally ill people do have dependants the churches can also play a great role in supporting the dependants by giving them counselling and support, especially during times of crisis.

Finally churches could help in the fight to de-stigmatize mental illness by letting people know that it is not wrong to have a mental illness. It is often not their fault. What is important is what one does to improve their health and to make sure that they live as healthily as possible. The government has committed itself to improve the mental health of the nation by improving the mental health service provision. To this effect they have committed large amounts of money and resources to dealing with this problem.

Structures are being improved or developed to ensure that treatment is easily accessible. One of the targets is to reduce suicide. The research has shown that a large number of people who do commit suicide have an underlying mental health problem. The majority of people who commit suicide have seen their General Practitioner recently. Also the majority of people who commit suicide have voiced their intentions to do so indirectly or directly for a number of months before doing so. Therefore it is important for people to try and take a preventative action when someone voices suicidal intentions i.e. provide support and refer to an organization or agency that could help.

> "Unfortunately the stigma associated with serious mental illness continues to influence people's attitudes, the social stigma that refers to the mentally ill as 'mad', 'lunatics' or as 'nutters', and the media's representation of the schizophrenic as 'dangerous' 'violent' 'murderers let loose on our streets', only serves to isolate the mentally ill further and widen the gap of mistrust. The Royal College of Psychiatrists have pointed out that suffers of schizophrenia are one hundred times more likely to kill themselves than others.*

The challenge facing the Christian community is to avoid these patronizing and prejudice social stereotypes of the mentally ill.

Regrettably at times preachers have added to this stigmatization by claiming the mentally ill are demon-possessed. The manifestations of serious mental illness are not necessarily a revelation that a person is demonized! The result of the church's stigmatizing of the mentally ill is that they and those they are dependent upon will simply stay away or those in the church with serious mental illness will suffer in silence, which often preludes many suicides.

Pastors and church counselors would do well to accept when they are out of their depth and rely on community resources such as Community Mental Health Teams and charities such as Mind or the National Schizophrenic Fellowship.

Those suffering serious mental illness and their families need to be loved, accepted and supported in the Christian community rather than ostracized and isolated. Often they need to be assured that their illness is most likely through no fault of their own. Telling a mentally ill person to "Snap out of it" or "Pull yourself together" just does not help."

TAKEN FROM AN ARTICLE BY JOE HAYES © 2001

AFFIRMATION

The following is a list of churches, organizations or individuals who are taking action to alleviate problems of mental illness. They will, we believe, be able to offer practical and professional advice to assist you in your efforts to minister to the mentally ill. (Please see appendix B.)

---

* © *Homicide by Mental Ill People*, by The Royal College of Psychiatrists.

TURNING POINT
NEWLOOM HOUSE
101 BACKCHURCH LANE
LONDON E1 1LU
TEL: 0207 702 2300

YOUNG MINDS
102-108 CLERKENWELL ROAD
LONDON EC1M 5SA
TEL: 0207 336 8445

MANIC DEPRESSION FELLOWSHIP
8-10 HIGH ST
KINGSTON UPON THAMES
SURRY KT1 1EY
TEL: 020 77932600
EMAIL: MDF@MDF.ORG.UK
WEBSITE: WWW.MDF.ORG.UK

MIND
(NATIONAL ASSOCIATION FOR MENTAL HEALTH)
15 STRATFORD BROADWAY
LONDON
E15 4BQ
TEL: 0208 5192122

GUIDEPOSTS TRUST LTD
TWO RIVERS
STATION LANE
WITNEY
OX8 6BH
TEL: 01993 772 886
FAX: 01993 778 160
EMAIL: GPT@GUIDEPOSTS.ORG.UK

THE MATTHEW TRUST
PO BOX 604
LONDON
SW6 3AG
TEL: 0207 736 5976
FAX: 0171 731 6961

POST GREEN COMMUNITY TRUST
SPARROW'S NEST
AST HOLTEN FARM
HOLTEN HEATH
POOLE
BH16 6JN
TEL: 01202 622 317
FAX: 01202 632 632
EMAIL: 1C0275.373@COMPUSERVE.COM

Books dealing with the issue of mental illness:

0950604259, *Breakdowns Are Good For You*, Robert Law, £9.95
0830723285, *Finding Hope Again*, Neil Anderson, £8.99
0800755561, *Healing The Scars Of Emotional Abuse*, Greg Jantz, £5.99
1852400528, *Healing Through Deliverance*, P. Horrobin, £9.99
0281050961, *Unwanted Guest*, J. Robertson, £6.99
0891078053, *Under His Wings: Mentally Disabled*, Robert Bittner, £8.99, Publisher CBUSA

EATING DISORDERS

AWARENESS

The following information is included to raise the social awareness and understanding of ministers and church leaders in relation to the contemporary issue of eating disorders.*

Eating disorders can be frightening patterns which may appear gradually over a period of time as a way of coping with life, but which very quickly take control, leaving the sufferer feeling as if there is no escape.

Women are more like to suffer from eating disorders than men. Often considered an adult problem, eating disorders often begin in teenage years while the sufferer is still living at home.

Anorexia

Anorexia means loss of appetite however, those who suffer this eating disorder have a normal appetite; they drastically seek to control their appetite.

Anorexics fear getting fat, they deliberately under-eat, they excessively lose weight, putting themselves through vigorous exercise programs and often monthly periods stop.

Anorexia effects one in every one hundred and fifty fifteen-year-old girls. They are predominately girls from professional type families and often other members of the family have a history of eating disorder problems.

Anorexia often begins with normal dieting, most anorexics are overweight before they begin dieting. Anorexics continue wanting to lose weight when their normal weight is achieved. Anorexics continue to eat quantities of fruit, vegetables and salads while taking in very few calories, continuing excessive exercise and taking sliming pills. Despite the eating disorder anorexics can have an obsessive interest in food and preparing it for others.

Bulimia

Bulimia occurs more among women in their early to mid-twenties who have been overweight as a child; many anorexics develop signs of bulimia using laxatives and vomiting to control their weight. The difference between anorexics displaying signs of bulimia is anorexics continue to have a very low weight while the weight of those suffering solely from bulimia fluctuates.

Bulimics like anorexics have a fear of getting fat, they also however, binge eat, abuse laxatives and induce vomiting, their weight can stay normal and their periods become irregular.

Around one in one hundred women suffer bulimia at some stage in their life.

* Thanks to Kainos Trust for their contributions to this section

Bulimics manage to maintain a normal weight because of binge eating and vomiting or laxative abuse. A bulimics weight can go up or down by around 10lb in a very short period of time.

The symptoms of bulimia trap many women in a vicious circle of guilt and depression, binge eating and vomiting.

Consequences of self-induced starvation; broken sleep patterns, constipation, regular difficulty with concentrating, depression, feeling cold, brittle bones, muscles wastage and finally death.

Consequences of self-induced vomiting; acids from the stomach destroy the enamel on teeth, swollen salivary glands cause a puffy face, irregular heart beat, kidney damage and epileptic fits.

Consequences of laxative abuse; continual stomach pains, swollen fingers and the possibility of long-term constipation due to bowel muscles being damaged.

The reasons why eating disorders develop vary from the social pressure to be thin, the self satisfaction from being able to control one's weight, problems during puberty, family tensions, depression or an emotional upset.

The following extracts from © Helena Wilkinson's book *Beyond Chaotic Eating*, describes a little of the battle of eating disorders.

Ever-Downward Spiral

The anorexic has a fear of weighing more than a certain weight (which is below average for her age and height). Sometimes anorexics believe in a 'magical' weight at which they consider that everything will be OK. When they achieve this weight and discover that nothing has changed they set another 'goal'. The pattern continues in an ever-downward spiral. The anorexic weighs herself frequently; the scales consistently tell lies. When she looks in the mirror a huge flabby figure stares back at her and her face, filled with horror, gives away how much she detests the sight. She examines herself with great precision. Her hands glide over her body searching for sharp angular bones. As her fingers feel the hardness she is reassured, but it is still not quite good enough.

Not eating causes restlessness and over-activity. The anorexic wakes early in the morning ready to move. She develops frantic exercise programs pushing her body to physical extremes. Exercise involves discipline and not only keeps her weight down but rids her of guilt and helps her to feel warmer without eating more. As with fasting, excessive exercise releases endorphins in the brain which causes the anorexic to feel 'high'.

Soon the anorexic begins to develop rituals dictating that things must be done in a certain order at a certain time. She becomes obsessive and often very concerned with cleanliness and tidiness. There is intense self-hatred when she fails to keep the harsh rules she has imposed. She can't allow herself to enjoy life and feels guilty when she does. Her body must not rest. She denies herself things which others consider to be the basics of life, calling them luxuries. She is hard-working, determined and very competitive. She buries herself in work, partly because achievement is so important and partly so that she has less time to eat. She becomes obsessively concerned with what other people think of her.

Dying on the Inside

The bulimic only appears to be confident; underneath she doubts herself and feels that she has failed. Her moods swing from despair to elation in a very short time. Charlotte looked healthy enough, she could laugh and smile, but on the inside she was dying. 'I was standing watching my friends enjoying themselves – watching but never fully joining in.'

At times the bulimic can eat a normal meal without getting rid of the food. On other occasions she feels overcome by guilt and chooses to induce vomiting. She may starve herself all day and then crave food in the evening or raid the fridge in the middle of the night. The foods she buys for binges are those which she usually avoids eating. Sometimes her desperation to binge and vomit is so great that she doesn't care what she eats. Raw vegetables, raw meat, dry cereal, sweet, savoury and half-cooked foods are all crammed in one after the other at great speed. Packets are ripped open and there is an urgency in her eating. The amount of calories consumed in one binge can be equal to what most people would eat in ten days, sometimes more. Her bingeing and vomiting may occur only twice a week or twenty times in a day. However frequently the pattern occurs it is usually her need for release of tension, rather than hunger, which drives her to binge.

After her binge she feels heavy, her stomach is distended as though it may burst open. She is hot and sweaty. She forces herself to vomit until she is sure that all the food has gone and she can return to a comforting state of emptiness. She feels tired and numb, but relaxed. Her bingeing and vomiting concludes with carefully cleaning the bathroom, tidying up and washing herself. Often after this she collapses exhausted. She must not let anyone know about her dreadful secret.

Sometimes the bulimic feels disgusted by what she does and vows that she will never do it again. In a fit of desperation she forgets her promise and repeats the cycle. At other times there is a love-hate relationship: whilst she is disgusted that she could be capable of such behaviour, there is also a sense of excitement.

Bulimia is very hard for family and friends to detect. Large amounts of food disappearing, money struggles, increased eating without weight gain, visiting the bathroom regularly after meals, spending a long time in the bathroom and fluctuations in weight can all be signs.

The bulimic may appear to have a puffy face due to swelling of the salivary glands, and be prone to throat infections. Perpetual vomiting can cause the esophagus to bleed, and the enamel on her teeth to erode. A disturbance in the balance of electrolytes (potassium, sodium, magnesium and calcium, etc) affects both the bulimic and the anorexic. This can cause muscle weakness, numbness, kidney failure, and an erratic heartbeat. In a small number of people it can result in epileptic fits or the heart stopping beating. Anemia or a decreased white blood cell count can also occur.

Some bulimics and anorexics resort to taking laxatives to get rid of the guilt of eating or to 'cleanse' themselves. The body becomes used to relying on the laxatives and they cease to be as effective, forcing the sufferer to increase the amount. In addition she may use diuretics to get rid of water and so feel lighter. Abuse of laxatives can result in abdominal pain, nausea, muscle spasms, and chest pain. The weight loss is nearly all fluid and yet the sufferer feels panic-stricken if forced to give up her addiction.

When anyone with an eating disorder becomes desperate enough for food or laxatives, but cannot afford them, they may turn to shoplifting. In addition, they may alter their behaviour in ever more harmful ways. Drug and alcohol abuse is not uncommon in people with eating disorders, but it is more often the bulimic who turns to this additional form of addiction.[5] Self-harm is also more common in the bulimic. Cutting or burning herself is frequently misunderstood as attention-seeking. But usually it is done in secret and is a way of releasing tension and suppressed feelings, or a way of enabling the sufferer to feel 'alive'. Sometimes people can become addicted to the shot of adrenalin which self-harm causes. Other forms of self-harm which are adopted by all types of sufferers are: bruising; biting; scratching; pulling out her hair; purposely getting very cold. Overdoses which are not serious suicide attempts are also taken as an expression of self-harm.

References

4. M. Duker and R. Slade, *Anorexia Nervosa and Bulimia: How to Help* (Open University Press, Milton Keynes, 1988).
5. J. Yager, H. E. Gwirtwman and C. K. Edelstein (eds), *Special Problems in Managing Eating Disorders* (American Psychiatric Press, Washington, DC, 1992).

M. LAWRENCE (ED), *FED UP AND HUNGRY*, THE WOMEN'S PRESS

ASSESSMENT

The following are some of the most up-to-date statistics in relation to the issue of eating disorders. (Please see appendix A.)

- At any one time there are an estimated 60,000 people with eating disorders in the UK. One in ten sufferers are male but the majority are young women.
- Anorexia nervosa affects 1–2% of the UK female population between the ages of 15 and 30 and of these between six and ten of every one hundred patients die as a result of their disorder. The report states: "The crude mortality rate for anorexia nervosa at 20 years follow-up may be as high as 15–20%". (p.8)

BMA REPORT INTO EATING DISORDERS. *EATING DISORDERS BODY IMAGE AND THE MEDIA*, PRICE £7.95 FROM BMJ BOOKSHOP

ADDRESSING

The following is a list of practical suggestions that may enable churches and organizations to minister effectively to those who have suffer from eating disorders.

- ☆ Be understanding, the cause of the disorder is because a person does not feel understood and want to be loved.

- ☆ Be aware that parents and those close to a person with an eating disorder may be the first to notice the problem.

- ☆ Be prepared to be supported by statutory service such as GPs and hospitals, don't get out of your depth when counselling.

AFFIRMATION

The following is a list of churches, organizations or individuals who are ministering to those who suffer from eating disorders. They will, we believe, be able to offer practical and professional advice to assist. (Please see appendix B.)

KAINOS TRUST
THE LOWER GEORGE HOUSE
HIGH ST
NEWNHAM-ON-SEVEN
GLOUCESTERSHIRE
GL14 1BS
TEL: 01594 516284
WEBSITE: WWW.KAINOSTRUST.CO.UK

ANOREXIA & BULIMIA CARE
P.O BOX
ORMSKIRK
L39 5JR
TEL: 01695 422479
WEBSITE: WWW.ANOREXIABULIMIACARE.CO.UK
HELPFUL WORLD WIDE WEB SITES. BBC ONLINE SITE AN EXCELLENT EATING DISORDERS MESSAGE BOARD ON THE BBC ONLINE SITE. WHEN REGISTERING REMEMBER YOU DO NOT HAVE TO USE YOUR REAL NAME.

WWW.BBC.CO.UK/HEALTH/FEATURES/EATING_DISORDERS.SHTML INFORMATIVE BBC SITE ON EATING DISORDERS

WWW.MIND.ORG.UK MIND (NATIONAL ASSOCIATION FOR MENTAL HEALTH)

WWW.COUNSELLING.CO.UK THE BRITISH ASSOCIATION FOR COUNSELLING WEBSITE

WWW.CAFAMILY.ORG.UK CONTACT A FAMILY IS AN ORGANIZATION HELPING FAMILIES WITH CHILDREN WITH DISABILITIES

WWW.ANOREXIABULIMIACARE.CO.UK ANOREXIA & BULIMIA CARE ARE A CHRISTIAN ORGANIZATION FOR PEOPLE WITH EATING DISORDERS

Books that deal with the issue of eating disorders

Talking About Anorexia, M. Monro, Published by Sheldon, 1996

Let's Discuss Anorexia and Bulimia, P. Sanders and S. Myers, Published by Watts, 1995

Dealing With Eating Disorders, K Haycock, Published by Wayland, 1994

Getting Physical: A Teenage Health Guide, A. Sigma, Published by BBC Books, 1992

Anorexia Nervosa And The Wish To Change By A Crisp, N. Joughin, C. Balek and C. Bowyer, Published by Lawrence Elbaum, 1989

Coping With Bulimia, B. French, Published by Thorsons, 1994

I Look In The Mirror And Screamed, L. Ojeda, Published by Piccadily, 1993

ALTERNATIVE SEXUALITY

Awareness

The following information is included to raise the social awareness and understanding of ministers in relation to the contemporary issue alternative sexuality.

The fact that the Church is facing the social issue of "alternative sexualities" such as 'homosexuality' bisexuality' 'trans-sexuality' and 'lesbianism' is perhaps nothing new. What is new is that preachers can no longer condemn "alternative sexualities" and be appalled for it. Proponents of "alternative sexualities" have marshalled the language of equality in their favor and thus increased their civil rights and social acceptability.

The social values and morals of our generation have taken a major paradigm shift and to the Christian the moral decline of our society is so evident. To the non-Christian the changes are simply the progression of a modern society, that teaches all men and women are equal and thus allows every one the freedom to do as they please as long as it does not harm any one else.

The issue of "alternative sexualities" is about people trapped in a sinful life style. We have all heard the phrase, "God hates the sin but loves the person" especially when Christians come into contact with those in our society who practice an "alternative sexuality".

There is no doubt that God demonstrated His love in Jesus for the homosexual community as much as He did for the heterosexual community. Homophobic Christians who either avoid or condemn those practising an "alternative sexuality" as an abomination unto the Lord do little to win these people to the Lord. Jesus' greatest rebuke when upon this earth was for the self-righteous religious hypocrites who sought to bolster their righteousness by highlighting and condemning the sins of others.

Our media-saturated society influences and determines the social values and morals of our generation and so every soap opera on our television screens seems to have a "alternative sexuality" storyline that supports the homosexual plight as a misunderstood and persecuted minority.

This increasing social acceptance of homosexuality has left many young people confused about their own sexuality and when confronted by the macho-sarcasm and hypocritical condemnation from homophobic Christians their only source of comfort and understanding at times is to turn to members of the "alternative sexualities" community.

The Bible clearly teaches that sexual preference for and sexual behaviour between members of the same sex (whether they call it "homo-", "trans-", or "bi-" sexual behaviour) is considered to be an immoral lifestyle. Only heterosexual preference and behaviour patterns are approved in Scripture as conforming to

God's plan in the creation of man and woman. All sexual behaviour is to take place in the context of marriage. Sex is considered good so long as it takes place within these parameters. Leviticus 18: 22–24; Leviticus 20: 13–16; Romans 1: 24–32; 1 Cor. 6: 9–11; 1 Tim. 1: 8–11

The Bible says little or nothing about transsexuality other than "God created us male and female" and also that it is an abomination to cross-dress, Deu 22: 5. We must conclude then that it is as abhorrent in the eyes of God to cross over to the opposite gender.

However, before passing judgment we must with Christian compassion take into account those individuals who suffer from pseudo-hermaphroditism, a physical and genetic abnormality which means an individual is born with both the male and female chromosomal biological makeup. Pseudo-hermaphroditism is often not discovered until puberty and can only be treated with medical intervention, as with those cases discovered at birth.

Assessment

The following are some of the most up-to-date statistics in relation to the issue of "alternative sexuality." (Please see appendix A.)

Attitudes towards sexual relations 1998 Great Britain							
Scenario	Always wrong	Mostly wrong	Sometimes wrong	Rarely wrong	Not wrong	Other	Total
A man and a woman having sexual relations before marriage	8	8	12	10	58	4	100
A married person having sexual relations with someone other than their spouse	52	29	13	1	2	3	100
A boy and a girl having sexual relations under 16	56	24	11	3	3	3	100
Sexual relations between two adults of the same sex	39	12	11	8	23	7	100

Social Trends 30, © Crown Copyright 2000

The above table reveals that in 1998 two-thirds of people aged 65 and over thought sexual relations between two adults of the same sex were always wrong compared with less than a fifth of people aged 18–24. Overall almost two in five people thought such relationships were always wrong, with about one in five thinking they were not wrong at all. Four in five people thought it always or mostly wrong for a married person to have sexual relations with someone other than their spouse, and a similar proportion thought that sex between a boy and a girl aged under 16 was always or mostly wrong.

Gay couples 'too few to be counted'

By Steve Doughty, Social Affairs Correspondent

An official survey to discover how many homosexuals live together as couples was shelved – because it found so few. Analysts dropped the project when out of 9,700 households, they found only 14 avowedly gay male or female couples. Homosexual pressure groups frequently cite claims that one in ten of the population is gay and are pressing heavily for homosexuals to be given the right to marry.

But according to figures collected for the Government's General Household Survey, which is intended to give a definitive picture of how Britons live, only 0.0014 per cent of the population lives in a homosexual household. The figures, revealed yesterday, were collected two years ago, when interviewers spoke to more than 18,000 people in 9,700 homes.

Statisticians planned to include figures on gay households when the full results were published earlier this year but the idea was dropped, they said, because the researchers found so few. John Haskey, of the Office for National Statistics, which conducts the survey, said: 'We were surprised by the small number of homosexual couples. It is possible people didn't want to reveal the information. But we know that in the past some such couples have definitely wanted to record the information.'

The 'gay' question, directed at people of the same sex, was: 'Are you living together as a couple?' If the answer was Yes, interviewers noted the couple as 'same sex co-habitants'.

Mr Haskey said: 'It was a pretty neutral question. People know what it means. They don't misinterpret it.' In a survey calibrated to take in all regions and all social groups, the researchers found one gay couple for every 692 homes they visited – one-seventh of one per cent of all homes. If the same applies to the country as a whole, fewer than 100,000 out of a population of 55.4 million are living in stable homosexual relationships.

(c) *The Daily Mail* September, 1997

ADDRESSING

The following is a list of practical suggestions that may enable churches and organizations to minister effectively to those claiming an "alternative sexuality".

- ✝ Whatever a person's professed sexuality they remain people whom Jesus loves and died for. The barriers to reaching out and ministering to those professing an alternative sexuality are simply expressed differently to heterosexuals.

- ✝ The greatest barrier to reaching out to members of the 'homosexuality' 'bisexuality' 'transsexuality' and 'lesbianism' communities are Christian's negative attitudes, often expressed in embarrassment, distancing, hostility and even prejudice.

- ✝ What is sometimes termed "friendship evangelism" is perhaps the best way to reach out to these people. Literature designed to explain the evils of 'homosexuality' 'bisexuality' 'transsexuality' and 'lesbianism' only serve to distance the Christian from these people even more and reinforce negative attitudes.

- ✝ Many members of alternative sexuality communities have been treated badly by Christians in the past and the best way to break down the barriers is offer

- ✞ the hand of friendship and minister practically unto these people as Jesus did for the "woman at the well" John 4.

- ✞ It is possible for members of the 'homosexuality' 'bisexuality' 'transsexuality' and 'lesbianism' communities to change, many of these people are not aware that they can change to God's ordained sexuality.

- ✞ It is possible for members of alternative sexuality communities to relapse to their old lifestyle after they have become a Christian. Many people involved in reaching out to 'homosexuality' 'bisexuality' 'trans-sexuality' and 'lesbianism' say they see these people become Christians, but keeping them in the church is very difficult. The temptation to return to their gay friends and lifestyle, where they felt loved and understood is a massive temptation.

- ✞ Bear in mind that marriage is not the cure for those of an alternative sexuality. Heterosexuality may be the ultimate aim but never the immediate goal.

- ✞ Provide balanced and loving literature concerning 'homosexuality' 'bisexuality' 'transsexuality' and 'lesbianism' for Christians to read and pass on to their family and friends involved in these communities.

- ✞ Make contact with the recommended counselling agencies who seek to minister to these communities.

AFFIRMATION.

The following is a list of churches, organizations or individuals who are ministering to homo-, trans-, or bi- sexuals. They will, we believe, be able to offer practical and professional advice to assist you in your efforts to minister to those caught in the trap of "alternative sexuality". (Please see appendix B.)

THE INSTITUTE FOR THE STUDY OF CHRISTIANITY & SEXUALITY
OXFORD HOUSE
DERBYSHIRE STREET
LONDON
E2 6HG
TEL: 0207 739 1249
EMAIL: LGCM@LGCM.ORG.UK
WWW.LGCM.ORG.UK

CHRISTIAN INITIATIVE ON TEENAGE SEXUALITY
(A MINISTRY OF CARE FOR THE FAMILY)
GARTH HOUSE
LEON AVENUE
CARDIFF
CF4 7RG

TRUE FREEDOM TRUST
PO BOX 13
PENTON
WIRRAL
CH43 6YB
TEL: 0151 653 0773 FAX: 0151 653 7036
WEBSITE: WWW.TFTRUST.U-NET.COM
EMAIL: MARTIN@TFTRUST.U-NET.COM

U-TURN ANGLIA TRUST
PO BOX 138
WITNESHAM
IPSWICH
IP6 9EP
TEL: 01473 785 129

HELPFULWORLD.WIDE.WEB.SITES

EXODUS INTERNATIONAL EUROPE
HTTP://WWW.EXODUSEUROPE.ORG

EXODUS NORTH AMERICA
HTTP://WWW.EXODUSNORTHAMERICA.ORG

AN INTERNATIONAL DIRECTORY OF MINISTRIES AROUND THE WORLD. EXCELLENT FOR FINDING HELP IF YOU ARE NOT IN THE UK
HTTP://GEOCITIES.COM/EXGAYLINKS

COURAGE, UK
HTTP://WWW.COURAGE.ORG.UK

PARAKALEO, UK (MINISTRY FOR THE GENDER CONFUSED)
HTTP://WWW.PARAKALEO.CO.UK

ENCOURAGE (UK): A MINISTRY FOR CATHOLICS FACING HOMOSEXUAL ISSUES
HTTP://WWW.ENCOURAGETRUST.ORG.UK

NATIONAL ASSOCIATION FOR RESEARCH & THERAPY OF HOMOSEXUALITY (NARTH)
HTTP://WWW.NARTH.COM

FREETOBEME : AN EXCELLENT SITE FOR YOUNG PEOPLE DEALING WITH HOMOSEXUAL ISSUES
HTTP://WWW.FREETOBEME.COM

EXODUS YOUTH: A SITE FROM EXODUS NORTH AMERICA FOR TEENAGERS, PARENTS AND YOUTH WORKERS
HTTP://WWW.EXODUSYOUTH.NET

CHRISTIAN COUNSELLORS UK : A COMPREHENSIVE DIRECTORY OF COUNSELLORS, SUPERVISORS, TRAINERS & RESOURCES IN THE UK
WWW.DOVEUK.COM/CCUK

CHRISTIAN CHAT UK: A CHRISTIAN WEB-SITE WHERE PEOPLE CAN MEET TOGETHER AND CHAT ABOUT VARIOUS ISSUES OVER THE INTERNET
WWW.CHRISTIANCHAT.CO.UK

Books that deal with the issue of alternative sexuality

1-85424-318-7, *Setting Love In Order*, Mario Bergner, Monarch Publications
1-85424-115-X, *Pursuing Sexual Wholeness*, Andrew Comiskey, Monarch Publications
0-89693-935-9, *Homosexual No More*, Dr William Consiglio, Victor Books (Scripture Press Publications)
0-8500-9329-5, *Healing the Masculine Soul*, Gordon Dalbey, Word Publishing
0-8407-3450-6, *Father & Son*, Gordon Dalbey, Thomas Nelson Publishers
0-89081-897-5, *Desires In Conflict*, Joe Dallas, Harvest House
1-56507-431-9, *A Strong Delusion*, Joe Dallas, Harvest House
0-340-64188-6, *Coming Out of Homosexuality*, Bob Davies & Lori Rentzel, Hodder & Stoughton
0-86065-880-5, *The Truth About AIDS*, Dr Patrick Dixon, Kingsway Publications
0-340-62772-7, *The Rising Price of Love*, Dr Patrick Dixon, Hodder & Stoughton
0-9645000-0-0, *Sexual Healing*, David Kyle Foster, Mastering Life Ministries, USA
0-340-65152-0, *Out of the Blue*, Martin Hallett, Hodder & Stoughton, UK
1-851-74339-1, *Sexual Identity and Freedom in Discipleship*, Martin Hallett, Grove Books Ltd, UK
1-85424-101-X, *Love Is A Choice*, Robert Hemfelt, Frank Minirth and Paul Meier, Monarch Publications
1-85424-166-4, *Out Of Egypt*, Jeanette Howard, Monarch Publications
0-87123-606-0, *Where Does A Mother Go To Resign?*, Barbara Johnson, Bethany House Publishers
0-7852-7406-5, *When Men Think Private Thoughts*, Gordon MacDonald Thomas, Nelson Publishers, USA
0-227-67850-8, *Homosexuality: A New Christian Ethic*, Elizabeth Moberley, James Clarke & Co. ISBN
0-87668-545-9, *Reparative Therapy of Male Homosexuality*, Joseph Nicolosi, Jason Aronson Inc.
0-8054-6156-6, *Unwanted Harvest?*, Mona Riley & Brad Sargent, Broadman & Holman Publishers, USA
0-8010-5625-X, *Homosexuality and the Politics of Truth*, Jeffrey Satinover, MD Baker, USA
0-89109-711-2, *False Intimacy*, Dr. Harry W. Schaumburg, Navpress
0-85111-157-2, *Straight and Narrow?*, Thomas Schmidt, Intervarsity Press
0-8308-1982-7, *Someone I Love is Gay*, Anita Worthen & Bob Davies, InterVarsity Press, USA
0-945611-00-5, *Steps Out Of Homosexuality*, Frank Worthen, New Hope Ministry
0-945611-01-3 and 0-945611-03-X, *A Step Further*, Volumes I and II, Frank Worthen, New Hope Ministry

Sexual Behaviour in Britain
0-14-015814-6, *The National Survey of Sexual Attitudes & Lifestyles*, Penguin, £15.00

WORK AND UNEMPLOYMENT

AWARENESS

The following information is included to raise the social awareness and understanding of ministers in relation to the contemporary issue of work and unemployment.

Work takes various forms: such as paid employment; voluntary work; fulfilling unpaid family commitment such as caring for children/elderly and managing a home. All of these are equally important and of equal value as paid work.

Work finds a place in God's perfect social and spiritual order, for example in the beginning God worked and rested, He ordained that mankind should do the same.

Exodus 20: 8–10: 'Remember the Sabbath day, to keep it holy. Six days shall thou labor, and do all thy work: But the seventh day is the Sabbath of the Lord thy God: in it thou shall not do any work.'

The apostle Paul also encouraged the concept of working for one's sustenance;

2 Thes. 3: 10–12: 'For even when we were with you, this we commanded you, that if any would not work, neither should he eat. For we hear that there are some which walk among you disorderly, working not at all, but are busybodies. Now them that are such we command and exhort by our Lord Jesus Christ, that with quietness they work, and eat their own bread.'

The value of work can be viewed in three ways, a means of "Self Satisfaction" Ecc 3: 17, "Service unto God" and Col 3: 23 "Supporting the Community".

The concept of a "Job for Life" has become a thing of the past as a result of the social, economic and technological changes of the western world.

Before the industrial revolution natural disaster in agricultural societies was the main cause of unemployment. Since the industrial revolution the present and continuing technological revolution has meant less manpower and thus resulted in traditional skills being made redundant. Globalization has made it possible for multinational companies to take advantage of cheap labor in third world countries. Economic changes in supply and demand can also result in redundancy.

When a person's self esteem is wrapped up in their career, unemployment is often taken personally. John Stott makes the following point; 'It is a shocking experience to be declared "Redundant" and still worse to think of oneself thus.' (*Issues Facing Christians Today*, 1984, p.163) 'Redundant' communicates the impression of no longer being needed, wanted or of use, the shock of redundancy often damages a person's self-esteem. For those whose self-worth is wrapped up in their employment, redundancy and unemployment often lead to periods of depression and despair.

Assessment

The following are some of the most up-to-date statistics in relation to the issue of work and unemployment. (Please see appendix A). Employment statistics change so rapidly it is advisable to request this information from the Department for Employment for the most up to date figures.

Addressing

The following is a list of practical suggestions that may enable churches and organizations to minister effectively to the unemployed:

- **Open empty church buildings to be used for Job Clubs, providing newspapers, telephone, letter writing materials, advice on CVs, access to computers. Job Centers will give advice on Job Clubs.**
- **Use the church building as a drop-in center for the unemployed.**
- **Teach on a person's value in Jesus rather than in their occupation.**
- **Provide opportunities for the unemployed to do voluntary work in the community.**

Affirmation

The following is a list of churches, organizations or individuals who are ministering to the unemployed. They will, we believe, be able to offer practical and professional advice to assist. (Please see appendix B.)

NATIONAL YOUTH AGENCY (NYA)
17-23 ALBION STREET
LEICESTER
LE1 6OD
TEL: 0116 285 3700
FAX: 0116 285 3777
EMAIL: NYA@NYA.ORG.UK
WEBSITE: WWW.NYA.ORG.UK
THE NATIONAL YOUTH AGENCY AIMS TO ADVANCE YOUTH WORK TO PROMOTE YOUNG PEOPLE'S PERSONAL AND SOCIAL DEVELOPMENT, AND THEIR VOICE, INFLUENCE AND PLACE IN SOCIETY. IT PROVIDES RESOURCES TO IMPROVE WORK WITH YOUNG PEOPLE AND ITS MANAGEMENT; AND SECURES STANDARDS OF EDUCATION AND TRAINING FOR YOUTH WORK.

PRISON REFORM TRUST
THE OLD TRADING HOUSE
2ND FLOOR
15 NORTHBURGH STREET
LONDON
EC1V OJR
TEL: 0207 2515070

FAX: 0207 251 5076
PUBLISHES A WIDE RANGE OF PUBLICATIONS INCLUDING A PRISON REPORT, A QUARTERLY MAGAZINE. ASK FOR THEIR PUBLICATIONS LIST.

EQUAL OPPORTUNITIES COMMISSION
OVERSEAS HOUSE
QUAY STREET
MANCHESTER
M3 3HN
TEL: 0161 833 9244
FAX: 0161 835 1657
THE WORK AND FAMILY UNIT EQUAL AT THE OPPORTUNITIES COMMISSION PROVIDES INFORMATION PACKS AND BRIEFINGS (SOME FREE) ON A RANGE OF ISSUES RELATING TO WOMEN AND MEN IN THE WORKPLACE.

FAWCETT SOCIETY
46 HARLEYFORD ROAD
LONDON
SE11 5AY
TEL: 0207 628 4441
TO INFLUENCE PARLIAMENT AND PUBLIC OPINION TO ACCEPT EQUAL STATUS FOR WOMEN IN THE HOME AND PUBLIC LIFE, AND EQUAL EDUCATIONAL AND JOB OPPORTUNITIES. PUBLISH TOWARDS EQUALITY, A QUARTERLY PUBLICATION. TO SUBSCRIBE TO TOWARDS EQUALITY AND OTHER PUBLICATIONS SEND £25.00 TO: FAWCETT SOCIETY, FREEPOST FE 6903, LONDON, BC2B ZJD

NATIONAL COUNCIL FOR ONE PARENT FAMILIES
255 KENTISH TOWN ROAD
LONDON
NW5 2LX
TEL: 08000185026
FAX: 0207 4824851
THE NATIONAL COUNCIL FOR ONE PARENT FAMILIES HAS PIONEERED THE DEVELOPMENT OF 'RETURN-TO-WORK' TRAINING FOR LONE PARENTS. THEY PRODUCE PUBLICATIONS INCLUDING THE RECENT RETURNING TO WORK: A GUIDE FOR LONE PARENTS (1996) AND PROVIDE TRAINING COURSES.

NEW WAYS TO WORK
309 UPPER STREET
LONDON
N1 2TY
TEL: 0207 226 4026
FAX: 0207 354 2978
ADVANCES KNOWLEDGE ON NEW FLEXIBLE WORKING SCHEMES I.E. WORKING PATTERNS.

PARENTS AT WORK
77 HOLLOWAY ROAD
LONDON
N7 8JZ
TEL: 0207 628 3578
(PREVIOUSLY WORKING MOTHER'S ASSOCIATION). TO PROVIDE INFORMATION AND ADVICE ABOUT CHILD CARE PROVISION TO ENABLE WORKING PARENTS TO MAKE THE BEST POSSIBLE CHOICE OF CHILD CARE FOR THEIR CHILD. HELPLINE OPEN FROM 11: 00AM-1: 00PM & 2: 00PM-4: 00PM TUESDAYS AND THURSDAYS.

THE INDUSTRIAL SOCIETY
ROBERT HYDE HOUSE
48 BRYANSTON SQUARE
LONDON
W1H 7LN
TEL: 0207 262 2401
FAX: 0207 724 3354
PRODUCES RANGE OF BOOKLETS AND INFORMATION PACKS ON ALL SORTS OF WORK RELATED ISSUES INCLUDING: WORKING MOTHERS, RACIAL AND SEXUAL HARASSMENT, SMOKING AND ALCOHOL POLICIES. THEIR LIBRARY INCLUDES A WIDE RANGE OF PRESS CUTTINGS AND EMPLOYMENT STATISTICS.

WOMEN'S EDUCATIONAL TRAINING TRUST (WEIT)
BLACKBURN HOUSE CENTER FOR WOMEN
HOPE STREET
LIVERPOOL
L87 PE
TEL: 0151709 4356
FAX: 0151709 8293
WWW.BLACKBURNWHOUSE.CO.UK
ESTABLISHES AND PROMOTES EQUAL OPPORTUNITIES IN EDUCATION AND TRAINING. TO ENCOURAGE WOMEN INTO NON-TRADITIONAL JOBS. PRODUCES PUBLICATIONS.

WOMEN'S RETURNERS NETWORK (WRN)
100 PARK VILLAGE EAST
LONDON
WC1 3SR
TEL: 0207 468 2290
A NATIONAL INDEPENDENT ORGANIZATION WHICH IS CONCERNED THAT THERE IS NO NATIONAL RECOGNITION OF THE NEEDS OF THE INCREASING NUMBER OF WOMEN SEEKING TO RETURN TO WORK. THEY HAVE A HELPLINE, PUBLISH RESOURCE SHEETS WHICH PROVIDE USEFUL CONTACTS ON ISSUES RELATING TO WOMEN RETURNING TO WORK, PRODUCE A QUARTERLY NEWSLETTER AND CONDUCT RESEARCH PROJECTS.

Books that deal with the issue of work and unemployment

1901949060, *Being Unmistakably Christian at Work*, Latham, £3.50,
0851692389, *Unemployment and the future of work*, Anton Baumol, CCBI, £8.50
0862099706, *Lifelines for the unemployed*, Susan Hardwick, KW, £2.99
0853648808, *"Just Business"*, A. Hill, £9.99
084993564, *Answers To Life's Problems*, Billy Graham, £6.99
0853648069, *Changing Values*, David Attwood, £9.99
0851106838, *Work And Leisure*, Leland Ryken, £9.99
0851111513, *Work And Worship*, Ben Patterson, £6.99
1860243401, *Work, Prison, Or Place Of Destiny*, David Oliver, £6.99
1576830241, *Work: Serving God On The Job*, NAV, £4.25
0902548284, *Help! I'm Redundant*, Brian Edwards, £8.50

AGEISM

Awareness

The following information is included to raise the social awareness and understanding of ministers/church leaders in relation to the contemporary issues of ageing and ageism. Ageing is the unavoidable destiny of everyone. It of course becomes more apparent in the latter stages of life.

© Bromley in his study *The Psychology of Human Ageing* states the following:

> Ageing is a complex sequence of changes. The organs and functions of the body are impaired. Some people suffer mild or severe psychological disorders brought on by degenerative disease or other causes. There are changes in sensory and motor capacities, in the central processing functions associated with intelligence, and in its physical basis – the nervous system. People's position in society changes; their beliefs, attitudes and personal qualities alter, as does their behaviour. The content and organization of their experience changes... These changes lead to greater deterioration, and culminate in death.

* **Biblical insights on ageing 2 Sam 19: 35, Ecc 12: 2ff, Ps 90: 10**
* **Ageing is an enviable process of losses**
* Physical Independence, **dependency upon social services, neighbors and family.**
* Mental Independence, **memory loss**
* Financial Independence, **retirement is often forced to make way for younger people**
* Social Independence, **bereavement of direct family members and their net work of social friends**
* **Ageism is not the study of elderly people! Ageism is the same as racism or sexism. Ageism is to hold prejudices or show discrimination towards those who are older**
* Institutional or economic ageism. **Age discrimination occurs when employers make decisions affecting procedures for advertising, recruitment, selection, promotion, training and development on the basis of individuals' age rather than their skills, abilities, qualifications and potential**
* **Much research is concerned with discrimination against the over 50s but job adverts frequently give age limits of 40, 35 or even 30**

✴ Reasons for age discrimination are:

- ✞ Recession – organizations' reductions in the size of the workforce concentrated on early retirement first and targeted redundancy at older workers
- ✞ Younger workers are generally cheaper to employ
- ✞ Young employees are thought to be more flexible, more skilled in technology
- ✞ Older workers are thought to be more costly for benefits, such as sick leave and pensions as well as salary
- ✞ **Stereotypical** ageism. The value of an individual within the capitalist west is often based upon their ability to produce and be self-sufficient

However, organizations are now beginning to see the results of age discrimination:

- ✞ When older workers leave, their knowledge, skills and experience go too
- ✞ Older employees tend to stay longer, give greater commitment and loyalty and have less absenteeism
- ✞ Mixed age groups provide balance

Old age does not automatically mean a person has little or nothing to contribute to society, or the life of a local church.

The effects of ageing upon an individual are sometimes dependent upon the value that a society (or a social group) places upon its elderly population.

A discriminatory attitude towards the elderly is that those on the "edge of life" can be considered and kept on the "edge of things" excluding them from full participation in society (or a social group).

Medical ageism: Disengagement theories were pioneered in the 1950s by Cummings and Henry, suggesting that the elderly withdraw from the world to prepare for death; the theories are currently unpopular, being regarded as justifying social structures which cause elderly people to withdraw whether or not they wish to do so.

However, a more contemporary concern has to be the increasing acceptance and demand for legalized euthanasia within medical and political bodies.

✞ The majority of doctors want to be able to help patients end their lives

Opinion polls reveal strong support for the legalization of Physician Assisted Suicide among the medical profession, and among the population at large. A majority of medical practitioners (54%) are in favor of changing the law to allow PAS in some circumstances, with only 36% of respondents opposing such a change. 55% felt that this should be permissible if the person had a terminal condition or was in a state of extreme mental or physical suffering. (© *Glasgow University Physician Assisted Suicide Report*, 1996.) Ageing and Ageism of course do not go together.

Assessment

The following are some of the most up-to-date statistics in relation to the elderly. (Please see appendix A). According to government statistics:

- For men aged 50 to 64 the activity rate was 68.4% in 1995 (in 1975 the rate for men aged 55 to 59 was 94%).
- For women aged 50 to 59 in 1995 the rate was 63.9% but this rate is not declining – due perhaps to the increase in job opportunities, particularly part time, for women.
- Rates for those over retirement age drop dramatically: men – 9%, married women – 5%; and non-married women – 3%.
- Of those who do work, older people are more likely to work part-time. In 1994:
    - Of those aged 50 to 59 more than a quarter of those who worked were part-time.
    - Of those aged 60 to 64, 35.5% were part-time.
    - For the over-65s, 70.4% were part-time.
    - Older people are more likely to be self-employed: of those aged 50 to state pension age, 17% were self-employed (all employees: 12.8%).

Expectation of Life at selected ages, by gender

	1911	1931	1951	1971	1991	1997	2011	2021
Males								
At birth	50.4	58	66.1	68.8	73.2	74.6	77.4	78.6
At Age 20	44	46.5	49.4	50.9	54.2	55.5	58	59.1
At Age 40	27.5	29.5	30.8	31.8	35.2	36.4	39	40
At Age 60	13.7	14.5	14.8	15.3	17.7	18.8	21	22
At Age 80	4.9	4.8	5	5.5	6.4	6.7	7.7	8.3
Females								
At birth	53.9	62	70	75	78.8	79.6	81.6	82.7
At Age 20	46.4	49.4	53.6	56.7	59.6	60.3	62	63.1
At Age 40	29.8	32.2	34.9	37.3	40	40.8	42.5	43.5
At Age 60	15.3	16.4	17.8	19.8	21.9	22.6	24.1	25.1
At Age 80	5.6	5.6	5.9	6.9	8.4	8.5	9.1	9.9

UNITED KINGDOM, SOCIAL TRENDS 30 © CROWN COPYRIGHT 2000

The above table reveals large improvements in the expectancy of life at birth have been seen over the past century for both males and females. In 1911 life expectancy for males was just over 50 years and 54 years for females while in 1997 life expectancy for males was 75 years and 80 years for females.

It may be that because of the devaluing of the elderly in some sections of society that they are accepting euthanasia as the inevitable conclusion to their life. The following survey suggests that the elderly no long value their life:

> Support for voluntary euthanasia is even stronger among the elderly. Anti-v.e. groups often base their opposition upon the assertion that legalization of euthanasia or assisted suicide would pose a threat to the most vulnerable in society – in particular, the elderly and the disabled. It is interesting to note, therefore, that support among members of such groups is actually higher than among those not deemed to be at special risk. In what is believed to be the first such poll specifically targeted at pensioners, 92% of those surveyed replied that doctors should be allowed to end the life of terminally ill patients who want to die. Only 29% agreed with the statement that legalizing euthanasia posed a realistic risk of allowing the unscrupulous to end a patient's life without consent.
>
> © *Yours* magazine – November 1994

Elderly Top List of Abused

by Kirsty Walker
Social Affairs Correspondent

PENSIONERS are the most abused people in society, according to research. Some have been physically attacked by children as young as nine. Others suffer emotional abuse from family members. But one of the main forms of abuse is financial, with relatives stealing money or possessions. Two-thirds of the abused adults in a survey of three social services departments were elderly, according to a report from the Joseph Rowntree Foundation. Most of them were women over 75. Some reported that their tormentors were strangers or local children who delighted in making their lives a misery. Others were trapped in abusive relationships with spouses or children. But despite the fact that so many elderly people suffer day-to-day abuse, the report found that victims are not receiving the kind of long-term help they need. It says social workers and care professionals often lack the skills and knowledge to deal with cases where older people are being abused. In many cases there is a belief that little can be done to help victims, so there is an emphasis on short-term "rescue" rather than long-term support. The study was based on interviews with more than 300 people. In one case a 60-year-old woman had been abused for years by her husband, and a 78-year-old woman had her jewellery and possessions stolen by her grandson to buy drugs. The report says social workers' attitudes are predominantly negative, mainly because many have insufficient experience or understanding to identify abuse. "With appropriate support, elder women can take the decision to leave an abusive relationship, even when they have lived in it for a large part of their lives," the report said. It recommends that pensioners should be given help in finding new accommodation to get away from an abuser, and access to money. But it says many do not know where to go for help. Report author Jacki Pritchard said: "After leaving an abusive situation, victims often encountered problems with the length of time taken to sort out their financial entitlements. Help was needed on practical problems which worried victims, such as retrieving possessions and clothes from their previous home and obtaining new furniture." *The Daily Express* Respect campaign has highlighted the plight of vulnerable elderly people who are victims of neglect or ill treatment by poorly-qualified or untrained staff in old people's homes. kirsty.walker@express.co.uk

© Express Newspapers, 2000

Addressing

The following is a list of practical suggestions that may enable churches and organizations to take action that will alleviate the problems of ageism in their locality.

- **Elderly people are not "yesterday's church" just as young people are not "tomorrow's church". All the members of our congregation should be encouraged to consider every member as an integral part of the community of faith at every stage of life.**
- **Encourage congregations to respect and honour those who are elderly.**
- **Acknowledge that experience of life does bring a natural wisdom concerning the things of this world.**
- **Be careful not to push the elderly to the sidelines of church activity offering them a luncheon club.**
- **Open your building up to the community. A church building that is empty Monday – Saturday could be an asset to community groups supporting the elderly.**
- **One danger in dealing with the elderly in the church is to assume that they become a powerhouse of prayer because of their lack of physical ability.**

© G Keyes *Prayer in the second half of life* makes the following observation

- **"Expectations are that prayer supersedes activity and guards against loneliness, in reality ageing brings new difficulties to praying, and that expectations are self-serving projections placed on the elderly by those who feel they are too busy to pray themselves. Some older people are less at ease with their faith as they find church practice changing around them, and find faith harder to express if the familiar traditions and language are no longer available to them."**

© Daves D (ed) *Studies in Pastoral Theology and Social Anthropology*
(Birmingham University Press 1986)

Affirmation

The following is a list of churches, organizations or individuals who are taking action to alleviate ageism. They will, we believe, be able to offer practical and professional advice to assist you in your efforts to take action against ageism and minister to the elderly. (Please see appendix B.)

Help the Aged (HTA)
207-211 Pentonville Rd
London
N1 9UZ
Tel: 0207 2781114
Website: http://www.helptheaged.org.uk
HTA can provide the most up to date information on issues relating to the elderly.

Christian Vocations
St James House
Trinity Rd
Dudley
W. Midlands
Tel: 01384 233711
www.christianvocations.org
Email: info@christianvocations.org

KEY CHANGE
5 ST GEORGE'S MEWS
43 WESTMINSTER BRIDGE ROAD
LONDON
SE1 7JB
TEL: 0207 633 0533
EMAIL: KEYCHANGE@KEYCHANGE.ORG.UK

PILGRIM HOMES
NASMITH HOUSE
175 TOWER BRIDGE ROAD
LONDON
SE1 2AL
TEL: 0207 407 5466
FAX: 171 403 5433
EMAIL: PILGRIMHOMES@COMPUSERVE.COM

CHRISTIAN COUNSEL ON AGEING
EPWORTH HOUSE
STUART STREET
DERBY
DE1 2EQ
TEL: 01335 296200

ELDER ABUSE RESPONSE LINE
(ACTION ON ELDER ABUSE)
ASTRAL HOUSE
1268 LONDON ROAD
LONDON SW16 4ER
TEL: 0203 765 7000 (2–4.30 PM MON–FRI AND UNTIL 7.30 PM TWO EVENINGS A WEEK)
SERVICE PROVIDED BY ACTION ON ELDER ABUSE. CALLERS MAY INCLUDE: THE ABUSED OLDER PERSON, THE ABUSER, RELATIVES, FRIENDS, NEIGHBOURS, PROFESSIONAL STAFF (NURSES, DOCTORS, SOCIAL WORKERS, THERAPISTS, POLICE, SOLICITORS), VISITORS (HOME HELPS, VOLUNTARY ORGANIZATIONS), RESIDENTS OF HOMES AND SHELTERED HOUSING. OFFERS CONFIDENTIALITY, AN OPPORTUNITY TO TALK THROUGH CONCERNS, INFORMATION ON WHO TO CONTACT AND GUIDANCE ON LEGAL IMPLICATIONS. THE SERVICE IS AVAILABLE TO CALLERS IN ENGLISH AND HINDI.

Books that deal with issues facing the elderly

0715206400, *Old Age-Guide for professional carers*, £5.95, Maclennan St Andrews Press

0800792076, *Caring For Your Elderly Parents*, Pushland, £7.50

0715206400, *Old Age*, W. J. McLennan, £5.95

0736900020, *Over The Hill And On A Roll*, Bob Phelps, £3.99

0281046468, *Being Your Age, Pastoral Care for Older People*, £8.99

RACISM

Awareness

The following information is included to raise the social awareness and understanding of ministers/church leaders in relation to the contemporary issue of racism.

- Racism is prejudice against people of another race or ethnic group. Prejudice means pre-judging: making up your mind about someone or something when you have not considered the facts or the evidence.

- Racists believe that human beings can be divided up into racial groups. Most groups will be inferior; the racists' own group will of course be the superior race.

- Colour prejudice is a form of racism based upon the colour of another person's skin.

- Racial discrimination puts racism into practice, this is when a person is treated badly or unfairly because of the colour of their skin or because they are from a different ethnic group.

- Every day on the streets of Britain, in playgrounds, classrooms, shops or at work, black people are racially harassed. This can take any form from a racist remark to a physical attack. Even in their homes, families are not safe. Houses are daubed with racist messages, windows are broken and firebombs are pushed through letterboxes in the dead of night.

- Racism is learned, no one is ever born a racist. Parents, peers and significant people in a child's up-bringing influence their attitudes to people different from them.

- Racism can often be a result of wanting someone to blame for personal hardship and the following comments are often made. "It's their fault, coming over here and taking our jobs, they should go back to where they belong."

- According to Human Rights Watch, the UK now has one of the highest levels of racial violence anywhere in Europe.

- Racial attacks are hard to prevent because even the fact of their existence is not often acknowledged by the police, the courts and the press. Sometimes the racial dimension of an attack is just not understood, sometimes the seriousness of harassment is not appreciated, sometimes wrong advice is given to the victims. And very few of the culprits have been brought to justice.

- Leviticus 19: 33–34 "When an alien lives with you in your land, do not mistreat him. The alien living with you must be treated as one of your native-born.

Love him as yourself, for you were aliens in Egypt. I am the Lord your God."
(see also LL 7: 1–10, 10: 25–37, Acts 11: 1–18)

➡ Racism finds no place in the heart of God, His Son died that all might be saved.

ASSESSMENT

The following are some of the most up-to-date statistics in relation to the problem of racism. (Please see appendix A.)

In the year 1995/6, 12,199 racial attacks were reported to the police. Between 1989 and 1996, the number of incidents reported to the police increased by 275%.

The number of attacks reported to the police is much smaller than the actual number of incidents.

The 1991 British Crime Survey suggested that 32,500 violent assaults and 26,000 acts of vandalism were racially motivated.

The Survey concluded that 18% of all crimes against black people were considered to be racially motivated. And, in 1993, the Minister of State at the Home Office told a select committee that there might be 140,000 such attacks a year and that the 'true figure' could be as high as 330,000. Between 1992 and 1996 alone, 18 people lost their lives in racial attacks.

ADDRESSING

The following is a list of practical suggestions that may enable churches and organizations to take action that will alleviate the problem of racism in their locality.

❖ **Preach and teach the value of every person despite ethnic background.**

❖ **Acknowledge and celebrate the diversity of cultural background (music, dance, dress and food) when possible within your congregation and community.**

❖ **It is not popular in our postmodern world to disagree with the religious teaching of other groups, however, nor is it racist.**

❖ **Avoid being sucked into the "political correctness vacuum" by thinking you must have ethnic minorities in leadership roles within the church. The colour of our skin does not qualify any one for leadership within the Body of Christ, look for calling and anointing upon a person.**

AFFIRMATION

The following is a list of churches, organizations or individuals who are taking action to alleviate abortion. They will, we believe, be able to offer practical and professional advice to assist you in your efforts to take action against racism. (Please see appendix B.)

CHURCHES COMMISSION FOR RACIAL JUSTICE
INTER-CHURCH HOUSE
35 LOWER MARSH
LONDON
SE1 7RL
TEL: 0207 620 4444
FAX: 0171 928 0010

EVANGELICAL CHRISTIANS FOR RACIAL JUSTICE
29 TRINITY ROAD
ASTON
BIRMINGHAM
B6 6AJ

AFRICAN AND CARIBBEAN EVANGELICAL ALLIANCE
WHITEFIELD HOUSE
186 KENNINGTON PARK ROAD
LONDON
SE11 4BT
TEL: 0207 735 7373
FAX: 0171 735 7275
EMAIL: ACEA@EAUK.ORG
WEBSITE: WWW.EAUK.ORG/ACEA

KICK IT OUT
C/O BUSSINESS DESIGN CENTRE
52 UPPER ST
LONDON
N1 0QH
TEL: 0207 2886012
EMAIL: KICK-RACISM@KICK-IT-OUT.DEMON.CO.UK
WWW.KICKITOUT.ORG

BLACK INFORMATION LINK
THE 1990 TRUST
9 CRAMMER ROAD
LONDON
SW9 6EJ
TEL: 020 7582 1990
EMAIL: BLINK1990@GN.APC.ORG
WWW.BLINK.ORG.UK

COMMISSION FOR RACIAL EQUALITY
ELLIOT HOUSE
10-12 ALLINGTON ST
LONDON
SW1E 5EH
TEL: 020 7828 7022
EMAIL: INFO@CRE.GOV.UK
WWW.CRE.GOV.UK

SHOW RACISM THE RED CARD
PO BOX 141
WHITLEY BAY
TYNE AND WEAR
ME26 3RG
TEL: 0191 291 0160
EMAIL: INFO@THEREDCARD.ORG
WWW.SRTRC.ORG

Books that deal with racism
0062505521, *I Have A Dream*, King, HARCOL
Racism (video), ttv11, £9.99, Carman

© *UNJUSTIFIED ASSUMPTIONS PROMOTE RACISM.*

The following is a list of assumptions and the facts in relation to ethnic minorities in Britain. (Provided by the Commission for Racial Equality.

They say...
They're still flooding in when the country's crowded with millions of them.

Fact
Immigration is strictly controlled and relatively few people are allowed in to settle. More people leave Britain to live abroad than come to live here.

Of those who have come to live in Britain 61% are white.

Only 1 in 20 people living in Britain are black or Asian, that's 5%

Some – including politicians – would have you believe there is massive immigration into this country. It's nonsense, Britain has some of the strictest immigration controls in the world and it's been like that for a quarter of a century.

Others would have you think that there are many millions of black and Asian people living in this country. Untrue. The figures speak for themselves. The total number of black and Asian people living in Britain is now 3 million or 5.5% of the total.

In the 32 years since records started, only in five years have more people settled in Britain than have gone abroad. They are 1962, 1972, 1983, 1984, 1985.

They say...
They should learn to be British like us.

Fact
Nearly half the black and Asian people living here were born in Britain.

This country is their home as much as it is that of anyone else born here. Everyone living here has a right to be treated decently and fairly. And anyway, who is 'British?' Is it the Scots, or the Welsh or the English? Or is it those from Yorkshire or those who speak like a Cockney?

We are all proud of ourselves, of who we are and where we come from.

The differences are what makes life in Britain so rich and exciting. We don't all have to be the same to be able to share pride in the people of this country – and pride in working together to make it a better place.

People abroad are quite clear who they see as 'British.' They don't say you can't be British unless you support the English cricket team. For them the British person they know is now as likely to be Linford Christie winning a gold medal in the Olympics as it is to be John Major.

Of course, it is not always easy to get on with new differences. But Chinese take-aways, black music and the Asian shops are in our streets and communities because they are needed.

They say...
They're taking our jobs...

Fact
Black, Asian or Irish people are more likely to be unemployed than the average. They are also more likely to be in a lower paid job and one using lower skills.

Far from 'taking our jobs,' such workers are often doing jobs others have chosen not to do, perhaps because they are too dirty, too hard or the wages are too low.

Asian or black people are not stuck in these jobs because they do not have the skills or the education to do better. People in groups such as Bangladeshis are four times more likely than whites to end up in the dole queue. And figures show that the gap between unemployment rates for whites on the one hand and black and Asian groups on the other, gets larger as one goes up the skills ladder.

So, for instance, 22% of Pakistanis with A-levels or above are unemployed. For whites the figure is only 5%.

They say…
The race relations laws give special favours to black and Asian people.

Fact
Each year white people win cases in courts and tribunals using the Race Relations Act. It gives privileges to no one, only rights to all.

In this country there are no quotas for jobs, no reserved places. People who have jobs where things have been run properly under the Race Relations Act have them because they deserve them. The Act makes discrimination against the law – you can't be denied a job because you are Asian or because you are white.

Only in exceptional cases does it let someone get a job because they are white, black, Chinese or whatever. These are simple things like being a waiter in a Chinese restaurant, acting the part of Winston Churchill or taking care of elderly Bangladeshi women who speak very little English.

It's where the Act is ignored that things become unfair. Companies which follow real equal opportunities are the most efficient, get the best staff for the job, treat all their staff better and are the ones on the look out for the ways to get better still.

They say…
They're sponging off the welfare state

Fact
Asian and black people use the benefit system less than whites – and they are less likely to claim the benefits they have a right to.

People from ethnic minorities come off worse throughout the benefits system.

They are less likely to be claiming benefits like pensions because they are generally younger than whites but when they do go to the benefits system they run into all sorts of problems.

Research has shown that they are less likely to be claiming the benefits they have a right to – for some this will be because of the difficulty of filling in complex forms in English when it is not their first language, for others it may be because of racism in the benefits system.

Black and Asian people are more likely to be refused benefits than whites and face longer delays than white claimants before they get a decision in their favour.

They say...
They jump the housing queues.

Fact
Local councils and housing associations give homes on the basis of careful rules, which means homes go to those who need them, white or black.

If there is a problem it is the other way round – black and Asian people get a rougher deal. They're more likely to end up homeless. The homes they do get are more likely to be run down or overcrowded. Sometimes the rules that local councils lay down have made it harder for them to get decent housing than is the case for whites.

Just take one figure – that for households with one or more bedroom below standard. For whites only 2% of households are covered. For Pakistanis and Bangladeshis the figure soars to 28%.

If you are black or Asian you are more likely than a white person to be living in a home built before 1945, one that is terraced rather than semi-detached or detached, and one that is overcrowded. That last problem affects 35% of Asians but only 3% of whites.

They say...
They have too many children.

Fact
Family sizes are falling for all groups except Bangladeshis – for some Afro-Caribbeans the number of children for each adult is now lower than for whites.

Families come in all sorts of shapes and sizes – some of us, white or black, live with in-laws, grand-parents, and cousins while others live on their own. Some cannot understand how people can cope with more than two adults in the same house, others don't understand what they see as the cruelty of pushing the elderly into the lonely life of a single flat.

Only in the case of Bangladeshis have families grown in size over the past ten years. For all other ethnic minorities family sizes are falling faster than for whites.

They say.

They are not as bright as we are...

Fact

School exam results now show that whites are no longer always in the lead other groups are there with them. Some studies show Afro-Caribbean girls do best of all.

The one about the thick Paddy still gets a laugh, but the days are long gone when anybody seriously suggested that it was actually true. Many people from different minority groups still have problems in the education system – discrimination and different treatment has not been overcome.

But at the end of the day the exam results tell their own tale.

They say...

They're all muggers or crack dealers.

Fact

Black and Asian people are more likely to be victims of crime and less likely to be criminals than whites.

Crime is one of the big problems in this country today. It affects us all. The figures show that people who are black or Asian are more likely to be the victims of crimes. And they are the targets of a particular problem – racial violence. The latest Home Office figures show that black and Asian people in Britain suffer some 110,000 racially motivated assaults, threats or acts of vandalism each year with many, many more acts of abuse and harassment that go unrecorded.

People are still being attacked and seriously injured, in some cases even murdered, solely because of the colour of their skin.

Yet police figures show that some, particularly young black men, are more likely than whites to be stopped and questioned but never charged with any offence.

Don't just listen...

Don't just sit and listen to the things people say. Take it up with them and try to get them to think and not just repeat prejudices they have picked up from others.

1. **Insults**

    If you hear someone using racist insults or even threatening and harassing others just because of their colour, don't ignore it. Let both sides know that you disagree with racism. Let the person who is doing it know they are doing something you think is wrong. Let the victims know they are not on their own and that you will help them if necessary.

2   **Discrimination**
    If you think your employer is discriminating against someone because of their race, raise the matter with a trade union, the personnel manager – or with the person you think is the target of the discrimination. Make a careful note of what happened, it could help someone gain their rights.

3   **Harassment**
    Racial attacks are crimes. If you see acts of violence or intimidation directed against people because of their race go to the police and act as a witness.

4   **Be sensible**
    Don't try to solve all the problems of the world on your own. If you respond to someone who is using racial insults against a colleague at work or someone in the street, do so with care and dignity. Remember that you are trying to help the person the abuse is directed against.

5   **Get advice**
    There are many specialist advice centres which can help – there is usually a Citizens Advice Bureau within reach, many towns have a racial equality council and you can always ring the Commission for Racial Equality.

SEXISM

AWARENESS

The following information is included to raise the social awareness and understanding of ministers in relation to the contemporary issue of sex discrimination.

Sex discrimination or sexism like racism or ageism is all about prejudice towards a person because of their gender. Most sexism is from men toward women. Sex discrimination at work, under the Sex Discrimination Act 1975, means discriminating on the grounds of sex or marital status in terms of:

- recruitment and selection;
- terms and conditions of employment offered and provided;
- access to promotion, transfers and training;
- other benefits and services;
- dismissal;
- subjecting the person to any other detriment.

Sadly the major voice on issues of sexism has been from feminist movements who have by and large a negative attitude toward men as a result of male sexist attitudes.

Feminism is a broad set of ideas and not all feminists are "men-hating lesbians" many are good Christian women with a concern for those who are being mistreated simply because of the their gender.

Feminists are united in arguing that from a socio-structural point of view that the Western world is patriarchal or male-dominated and thus favored towards men in the home and out in the labor market. Their argument is not with individual men but with the social systems in public and private life that favors men. For example women could not vote in the UK on equal terms with men until 1928 and more recently women were only considered of equal value in the labor market in 1975 with the introduction of the 1975 Sex Discrimination Act.

Despite legal changes that say women are equal male attitudes and treatment is far from equal.

Socio-economic treatment of women by men has often resulted in many women doing what social scientists have termed the "Double Shift" where women have been taken on as cheap and casual labor in factories, shops and offices and then expected to return to the home in unpaid labor as the "home makers" caring for children and husband, the real "breadwinner".

Social stereotyping of women as "sex objects" and "domestic helpers" often condition men to think and treat women in a sexist manner.

Many feminists are often anti-Christianity believing that its message only serves to reinforce male dominance.

Some feminists argue that Jesus was sexist for a number reasons;

- ☆ None of Jesus' chosen disciples were female.
- ☆ Jesus refers to God as "Father" suggesting that if God is spirit neither male nor female, how could Jesus call him by a male term.
- ☆ Some feminists argue that the institution of the Church is anti-female due to;
  - ✳ Its anti-abortion stance.
  - ✳ Its leadership being predominantly male
  - ✳ Its focus on the traditional family reduces women to mothers and home makers.

The Bible of course presents a very different picture of God and his attitude towards women.

- ☆ Both male and female were made in the image of God, Gen 1: 27.
- ☆ Both male and female are equal in the eyes of God, Gal 3: 27–28.
- ☆ Women play important roles in the Judeo–Christian history such as Deborah, Esther, Ruth and Mary who sat at the feet of Jesus.
- ☆ Several times God is revealed in female terms, see Isaiah 49–15–16.

Assessment

The following are some of the most up-to-date statistics in relation to the issue of sex discrimination. (Please see appendix A). Some key findings from the Equal Opportunities Commission (EOC); their address can be found at the end of this section:

> Since 1993, the ceiling on compensation in sex discrimination cases has been abolished.

> The EOC helped applicants in discrimination cases to win a total of £711,832 Out of 71 cases last year, 10 were successful, 19 were unsuccessful and 42 were settled outside court.

> In those cases that were settled, half the employers have agreed to change policies and practices.

> Three-quarters of complaints were from women, and there has been an increase in the number of women complaining that they are denied access to training.

> The EOC says women are paid, on average, 20% less than men, with fewer opportunities to take up overtime, shift work and bonuses.

Women who work part-time earn less than half the hourly pay of male part-timers.

There is still discrimination against men who want to work in traditional women's work.

The proportion of women in the workforce is growing faster than that of men. From 1994 to 2001, the numbers of women and men being 'economically active' will grow by 11% and 3% respectively Current figures are 71% of women of working age and 85% of men 44% of women work part-time and only 6% of men, but this rate is increasing twice as fast as that of women.

Citizens Advice Bureau (CAB) made the following comments in relation to sex decimation in the work place:

CAB advisers deal with some 700,000 employment enquiries every year – and the trend is upwards. Amongst this case load are tens of thousands of women, and a growing number of men, seeking advice on their maternity or parental rights at work.[1] In the great majority of these cases, the worker has been denied one or more of these rights.

Such non-compliance includes: denial of time off work to attend ante-natal appointments; denial of the right to return to the same job after taking maternity leave; and denial of (unpaid) parental leave. It is frequently compounded by the denial of other basic employment rights, such as the rights to paid holiday, to sick pay, and to proper rest periods and breaks.

However, by far the most common problem reported by CAB is pregnancy-related dismissal or detrimental treatment.

Under current employment law, it is automatically unfair to dismiss a woman, select her for redundancy or subject her to detrimental treatment short of dismissal because of her pregnancy, or because she has taken or has sought to take maternity leave, parental leave or time off to care for dependants in an emergency.[2] There is no minimum length of service requirement (so a woman who is dismissed by her employer on such grounds can claim unfair dismissal before an employment tribunal, regardless of how long she has worked for the employer). In addition, the woman may also claim that the dismissal in such circumstances is unlawful sex discrimination contrary to the Sex Discrimination Act 1975.

© 2001 NATIONAL ASSOCIATION OF CITIZENS ADVICE BUREAU, *BRITH RIGHT* 2000

ADDRESSING

The following is a list of practical suggestions that may enable churches and organizations to minister effectively to those claiming sex discrimination/sexism.

➢ Political correctness should not form our attitudes and treatment of women, the fruit of the Spirit should be so evident in our behaviour that militant feminists will point the men of this world to the Church as an example.

➢ Political correctness toward women should not influence whom the Church seeks to have in leadership, a person's gender is secondary to calling, anointing and Biblical principles.

➢ Avoid demeaning comment about women, set an example to young men in how they should treat women.

➢ Treat seriously any complaints about sexist attitudes from members of your congregation.

Affirmation

The following is a list of churches, organizations or individuals who are ministering to those who have suffered sexism/sex discrimination They will, we believe, be able to offer practical and professional advice to assist you in your efforts to minister to those suffering the effects of sex discrimination (Please see Appendix B).

EQUAL OPPORTUNITIES COMMISSION (EOC)
ARNDALE HOUSE
ARNDALE CENTRE
MANCHESTER
M4 3EQ
TEL: 0161 833 9244
FAX: 0161 835 1657
EMAIL: INFO@EOC.ORG.UK
WEBSITE: WWW.EOC.ORG.UK
WORKS TOWARD THE ELIMINATION OF UNLAWFUL SEX AND MARRIAGE DISCRIMINATION, TO PROMOTE EQUALITY OF OPPORTUNITIES BETWEEN WOMEN AND MEN GENERALLY AND TO KEEP THE SEX DISCRIMINATION ACT AND EQUAL PAY ACT UNDER REVIEW.

EQUAL OPPORTUNITIES COMMISSION –
SCOTLAND
ST STEPHEN'S HOUSE
279 BATH STREET
GLASGOW
SCOTLAND
G2 4JL
TEL: 0141 248 5833
FAX: 0141 248 5834
EMAIL: SCOTLAND@EOC.ORG.UK
WEBSITE: WWW.EOC.ORG.UK
THE EQUAL OPPORTUNITIES COMMISSION HAS THREE MAIN TASKS: WORKING TO END SEX DISCRIMINATION, PROMOTING EQUAL OPPORTUNITIES FOR WOMEN AND MEN, AND REVIEWING AND SUGGESTING IMPROVEMENTS TO THE SEXUAL DISCRIMINATION ACT AND THE EQUAL PAY ACT

FAWCETT SOCIETY
5TH FLOOR
45 BEECH STREET
LONDON
EC2Y 5AD
TEL 02076284441
FAX 020 7628 2865
E-MAIL. FAWCETT@GN.APC.ORG.UK
WEB SITE. WWW.GN.APC.ORG/FAWCETT
WORKS TO INFLUENCE PUBLIC OPINION TO ACCEPT EQUAL STATUS FOR WOMEN IN THE HOME AND PUBLIC LIFE, AND EQUAL EDUCATIONAL AND JOB OPPORTUNITIES PUBLISHES TOWARDS EQUALITY, A QUARTERLY PUBLICATION TO SUBSCRIBE TO TOWARDS EQUALITY AND OTHER PUBLICATIONS SEND £25 00 TO-FAWCETT SOCIETY, FREEPOST FE 6903, LONDON, EC2B 2JD

JOSEPH ROWNTREE FOUNDATION (JRF)
THE HOMESTEAD
40 WATER END
YORK
NORTH YORKSHIRE
YO30 6WP
TEL: 01904 629241
FAX: 01904 620072
EMAIL: INFOR@JRF.ORG.UK
WEBSITE: WWW.JRF.ORG.UK

THE FOUNDATION IS AN INDEPENDENT, NON-POLITICAL BODY WHICH FUNDS PROGRAMS OF RESEARCH AND INNOVATIVE DEVELOPMENT IN THE FIELDS OF HOUSING, SOCIAL CARE AND SOCIAL POLICY IT PUBLISHES ITS RESEARCH FINDINGS RAPIDLY AND WIDELY SO THAT THEY CAN INFORM CURRENT DEBATE AND PRACTICE.

NATIONAL FAMILY AND PARENTING INSTITUTE (NFPI)
430 HIGHGATE STUDIOS 5
8–79 HIGHGATE ROAD
LONDON
NW5 1TL
TEL: 020 7424 3460
FAX: 020 7424 3590
EMAIL: INFO@NFPI.ORG
WEBSITE: WWW.NFPI.ORG
THE INSTITUTE'S ROLE IS TO BRING TOGETHER ORGANIZATIONS, KNOWLEDGE AND KNOW-HOW TO ENHANCE THE VALUE AND QUALITY OF FAMILY LIFE, TO MAKE SURE THAT PARENTS ARE SUPPORTED IN BRINGING UP THEIR CHILDREN AND IN FINDING THE HELP AND INFORMATION THEY NEED

THE FUTURE FOUNDATION FIRST FLOOR
14–16 COWCROSS STREET
LONDON
EC1M6DG
TEL: 02072503343
FAX: 02072518138
EMAIL: INFO@FUTUREFOUNDATION.NET
WEBSITE: WWW FUTUREFOUNDATION.NET
THE FUTURE FOUNDATION IS A BUSINESS FOCUSED THINK-TANK SET UP IN JULY 1996 WHICH AIMS TO HELP ORGANIZATIONS IMPROVE THEIR PERFORMANCE THROUGH UNDERSTANDING, ANTICIPATING AND RESPONDING TO THEIR CUSTOMERS

THE INSTITUTE OF MANAGEMENT
3RD FLOOR
2 SAVOY COURT STRAND
LONDON
WC2R OEZ
TEL: 020 7497 0580
FAX: 020 7497 0463
WEBSITE: WWW.MST-MGT.ORG.UK
THE INSTITUTE OF MANAGEMENT REPRESENTS AROUND 86,000 INDIVIDUAL MANAGERS MAKING IT THE LARGEST BROADLY BASED MANAGEMENT INSTITUTE IN THE UK.

TRADES UNION CONGRESS – EQUAL RIGHTS DEPARTMENT (TUC)
CONGRESS HOUSE
23–28 GREAT RUSSELL STREET
LONDON
WC 1B3LS
TEL: 020 7636 4030
FAX: 020 7636 0632
EMAIL: INFO@TUC.ORG.UK
WEBSITE: WWW.TUC.ORG.UK
THE TUC HAS OVER 75 MEMBER TRADE UNIONS, REPRESENTING NEARLY SEVEN MILLION PEOPLE FROM ALL WALKS OF LIFE THEY CAMPAIGN ON CONCERNS IN THE WORLD OF WORK AND BUILD LINKS WITH ALL POLITICAL PARTIES, BUSINESS AND THE COMMUNITY

UNITED KINGDOM MEN'S MOVEMENT
P.O BOX 205
CHELTENHAM
GL510YL
TEL: 01242 691110
WEBSITE: WWW.UKMM.ORG.UK
THE UNITED KINGDOM MEN'S MOVEMENT WISHES TO PROTECT THE EQUITABLE RIGHTS OF MEN. THEY INVITE ALL MEN AND WOMEN TO HELP THEM IN THE RESTORATION OF OUR DECAYING SOCIETY

Books that deal with the issue of sexism or sex descrimination

1-85684-045-X, *Recovering Biblical Manhood & Womanhood*, John Piper & Wayne Grudem, Crossway Books, *A response to Evangelical Feminism*

Bilezikian, Gilbert, *Beyond Sex Roles: What the Bible Says About a Woman's Place in Church and Family*, (Grand Rapids: Baker Book House, 1986)

Evans, Mary J., *Woman in the Bible*, (Exeter: Paternoster, 1984)

Groothuis, R., *Good News For Women: A Biblical Picture of Gender Equality*, (Grand Rapids: Baker Books, 1997)

Hebblethwaite, Margaret, *Motherhood and God*, (London: Geoffrey Chapman, 1984)

Hebhlethwaite, Margaret and Elaine Storkey, *Conversations on Christian Feminism* (London: HarperCollins, 1999)

Hull, Gretchen Gaebelein, *Equal to Serve: Women and Men in the Church and Home,* (New Jersey: Fleming H. Revell, 1987)

King, Ursula, *Faith and Praxis in a Postmodern Age*, (London: Cassell, 1998)

Littauer, Florence, *Wake Up, Women! Submission Doesn't Mean Stupidity*, (Dallas: Word Publishing, 1994)

Lorde, A. 'An Open Letter to Mary Daly' in *Sister Outsider*, (New York: Crossing Press, 1984)

Malcolm, K.T., *Women at the Crossroads: A Path Beyond Feminism and Traditionalism*, (Downers Grove: Inter-Varsity Press, 1982)

Martin, Faith, *Call Me Blessed*, (Grand Rapids: Eerdmans, 1988)

Mbuga, Judy, *Our Time Has Come: African Christian Women Address the Issues of Today*, (Carlisle: Paternoster, 1994)

Mickelsen, Alvera (ed), *Women, Authority and the Bible*, (Downers Grove: InterVaristy Press, 1986)

Moltmann-Wendel, *Elisabeth and Jtirgen Moltmann, God: His and Hers*, (London: SCM, 1991)

Perriman, Andrew, *Speaking of Women: Interpreting Paul*, (London: Apollos, 1998)

Reid, John, Lesslie Newbigin and David L. Pullinger, Modern, *Postmodern and Christian*, (Carberry: Handsel Press,1997)

Ruether, Rosemary Radford, *New Woman New Earth: Sexist Ideologies and Human Liberation*, (New York: The Seabury Press, 1975)

To Change the World: Christology and Cultural Criticism, (New York: Crossroad, 1981)

Storkey, Alan, *The Meanings of Love*, (Leicester: IVP, 1994) Storkey, Elaine. *Contributions to Christian Feminism*, (London: Impact Publications, 1995) *Magnify the Lord*, (London: HarperCollins, 1997)

Stott, John, *New Issues Facing Christians Today*, (London: Marshall Pickering, 1999)

Torrance, T.F., *The Ministrsy of Women*, (Carberry: Handsel Press, 1992)

West, A., *Deadly Innocence: Feminism and the Mythology of Sin*, (London: Cassell, 1995)

DISABLED RIGHTS

Awareness

The following information is included to raise the social awareness and understanding of ministers in relation to the contemporary issue of disability.

It is often a lack of understanding that sets many disabled people at a disadvantage and robs them of the dignity of being considered a valued member of any social groups such as a local church. The world wide web sites listed below offer relevant advice to enable understanding of a vast number of disabilities.

Disabled people may need varying degrees of support, however, patronizing sympathy will never enable a disabled person to reach their potential in life or to simply make a contribution to the fabric of a social organization.

The following are comments from the Government's publication, *A Practical Guide for Disabled People.*

> The Disability Discrimination Act became law in November 1995 and many of its main provisions came into force on 2 December 1996. The Act has introduced new rights and measures aimed at ending the discrimination which many disabled people face. Disabled people now have new rights in the areas of employment; getting goods and services; and buying or renting property. Further rights of access to goods and services to protect disabled people from discrimination will be phased in. These require service providers to make reasonable adjustments to policies, procedures and practices; to provide auxiliary aids and services and, where premises are inaccessible, to provide these services by a reasonable alternative means (from October 1999); and to make reasonable adjustments to premises (from 2004).
>
> Under the Act, schools, colleges and universities must provide information for disabled people and their parents. The Act also allows the Government to draw up regulations which will require all new public transport vehicles and systems to be accessible.

For information about the Disability Discrimination Act telephone the DDA Information Line on 0345 622633 (local rate calls) or textphone 0345 622644; or write to: DDA Information Line, Freepost, MIDO 2164, Strafford-upon-Avon, CV37 9BR.

Assessment

The following are some of the most up-to-date statistics in relation to the issue of Disability. (Please see appendix A.) There are 8.5 million disabled people in the UK.[1]

- ✶ An average of 8.5 working days per year per employee are lost due to sickness.[2]

- ✶ Disabled people have lower levels of qualifications than non-disabled people.[3]

- ✶ More cases have been taken under the employment provisions of the Disability Discrimination Act in its first year, than under the employment provisions of the Sex Discrimination Act or the Race Relations Act in their first years.[4]

- ✶ Less than 5% of disabled people use wheelchairs.[5]

- ✶ Nearly one fifth (18%) of the UK working-age population (over 6.4 million people) have a long-term disability or health problem.[1]

- ✶ 15% of working-age people in the South East are disabled.[1]

- ✶ 24% of working-age people in the North East are disabled.[1]

- ✶ The unemployment rate for disabled people is twice as high as the rate for non-disabled people: 46% of disabled people are in employment, as opposed to 80% of non-disabled people.[1]

- ✶ Almost half (41%) of economically inactive people are disabled.[1]

- ✶ Only 49% of people with back, neck or limb problems are economically active.[1]

- ✶ Only 22% of people with mental illness are economically active.[1]

- ✶ A third of economically inactive disabled people (over 1 million people) would like to work.[1]

- ✶ Sickness absence costs UK businesses £10.2 billion per year.[2]

- ✶ Disabled people are more likely than non-disabled people to work in low-skilled occupations.[3]

Statistical Sources

1. Office for National Statistics, *Labour Force Survey*, 1998/99
2. Confederation of British Industry, *Focus on Absence*, 1999
3. Department for Education & Employment, *Employment of Disabled People*, 1998
4. Department for Education & Employment, *Monitoring the Disability Discrimination Act 1995*, 1999
5. Employers' Forum on Disability, *Update*, 1996

Addressing

The following is a list of practical suggestions that may enable churches and organisations to minister effectively to the disabled. The following is a list of practical considerations that may serve to support those in churches with disabilities.

† Provide freedom of access throughout the church building.

- † Provide disabled toilet facilities.
- † Large print Bibles and Songbooks.
- † Loop system for the hard of hearing, and where possible someone adept at sign language.
- † Get involved with organizations that support the disabled.
- † Host a befriending service.
- † Encourage those with disabilities to get involved in the life of the church.

Affirmation

The following is a list of churches, organization or individuals who are ministering to the disabled. They will, we believe, be able to offer practical and professional advice to assist. (Please see appendix B.)

MENCAP
123 GOLDEN LANE
LONDON
EC1Y 0RT
TEL: 02074540454
FAX: 02076083254
WWW.MENCAP.ORG.UK
EMAIL: INFO@MENCAP.ORG.UK

ST LOYE'S COLLEGE
TOPSHAM ROAD
EXETER
EX2 6EP
TEL: 01392 255428

CAUSEWAY PROSPECTS
PO BOX 351
READING
BERKSHIRE
RG1 7AL
TEL: 0118 950 8781
FAX: 0118 939 1683
WWW.PROSPECTS.ORG.UK/RESOURES.HTM
EMAIL: CAUSEWAY@PROSPECTS.ORG.UK
PROSPECTS OFFER ADVICE AND TRAINING TO MINISTER TO THOSE WITH LEARNING DIFFICULTIES.

THE FOLLOWING WORLD WIDE WEB SITES OFFER LINKS TO A VAST NUMBER OF SUPPORT GROUPS AND ORGANIZATIONS SEEKING TO HELP THE DISABLED.

WWW.PATIENT.CO.UK

WWW.SHAW-TRUST.ORG.UK
WWW.CROSSWAYS.CO.UK

OTHER SOURCES OF HELP AND INFORMATION:

THE PHONE BOOK FOR YOUR AREA LISTS NUMBERS FOR LOCAL AUTHORITY SERVICES, HEALTH AUTHORITIES AND NETS TRUSTS, GOVERNMENT DEPARTMENTS AND HELPLINES.

YELLOW PAGES HAS SECTIONS OF PARTICULAR INTEREST TO DISABLED PEOPLE AND AT THE FRONT LISTS HELPLINES AND LOCAL AUTHORITY SERVICES.

DIAL (DISABILITY INFORMATION ADVICE LINE) IS RUN MOSTLY BY PEOPLE WHO ARE THEMSELVES DISABLED. SEE PHONE BOOK FOR YOUR LOCAL DIAL OR CALL DIAL-UK ON (01302) 310123.

DISABLED LIVING CENTERS (DLCS) ARE LOCAL CENTERS WHERE YOU CAN SEE, TRY OUT AND GET INFORMATION AND ADVICE ON EQUIPMENT. THE DISABLED LIVING CENTERS COUNCIL (0171) 820 0567.

HEALTH INFORMATION SERVICE FOR INFORMATION ABOUT LOCAL HEALTH SERVICES AND PARTICULAR DISABILITIES, 10.00 A.M. TO 5:00 P.M., MONDAY TO FRIDAY. ALL CALLS ARE TREATED IN CONFIDENCE. PHONE FREE 0800 665544 VOICE AND TEXT.

HEALTH LINE WALES 0800 665544

CITIZEN'S ADVICE BUREAUS (CABS) PROVIDE ADVICE ON A WIDE RANGE OF MONEY, HOUSING, LEGAL AND OTHER PROBLEMS. SEE YOUR PHONE BOOK FOR LOCAL NUMBERS.

BENEFITS ENQUIRY LINE FOR ADVICE FROM THE GOVERNMENT

BENEFITS AGENCY ABOUT SOCIAL SECURITY BENEFITS PHONE FREE:
0800 882200; FOR HELP FILLING IN CLAIM FORMS PHONE FREE
0800 441144; DISABILITY BENEFITS HELPLINE 0345 123456

RADAR (THE ROYAL ASSOCIATION FOR DISABILITY AND REHABILITATION) HAS A WIDE SELECTION OF HELPFUL PUBLICATIONS.
TEL: 0171 250 3222;
TEXT PHONE: 0171 250 4119

DISABILITY SCOTLAND 0131 229 8632

DISABILITY WALES /ANABLEDD CYMRU
01222 887325

A GOVERNMENT PUBLICATION CALLED "A PRACTICAL GUIDE FOR DISABLED PEOPLE, WHERE TO FIND INFORMATION, SERVICES AND EQUIPMENT." CONTAINS A VAST AMOUNT OF INFORMATION ON ORGANIZATIONS SEEKING TO SUPPORT THOSE WITH DIFFERENT FORMS OF DISABILITIES. COPIES ARE FREE FROM;

"DEPARTMENT OF HEATH"
PO BOX 410
WETHERBY
LS23 7LN

USEFUL WORLD WIDE WEB SITES

ABILITYNET – HELPS MAKE MAINSTREAM COMPUTER TECHNOLOGY ACCESSIBLE TO DISABLED PEOPLE: HTTP://WWW.ABILITYNET.CO.UK

ARTHRITIS CARE – WORKS WITH AND FOR ALL PEOPLE WITH ARTHRITIS:
HTTP://WWW.ARTHRITISCARE.ORG.UK

BRITISH DYSLEXIA ASSOCIATION – NATIONAL ORGANIZATION FOR DYSLEXIA:
HTTP://WWW.BDA-DYSLEXIA.ORG.UK

BRITISH EPILEPSY ASSOCIATION – AIMS TO RAISE AWARENESS OF EPILEPSY:
HTTP://WWW.EPILEPSY.ORG.UK

BRITISH INSTITUTE FOR LEARNING DISABILITY – CHARITY WORKING TO IMPROVE THE LIVES OF ALL PEOPLE WITH A LEARNING DISABILITY:
HTTP://WWW.BILD.ORG.UK

CENTRE FOR ACCESSIBLE ENVIRONMENTS – PROVIDES INFORMATION AND TRAINING ABOUT MAKING BUILDINGS AND PLACES ACCESSIBLE TO ALL USERS: WWW.CAE.ORG.UK

COMPUTABILITY CENTRE – SHOWS HOW COMPUTERS, WITH THE APPROPRIATE 'GET ROUND' TECHNOLOGY, CAN HELP PEOPLE WITH ALL KINDS OF DISABILITIES:
HTTP://WWW.BCS.ORG.UK/COMPUTAB

DISABILITY ADVICE AND WELFARE NETWORK:
HTTP://WWW.DISABILITY-NETWORK.ORG.UK

DISABILITY NET – INTERNET RESOURCE FOR PEOPLE WITH DISABILITIES:
HTTP://WWW.DISABILITYNET.CO.UK

DISABILITY NOW – CAMPAIGNING NEWSPAPER FOR EVERYONE WITH AN INTEREST IN DISABILITY:
HTTP://WWW.DISABILITYNOW.ORG.UK

DISABLEDINFO.COM – A "ONE STOP SITE" FOR DISABLED PEOPLE, THEIR FAMILIES AND CARERS, WHO ARE LOOKING FOR HELP, ADVICE OR SHOPPING REQUIREMENTS: HTTP://WWW.DISABLEDINFO.COM/START/INDEX.HTM

DISABLED LIVING FOUNDATION – INFORMATION ON EQUIPMENT AND TECHNOLOGY TO INCREASE DISABLED PEOPLE'S INDEPENDENCE:
HTTP://WWW.ATLAS.CO.UK

DYSLEXIA INSTITUTE – AN EDUCATIONAL CHARITY FOR THE ASSESSMENT AND TEACHING OF PEOPLE WITH DYSLEXIA AND FOR THE TRAINING OF TEACHERS:
HTTP://WWW.DYSLEXIA-INST.ORG.UK

HEADWAY – THE BRAIN INJURY ASSOCIATION: HTTP://WWW.HEADWAY.ORG.UK

JOHN GROOMS – CHRISTIAN-BASED ASSOCIATION WORKING WITH DISABLED PEOPLE: HTTP://WWW.JOHNGROOMS.ORG.UK

LEONARD CHESHIRE – CHARITY PROVIDER OF SERVICES FOR DISABLED PEOPLE: HTTP://WWW.LEONARD-CHESHIRE.ORG

MENCAP – ORGANIZATION FOR PEOPLE WITH A LEARNING DISABILITY AND THEIR FAMILIES: HTTP://WWW.MENCAP.ORG.UK

MENTAL HEALTH FOUNDATION – CHARITY WORKING TO IMPROVE THE LIVES OF EVERYONE WITH MENTAL HEALTH PROBLEMS OR LEARNING DISABILITIES: HTTP://WWW.MENTALHEALTH.ORG.UK

MIND – MENTAL HEALTH CHARITY WORKING FOR A BETTER LIFE FOR EVERYONE EXPERIENCING MENTAL DISTRESS: HTTP://WWW.MIND.ORG.UK

MOTABILITY – CHARITY HELPING DISABLED PEOPLE TO GET AROUND: HTTP://WWW.MOTABILITY.CO.UK

NATIONAL AUTISTIC SOCIETY – CHARITY FOR PEOPLE WITH AUTISTIC SPECTRUM DISORDERS AND THEIR FAMILIES: HTTP://WWW.ONEWORLD.ORG

NATIONAL DEVELOPMENT TEAM – FOR PEOPLE WITH LEARNING DISABILITIES: HTTP://WWW.NDT.ORG.UK

NATIONAL SCHIZOPHRENIA FELLOWSHIP – AIMS TO IMPROVE THE LIVES OF EVERYONE AFFECTED BY SEVERE MENTAL ILLNESS: HTTP://WWW.NSF.ORG.UK

RADAR – A NATIONAL PAN-DISABILITY ORGANIZATION RUN BY AND WORKING FOR DISABLED PEOPLE: HTTP://WWW.RADAR.ORG.UK

REMPLOY – COMPANY WHICH CREATES EMPLOYMENT OPPORTUNITIES FOR PEOPLE WITH A WIDE RANGE OF DISABILITIES: HTTP://WWW.REMPLOY.CO.UK

ROYAL NATIONAL INSTITUTE FOR DEAF PEOPLE: HTTP://WWW.RNID.ORG.UK

ROYAL NATIONAL INSTITUTE FOR THE BLIND: HTTP://WWW.RNIB.ORG.UK

SAINSBURY'S CENTRE FOR MENTAL HEALTH – WAS ESTABLISHED TO DEVELOP EFFECTIVE WAYS OF DELIVERING MENTAL HEALTH SERVICES: HTTP://WWW.SAINSBURYCENTRE.ORG.UK

SCOPE – CHARITY WORKING WITH PEOPLE WITH CEREBRAL PALSY: WWW.SCOPE.ORG.UK

SKILL – PROMOTES OPPORTUNITIES FOR YOUNG PEOPLE AND ADULTS WITH ANY KIND OF DISABILITY IN POST-16 EDUCATION, TRAINING AND EMPLOYMENT: WWW.SKILL.ORG.UK/

WORKABLE – 'BRINGING TOGETHER EMPLOYERS AND DISABLED PEOPLE': HTTP://MEMBERS.AOL.COM/WORKABLEUK

GOVERNMENT DISABILITY SITES:

DISABILITY ON THE AGENDA – THE UK GOVERNMENT'S DISABILITY WEB SITE, INCLUDING INFORMATION ON THE DISABILITY DISCRIMINATION ACT: HTTP://WWW.DISABILITY.GOV.UK

DISABILITY RIGHTS COMMISSION – AN INDEPENDENT BODY WORKING TOWARDS THE ELIMINATION OF DISCRIMINATION AGAINST – AND EQUALISING OPPORTUNITIES FOR – DISABLED PEOPLE. PROMOTES GOOD PRACTICE TO EMPLOYERS AND SERVICE PROVIDERS; PROVIDES ADVICE AND INFORMATION; ADVISES THE GOVERNMENT ON IMPLEMENTING THE DISABILITY DISCRIMINATION ACT: HTTP://WWW.DRC-GB.ORG/DRC/DEFAULT.ASP

INTERNATIONAL:

EUROPEAN DISABILITY FORUM – AIMS TO ADVANCE DISABLED PEOPLE'S HUMAN RIGHTS AND PROMOTE EQUAL OPPORTUNITIES IN THE EU INSTITUTIONS AND MEMBER STATES IN ACCORDANCE WITH THE PRINCIPLES OF NON-DISCRIMINATION HTTP://WWW.EDF-FEPH.ORG

GLADNET – GLOBAL APPLIED DISABILITY RESEARCH AND INFORMATION NETWORK ON EMPLOYMENT AND TRAINING: WWW.GLADNET.ORG/

IPWH – INTERNATIONAL ORGANIZATION FOR THE PROVISION OF WORK FOR PERSONS WITH DISABILITIES AND WHO ARE OCCUPATIONALLY HANDICAPPED: WWW.DESARROLLO.TELESERVICIOS.COM

JOB ACCOMMODATION NETWORK – US-BASED SERVICE PROVIDING INFORMAT ON ABOUT JOB ACCOMMODATIONS AND THE EMPLOYABILITY OF DISABLED PEOPLE: HTTP://JANWEB.ICDI.WVU.EDU/

REHABILITATION INTERNATIONAL – A FEDERATION OF NATIONAL AND INTERNATIONAL ORGANIZATIONS AND AGENCIES WORKING FOR THE REHABILITATION OF PEOPLE WITH DISABILITIES: HTTP://WWW.REHAB-INTERNATIONAL.ORG/

A FEW MORE HELPFUL LINKS:

| TERRENCE HIGGINS TRUST – AIDS/HIV | ALZHEIMER INTERNATIONAL | ARTHRITIS CARE | BRITISH DYSLEXIA | BRISTISH EPILEPSY ASSOCIATION | CALIBRE RECORDED BOOKS | CAF – DISABLED KIDS HELP | CANCERHELP UK | CARERS UK | CHRISTIAN RECOVERY INTERNATIONAL | DEAF BLIND WEBSITE | DEMENTIA WEB | DEPRESSION ALLIANCE | DIAL UK – DISABLED HELP | EATING DISORDERS | GRIEFNET | HEARTBEAT INTERNATIONAL | LIFE FOR THE WORLD | MENCAP – LEARNING DISABILITIES | MENTAL HEALTH FOUNDATION | MULIPLE SCLEROSIS | NATIONAL AUTISTIC SOCIETY | PATIENT SELF-HELP | RADAR – DISABLED HELP | RE-SOLV – SOLVENT ABUSE HELP | SAMARITANS UK | SCHIZOPHRENIA UK SCOPE – CEREBRAL PALSY | SHAW TRUST – DISABLED HELP | THIS DIRECTORY OF MORE THAN 600 COUNSELLORS COVERS MOST AREAS IN THE UK. CHRISTIAN COUNSELLORS UK

Books that deal with the issue of disabled issues

0745931383, *Disability: Rights and wrongs*, Ted Harrison, Lion, £6.99
0891078053, *Under the wings : mentally disabled*, Robert Bittner, CB USA, £8.99
034074036X, *Look No Hands*, Brian Gault, £6.99
0006280935, *Problem Of Pain*, CS Lewis, £5.99
0852344341, *Overcoming Life's Difficulties*, Peter Jeffery, £4.95
080240336, *Overcoming Adversity*, Mark Bubeck, £7.50
1576736733, *When Life Hurts*, Phillip Yancey, £4.99

ANIMAL RIGHTS

Awareness

The following information is included to raise the social awareness and understanding of church leaders/ministers in relation to the contemporary issue "animal rights." This section in no way is an attempt to promote or demote the work of "animal rights" activists, it is simply included in this manual to increase the awareness of church leaders about an issue that concerns many thousands of people.

"Animals rights" is perhaps not an issue that has overly concerned the Church. It is however, an issue that many people feel passionate enough about to protest in their thousands and, at times, sadly, human life has been lost to save or improve the existence of animals.

"Animal rights" arguments are based upon the premise that animals are equal with humans. The basis of this argument of course finds no place in scripture. The Bible clearly teachers that animals were created by God and placed under the mastery of mankind. (Genesis 1&2)

Cruelty towards animals is considered an unrighteous act. "A righteous man regardeth the life of his beast: but the tender mercies of the wicked are cruel." Proverbs 12: 10 Some of the most common medical test that are performed on animals are listed below by the Advocates for Animal.

Draize eye test
A test substance is dripped into the eyes of rabbits who must suffer the effects over a period of up to seven days. This can eat away at the eye causing swelling, ulceration and even blindness. Normally no pain relief is given.

Skin test
Animals (often rabbits or guinea pigs) have their backs shaved or the hair pulled out with sticky tape. The test substance is applied to their broken skin, which can become extremely sore and blistered.

LD50 test
Groups of animals are fed (often by a tube forced down their throats) a test substance to find the dosage which will kill half of them. This dosage is then known as the Lethal Dose 50% (LD50). Reactions' can include vomiting, paralysis, convulsions and internal bleeding. Sometimes the animals have to be fed so much of a substance that they die not from poisoning, but from overloading and damaging the digestive system.

The LD50 test attempts to find out how poisonous a substance is for humans, but many scientists have criticised both this test and the eye and skin tests as being vastly outdated and unreliable.

Most household goods (like disinfectants and cleaners), pesticides, herbicides, food additives, environmental pollutants and industrial chemicals are also developed using these methods.

Psychology experiments

In psychology (or behaviour) experiments animals are given electric shocks, brain damaged, starved, separated from their mothers, deprived of water or made to go without sleep. They are tormented in many different ways and researchers observe their reactions.

The number of psychology experiments carried out is growing alarmingly. Researchers claim that animal experiments will help us understand human behaviour and mental illness.

But we can only find out about human behaviour by studying humans! And what we know about mental illness has been gained by observing and counselling mentally ill and disturbed people – not by cruel and inapplicable animal experiments.

Warfare experiments

Animals are irradiated, subjected to poisonous gases, shot, burned and blown up... all so that humans can learn more about warfare. In Britain animals are used in warfare experiments at the Porton Down Chemical Defense Establishment in Wiltshire.

© ADVOCATES FOR ANIMAL SEPTEMBER, 1994

Some benefits have been accomplished as a result of animal experimentation.

- o Discovery of vitamins and understanding of their significance in diet.
- o Control of bacterial infections by antibiotics and viral infections by vaccination, e.g. polio, smallpox and measles.
- o Determination of blood groups and development of blood transfusion.
- o Modern anesthetics and improved surgical techniques.
- o Control of high blood pressure with the reduction in kidney disease and strokes.
- o Treatment of neurological disorders, e.g. Parkinson's disease, epilepsy, and of mental illness, e.g. schizophrenia, depression.
- o Vaccines and medicines for distemper and hepatitis in dogs, influenza, enteritis and leukemia in cats, and for many other animal diseases including rabies and anthrax.
- o Treatment of childhood leukemia with chemotherapy, radiotherapy and bone marrow grafts.
- o Control of fertility with the contraceptive pill.
- o Hip and other joint replacements.
- o Development of the heart-lung machine and open heart surgery.
- o Renal dialysis for patients with kidney failure.
- o Organ transplantation and drugs to fight rejection.
- o Corneal transplants and other treatments for serious eye conditions.
- o Intensive care techniques for premature babies.

Assessment

The following are some of the most up-to-date statistics in relation to the issue of animal rights. (Please see appendix A.)

☆ There were about two and a half million scientific procedures using animals in 1998. The exact figure was 2,659,662. The number of animals used is slightly less as some animals are used more than once. This does not happen often, and is strictly controlled.

☆ The annual number of animal experiments has halved over the last 20 years. In 1997, the number was the lowest for 20 years. This is due to higher standards of animal welfare, scientific advances and stricter controls. Although there have recently been some small rises, e.g. in 1991, 1994, 1996 and 1998, the overall trend is downwards.

☆ A change in the law in 1986 led to "procedures," rather than "experiments," being counted. The definition of procedures is somewhat broader, including, for example, the use of animals to produce natural products for research or treatment (about 12% of all procedures).

Addressing

The following is a list of practical suggestions that may enable churches and organizations to deal with issues relating to animals that may concern those they are seeking to minister to.

This section has been included for information purposes and any actions that may be considered on this issue is of course a matter of personal choice.

The following list of organizations will be more that willing to assist with any advice that is required.

Affirmation

The following is a list of organizations who have a greater understanding of "animal rights" issues and will be able to help with any questions you have or action that you may wish to take. (Please see appendix B.)

ADVOCATES FOR ANIMALS
10 QUEENSFERRY STREET
EDINBURGH
EH2 4PO
TEL: 0131 225 6039
WEBSITE: WWW.ADVOCATESFORANIMALS.ORG.UK
EMAIL: ANIMAL@VERGIN.NET
PROTECTS ANIMALS FROM CRUELTY AND PREVENT THE INFLICTION OF SUFFERING. PRODUCES A WIDE RANGE OF BOOKLETS ON ANIMAL RIGHTS ISSUES.

ANIMAL AID
7 CASTLE STREET
TONBRIDGE
KENT TN9 1BH
TEL: 01732 364546
WEBSITE: WWW.ANIMALAID.ORG.UK
EMAIL: INFO@ANIMALAID.ORG.UK
OPPOSED TO ANY USE OF ANIMALS IN MEDICAL RESEARCH. PRODUCES A WIDE RANGE OF BOOKLETS ON ANIMAL RIGHTS ISSUES.

ANIMALS IN MEDICAL RESEARCH
12 WHITEHALL
LONDON
SW1A 2DY
TEL: 0207 5880841
SUPPORTS THE RESPONSIBLE USE OF ANIMALS IN MEDICAL AND BIOLOGICAL RESEARCH. PRODUCES LEAFLETS, VIDEOS, POSTERS ETC.

BRITISH FIELD SPORTS SOCIETY
59 KENNINGTON ROAD
LONDON
SR1 7W
TEL: 0207 928 4742
CAMPAIGNS TO ENSURE THE CONTINUATION OF FIELD SPORTS. THEY PUBLISH LEAFLETS AND STUDENT RESOURCES PACKS.

BIOMEDICAL RESEARCH EDUCATION TRUST
58 GREAT MARLBOROUGH STREET
LONDON
W1V 1DD
TEL: 0207 287 2818
WEBSITE: WWW.RDS-ONLINE.ORG.UK
EMAIL: ANIMAL@RDS-ONLINE.ORG.UK
SUPPORTS THE RESPONSIBLE USE OF ANIMALS IN MEDICAL RESEARCH. LEAFLETS, FACTSHEETS, VIDEOS, SPEAKERS AVAILABLE.

DR. HADWEN TRUST FOR HUMANE RESEARCH
22 BANCROFT STREET
HITCHIN
HERTS SG5 1JW
TEL: 01462 436819
WEBSITE: WWW.DRHADWEN.ORG.UK
EMAIL: INFO@DRHADWEN.ORG.UK
PROMOTES THE DEVELOPMENT OF HUMANE NON-VIVISECTIONIST TECHNIQUES OF RESEARCH WITHOUT THE USE OF LIVING ANIMALS IN ORDER TO REPLACE ANIMALS EXPERIMENTS IN SCIENCE AND MEDICINE.

FRAME (FUND FOR THE REPLACEMENT OF ANIMALS IN MEDICAL EXPERIMENTS)
RUSSELL & BURCH HOUSE
96-98 NORTH SHERWOOD STREET
NOTTINGHAM
NG4EE
TEL: 0115 9584740
WEBSITE WWW.FRAME-UK.DEMON.CO.UK
EMAIL:
WORKS TOWARDS REDUCING THE NUMBER OF ANIMALS USED, REFINING METHODS TO REDUCE SUFFERING AND REPLACING LIVE ANIMAL METHODS WITH RELIABLE ALTERNATIVE TECHNIQUES.

HUMANE RESEARCH TRUST (HRT)
BROOK HOUSE
29 BRAMHALL LANE
SOUTH BRAMHALL
CHESHIRE
SK7 2DN
TEL: 0161 439 8041
FAX: 061 439 3713
SUPPORTS MEDICAL AND SCIENTIFIC RESEARCH BY ADVANCED TECHNIQUES WHICH REPLACE THE USE OF LABORATORY ANIMALS.

LEAGUE AGAINST CRUEL SPORTS (LACS)
83-87 UNION STREET
LONDON SE1 1SO
TEL: 0207 403 6155
CAMPAIGNS FOR THE PROTECTION OF WILD LIFE AND TO OUTLAW HUNTING WITH DOGS.

LEAFLETS AND BOOKLETS AVAILABLE:

RSPCA (ROYAL SOCIETY FOR THE PREVENTION OF CRUELTY TO ANIMALS)
CAUSEWAY
HORSHAM SUSSEX
RH12 1HO
TEL: 08700 101181
WEBSITE: WWW.RSPCA.ORG.UK
PRODUCES A WIDE RANGE OF LEAFLETS AND OTHER MATERIAL ON ANIMAL WELFARE ISSUES.

Books that deal with the issue of animal rights from a Christian point of view
0340621508, *Animal Gospel*, Andrew Lizey, H&S, £8.99
0340669136, *Animal Rights and wrongs*, Tony Sargent, H&S, £8.99
0334027608, *Animal Rights*, Andrew Linzey,

ENVIRONMENTALISM

Awareness

The following information is included to raise the social awareness and understanding of ministers in relation to the contemporary environmental issues.

- Environmental issues like those of "animal rights," are issues that the Christian Church has generally been impassive about. Yet like "animal rights" environmental concern consumes the hearts of thousands of people in the world.

- From deforestation to industrial and nuclear pollution, there are few people in the Western World that are not unaware of environmental issues.

- The Church has remained largely uninvolved in environmental issues for a number of reasons.

  - The Church holds suspicions of the New Age Movement's association with green issues.

  - A "So What?" attitude, Green issues are considered irrelevant, all that matters is the Gospel.

  - The "As along as it's not in my backyard" approach to environmental problems.

- Children are bombarded in school and on Television with the green message, the earth is ours and we must care for it so we can pass it on to our children. Young people are becoming increasing involved with environmental groups.

- The environmental message is a very pessimistic message and offers little hope outside of enough individuals doing something about the environmental problem. Environmental groups are often influenced by New Age ideologies.

- Stewardship of the planet has always been a God-ordained responsibility for mankind. Adam and Eve were placed in a garden, the garden of Eden, 'to work it and take care of it' (Genesis 2.15). We are presented with a picture of the Earth as God's garden and humans as its 'gardeners'. The green message of course leaves God out, as the Earth is not ours, "the Earth is the Lord's". (Ps 8: 1–6,24: 1–2)

Assessment

The following are some of the most up-to-date statistics in relation to the issue of environmentalism. (Please see appendix A.)

- ⇨ Figures from the World Wide Fund for Nature show that an area of forest the size of England and Wales is disappearing each year.

- 62% of the world's total forest cover has been lost.
- 97% of UK's native woodland lost.
- Europe has lost 62% of original forest cover.
- Only 2% of Europe's remaining forest is protected.
- Even before the Indonesian fires 88% of Asia–Pacific forests had been lost.
- WWF and the World Bank are calling on all countries to protect a minimum of 10% of all forest types in their borders by 2000.
- Apart from the extinction of species the removal of trees always creates further problems and possibly changes in the climate. The huge smog in Indonesia in 1997 was followed by problems such as the rains washing soil and ash into the rivers which clogged them, killed the fish and caused flooding.

© Guardian October 9 1997

Worldwide Consumption

America has 6% of the world's population but consumes 30% of its resources. Worldwide, a fifth of the Earth's people take more than four-fifths of its resources, control over 50% of its wealth and produce the majority of its toxic waste and greenhouse gas emissions.

© Guardian 22.10.97

Addressing

The following is a list of practical suggestions that may enable churches and organizations to deal with environmental issues.

- ✝ Acknowledge the work of scientists that the world is facing environmental crises of unparalleled magnitude, including some on a global scale.
- ✝ Acknowledge that as Christians, looking after the Earth (or even our part of the planet) is a God-given responsibility, when teaching the doctrine of creation.
- ✝ Attempt to do something about the pollution in your locality. This could mean getting involved with an environmental group, allowing church car parks to be used for paper or bottle banks or even making it known that as a church you are teaching children the biblical principle for the Earth's stewardship.
- ✝ Our willingness to acknowledge and address environmental issues from a biblical perspective provides an enormous opportunity for the church which has too often ignored the Earth and the environment and neglected the importance of creation and its place in the overall Christian message.
- ✝ Much of the postmodern world is obsessed with green issues and so the church's acknowledgement of the issues and any attempts to lead in God ordained stewardship of the Earth could help to demonstrate the value of the

Christian faith to people who otherwise see no point in it and see no relevance in the spiritual message we want to bring.

AFFIRMATION

The following is a list of churches, organizations or individuals who are ministering to those who have suffered environmentalism. They will, we believe, be able to offer practical and professional advice to assist you in your efforts to understand environmental issues. (Please see appendix B.)

A ROCHA TRUST
CONNANS KNOWE
KIRKTON
DUMFRIES
DG1 1SX
TEL: 01387 710286
EMAIL: A_ROCHA@COMPUSERVE.COM
WEBSITE: WWW.AROCHA.ORG

CHRISTIAN ECOLOGY LINK
20 CARLTON ROAD
HARROGATE
HG2 8DD
TEL: 01423 871616
EMAIL: INFO@CHRISTIAN-ECOLOGY.ORG.UK
WEBSITE: WWW.CHRISTIAN-ECOLOGY.ORG.UK

THE JOHN RAY INITIATIVE
TEL 01242 543580
EMAIL: FOR DR CARLING: CARLING@TCP.CO.UK
EMAIL: FOR JRI ADMIN: INFO@JRI.ORG.UK
WEBSITE: WWW.JRI.ORG.UK

Books that deal with the issue

Al Gore, *Earth in the Balance*, Houghton Mifflin, 1992

Global Environmental Outlook 2000, United Nations Environment Program 1999, is available online at www.unep.org/geo2000/

The Care of Creation, ed. R J Berry, IVP, 2000

Ron Elsdon, *Greenhouse Theology*, Monarch, 1992

Lawrence Osborn, *Guardians of Creation*, Apollos, 1993

Colin Russell, *The Earth, Humanity and God*, UCL Press, 1994

John Houghton, *Global Warming: the complete briefing* (2nd edition) CUP, 1997

Ghillean Prance, *The Earth under threat: a Christian perspective*, Wild Goose Publications, 1996

0801058023, *Caring for Creation*, Calvin Dewitt, Baker, £8.50

185174195X, Caring for the Earth, Keith Innes, Grove, £2.25

1851743995, *Fair Trade as Christian Mission*, 2.25

2825413267, *Spiritual values for Earth Community*, 6.50

187167686X, *Creation in Crisis*, A. McDonald, £3.99

0521576318, *Environment, Christian Ethics*, M.Northcott, £15.95

0851109519, *Guardians of Creation*, L. Osborn, £9.99

1-900924-03-4, *Sustaining the Earth: A Christian Approach to Caring for the Environment*, Tim Cooper, £9.95, 1997

8066 3960, *This is the Earth that God Made,* Lyn Downey, £4.99

Earth Spirituality: Jesus at the Center, Edward Echlin, £5.99, Arthur James 1999

2-8254-1131-0, *Ecotheology: Voices from South and North,* ed. David Hallman, 1994

7459 2307, *Our World God's World*, Barbara Wood (Bible Reading Fellowship)

264 67281, *Preaching for our Planet*, Hugh Montefiore, 1992

0-232-5180-X, *God is Green*, Ian Bradley, £6.95, 1990

Whose Earth?, Chris Seaton, £4.99

ISSN 1363 7320, *Ecotheology*, a twice yearly Academic Journal published by Sheffield Academic Press, available on subscription

DRUG ABUSE

AWARENESS

The following information is included to raise the social awareness and understanding of ministers in relation to the contemporary issue of drug abuse.*

We live in a drug-taking society where drugs are taken legally and illegally on a daily basis. A person may decide to stop taking a drug but find they cannot, at which point they may seek help from the local minister or church. A drug is a chemical which people take initially for benefit and which has the power to change one's state of mind or mood. It is also a chemical on which the taker can become dependent. Drugs can be taken legally when they have been prescribed by a doctor, e.g. opiates, amphetamines and barbiturates, or those accepted by society e.g. alcohol, caffeine and nicotine.

Dependency usually involves:

- An over-powering desire to continue taking a drug.
- A tendency to increase the dose.
- A deterioration of the physical and emotional health of the individual.
- The appearance of withdrawal effects when the drug is discontinued or reduced below a certain level.
- A preoccupation with obtaining drugs, often at the expense of society.
- A psychological and often physical dependence on the effects of a drug.

Physical Safety

You and the drug abuser both need to be safe, think through potential problems and address a few questions.

- Where are you going to see the person?
- Will you be alone?
- Is help nearby?
- Is it appropriate to counsel the opposite gender?
- Could you cope with abusive, threatening, manipulative behaviour?

Disclosures

⇨ Avoid collecting negative information, especially about illegal activity, unless the person needs to disclose crimes to gain peace of mind.

* Thanks to Lesley Bellerby for her contributions to this section

⇨ Confidentiality should be kept unless the person or others are at risk. In such cases explain you cannot keep this information to yourself and that you will have no control over the consequences.

⇨ Think carefully before you disclose confidential things about yourself. The person does not have to maintain confidentiality and may not have integrity. They may be intimidating if they later regret confiding in you.

Coping with Failure

➢ It is very easy to feel that we have failed. When a drug abuser whom you have been ministering to commits suicide, contracts HIV, goes back to using drugs, goes to jail, die or simply disappears.

➢ It is also easy to think we have failed when we go to bed knowing a person you are ministering to is homeless or penniless.

➢ We have to have inner peace to know we have done what we can and then hand them over to the Lord, knowing it is He who changes lives. Matthew 6:

➢ General Advice, Luke 4: 18–19, 2 Corinthians 6: 6

Whatever the problems the main response must be harm reduction, deal with the underlying problem and treat withdrawal symptoms as they appear.

→ Encourage a proper diet, especially raw fruit and vegetables.

→ Help the body excrete toxins, encourage the client to drink plenty and bathe in Epsom salts.

→ Choose a time that is relatively stress-free.

→ Enlist the help of loved ones and sympathetic GPs.

→ Teach how to relax and breathe properly.

→ Encourage creative hobbies.

→ Work out an obtainable daily routine.

→ Expect setbacks, and start again.

Prescribing Reality

⇒ Twenty years ago, the benzodiazepines or tranquillizers were hailed as wonder drugs with no side-effects and in good faith were prescribed to relieve acute anxiety and to give the sufferer rest after a sudden shock or bereavement.

⇒ They were meant to be taken for a few weeks but many got repeat prescriptions and found when they eventually wanted to stop using them they couldn't, they had become addicted to them.

⇒ This affected many groups of people, the frightened young policemen, the isolated mum, the lonely old person to the harassed executive.

⇒ They put the emotions into cold storage and the person is unable to react normally to events in their lives, whether happy or sad.

⇒ Many people especially woman take them, some people in our churches are almost certainly using tranquillizers.

⇒ Withdrawal symptoms can include depression, increased anxiety, phobias, confusion, dizziness, headaches, rashes, personality changes and loss of balance.

They also have to cope with the world as it is not the world in its dampened-down form, we really are PRESCRIBING REALITY.

⇒ BEWARE, the person who stops taking tranquillizers may be a very different person, her family may need help to adapt and to accept that new person's opinions and needs. Bottled-up emotions are released, help may be needed to address and accept these.

⇒ Controlled withdrawal is important, fewer tablets should be prescribed, the client should not hoard spare tablets or take them erratically.

⇒ Drugs are a very emotive subject and for the majority of parents who discover that their child is taking drugs they are devastated and think the worst "My child is going to die."

⇒ In reality many young people experiment with drugs, they are the 1990s equivalent to a quick smoke behind the bike sheds, many will not enjoy the experience, many will shun it when they want to get a job or get married. It is not always, or even often, the first step on a slippery slope.

⇒ Some will choose to use it socially and recreationally and maintain a good lifestyle at the same time.

⇒ A small minority will go on to form a drug habit.

⇒ The parents may need support, advice and information. Knowledge can help alleviate fear and allow them to talk in an informed way with their children. Mixing with other parents in similar circumstances can help.

⇒ Parents should be challenged to look at their own drug taking to see what example they are setting.

⇒ COMMON DRUGS YOUNGSTERS TRY.

   Magic mushrooms, tobacco, alcohol, cannabis and solvents.
   These are all cheap, or free and widely available.

⇒ BEYOND THE LAW

   Jesus showed compassion to everyone and associated with all manner of people. Mark 2: 16–17

1. STREET DRUGS (Romans 13: 1–3)

- You do not know what you are buying, the drug's strength and purity are unknown.
- Often they are cut with other cheaper drugs or other contaminates.
- Many problems arise when money for drugs is owed and users are in the cycle of stealing to pay for their habit.
- Parents often have to ask their offspring to leave home as they are so disruptive, they should however go on showing love and parenting helping their offspring to find accommodation etc. (Luke 15: 22–24).
- To obtain street drugs is risky and costly and illegal. If you are charged with possessing or supplying drugs you can face severe fines, imprisonment and having your assets seized.
- Never look after drugs for a person, you could be charged with possession or supplying. If the person wants to leave the drugs with you, refuse, get them to destroy them or watch you destroy them.
- Confidentiality is of great importance there may be relationship problems to sort out, money problems, much guilt and often impending court cases.
- They may also only have drug user friends and will need to make new ones, perhaps having to even move to a new location and a fresh start.

2. COMMON ILLEGAL DRUGS

- Cannabis, tranquillisers, sedatives, anabolic steroids, stimulants, ecstasy, hallucinogens, heroin

3. INJECTING

- Injecting carries with it great risks:
- **OVERDOSE**, as a drug of unknown strength is being deposited into the blood stream.
- **INFECTION**, from contaminated/shared syringes, hepatitis and HIV are real risks.
- **ABSCESSES**, and thrombosis from injecting drugs never intended for injection.
- **GANGRENE**, from hitting an artery instead of a vein and blood poisoning caused by an infected wound.

4. HARM REDUCTION

- **CLEAN INJECTING EQUIPMENT**, while they reduce and stop injecting. Safe disposal of used equipment is also important.

➤ PRESCRIBED DRUGS, so that:
    a.   The dose of chemical is steady and controlled
    b.   The person is not breaking the law
    c.   Life is no longer consumed with looking for the next dose
    d.   There is no need to be involved in criminal activity to buy drugs
    e.   They have a less chaotic lifestyle so less disruption to work, college and family life.

➤ METHADONE HYDROCHLORIDE, usually prescribed as a non-injectable syrup. It is a clean, safe, legal substitute for street opiates. It is addictive but is given in a controlled dosage and reduction is monitored. Its availability differs around the country.

➤ REHABILITATION UNITS, at times residential care is the best option. Clients usually have to be drug-free, have funding and no outstanding court cases.

ASSESSMENT

The following are some of the most up-to-date statistics in relation to the problem. (Please see appendix A.)

The East Riding Drug Action Team in its latest report published very interesting figures. This body covers the East Riding of Yorkshire and Kingston upon Hull, an area of 88 nautical miles of coastland and a hinterland of 960.6 square miles with a population of 580,000. Over 1,000 users of substances use local drug services on a regular basis and many more are in less frequent contact. It is estimated that 1 in 4 of the population who are dependent on substances seek assistance.

In the last year there were 31 drug-related deaths, almost all involving an overdose of heroin. The local arrest referral scheme data shows that approximately 65% of all recorded crimes involve a drugs dimension.

Based on male and female clients over 13 years old of clients accessing treatment from April 99 to Sept. 99 the drug groups break down as below:

Heroin	54.4	Other Opiates	1.2
Alcohol	21.1	Solvents	0.9
Methadone	8.5	Other Drugs	0.5
Amphetamines	7.0	Cocaine	0.5
Benzodiazepines		Anti-depressants	0.4
Canabis	2.8	Ecstasy	0.3

British teenagers are the most socially irresponsible in Europe according reports published in the *British Medical Journal*. They take more illegal drugs and have more unwanted pregnancies and abortions than any of their contemporaries in Western Europe. They are also more likely to develop smoking and drinking-related problems and sexually-transmitted diseases. Martin McKee, professor of European public health at the London School of Hygiene and Tropical medicine blamed 'social development which is more American than European.' He cited poverty, second-rate education, long working hours and poor skills as major factors.

He also suggested that a key element was the breakdown of the traditional family which had left children without the level of parental support they might once have had. 'Another clue could lie in the amount of time families spend together.'

One abortion in five involves a teenage girl, as do nine per cent of births.

In Britain teenage girls had higher rates of gonorrhoea, genital warts and chlamydia than any other group of women. They also had the second highest level of herpes.

Britain's teen pregnancy rate is double that of Germany, four times that of France and seven times that of Holland.

British teenagers have the worst record for illegal drug use, particularly solvent abuse.

42% of 15 and 16-year-olds in the UK have tried drugs, almost three times as many as in France.

Cannabis use is higher than in Holland and ecstasy and LSD are also major problems.

British youngsters are also more likely to smoke and to drink. Professor McKee said: "Alone, each of these facts is worrying, but, taken together do they indicate a more fundamental malaise? On a range of issues, British teenagers are doing worse than their European neighbours and we need to know why."

Cornelia Oddie, of Family and Youth Concern said it was no coincidence that Britain also had the highest levels of divorce in Europe. "Girls from divorced families are twice as likely to become teenage mothers. Children need more attention. If parents work long hours they can be too tired to supervise homework. If children have goals and ambitions they're less likely to go off and have sex or take drugs."

© The Daily Mail 14.5.99.

Addressing

The following is a list of practical suggestions that may enable churches and organizations to take action that will alleviate the problem of drug abuse in their locality.

☆ The drug-dependent person may well present at the church or to the minister wanting help. They could be taking illegal drugs or prescribed drugs but have reached a point where they want to stop using.

☆ The minister can help by listening and treating the person with dignity and in finding out local services, often the situation is complex with legal, housing and benefits needing sorting out.

- ☆ Christian counselling can help and much support can be given by the church if the person is determined to be drug free, especially on hard days.
- ☆ The church can help with practical care during the initial withdrawal period. In the case of people withdrawing from tranquillizers friendship and a listening ear by sympathetic members is of great help.
- ☆ Confidentiality is of importance, the person may not wish their drug habit to be common knowledge.

Affirmation

The following is a list of churches, organizations or individuals who are taking action to alleviate alcohol/drug abuse. They will, we believe, be able to offer practical and professional advice to assist you in your efforts to take action against drug abuse. (Please see appendix B.)

EVANGELICAL COALITION ON DRUGS (ECOD)
WHITEFIELD HOUSE
186 KENNNINGTON PARK ROAD
LONDON
SE11 4BT
TEL: 0207 207 2114
FAX: 0171 207 2150
EMAIL: TKILLOCK@EAUK.ORG

CALAB HOUSE
21 VICTORIA ROAD
CLEVEDON
NORTH SOMMERSET
BS21 7UR
TEL: 01275 341112
WEBSITE: WWW.LIFEFORTHEWORLD.COM
THIS IS A CHRISTIAN REHABILITATION CENTER FOR MEN AGED 20–40 YEARS.

HOPE UK
25F COPPERFIELD STREET
LONDON
SE1 0EN
TEL: 0207 928 0848
FAX: 0171 401 3477
WEBSITE: WWW.HOPEUK.ORG

CRISIS CENTER MINISTRIES
12 CITY ROAD
ST PAUL'S
BRISTOL
BS2 8TP
TEL: 0117 942 3088
FAX: 0117 924 1799
EMAIL: DWGROVES@SAQNET.CO.UK

KENWARD TRUST
KENWARD HOUSE
YALDING
MAIDSTONE
ME18 6AH
TEL: 01622 814 187
FAX: 01622 814 187
WEBSITE: WWW.KENWARDTRUST.ORG.UK

TACADE (THE ADVISORY COUNCIL ON ALCOHOL AND DRUG EDUCATION)
1 HULME PLACE
THE CRESCENT
SALFORD
M5 4QA
TEL: 0161 745 8925
FAX: 0161 745 8923
WEBSITE: WWW.TACADE.COM

Books dealing with the issue of drug abuse

0851115993, *Use and misuse*, Ollie Batchelor, Inter-Varsity Press
0002740389, *Help your Kids Stay Drug-Free*, Francis, COL
0851115993, *Use and Misuse*, Batchelor, IVP
0830717714, *Drug-Proof your Kids*, Arteburn/Burns, Regal
0830713328, *Issues in Focus*, Rosenberger, Regal

ALCOHOL ABUSE

AWARENESS

The following information is included to raise the social awareness and understanding of ministers in relation to the contemporary issue of alcohol abuse.

Alcohol Addiction is the single biggest drug addiction problem in western society; commonly called alcoholism and the addict referred to as an alcoholic. The World Health Organization rates alcoholism as the third largest killer in the Western World. It is the most readily available drug in economic terms. It is legally sold under licence and generally socially acceptable in our culture.

How alcohol affects the body depends upon things such as:

- body weight
- whether the person drinking is male or female
- how quickly the person drinks
- the length of time since his or her last meal
- whether or not the person is taking another drug.
- The same amount of alcohol may have different effects upon different people.
- Alcohol is a depressant drug. It depresses (or slows down) the way body systems work.
- In small amounts alcohol may produce feelings of relaxation, fun and laughter

Who are alcoholics? "Alcoholic" is a term often used by people to describe the drinking habits of some people. There are two sorts of problem drinkers; those who abuse alcohol and those who are dependent on it. People who abuse alcohol may sporadically drink too much and incur problems; people who are dependent have effectively lost control. They may not necessarily drink every day, but when they do drink, they usually fail to limit their consumption to a reasonable level, despite the fact that they know their drinking is damaging and dangerous.

The Royal College of Physicians report summarizes the medical complications of excess alcohol as follows:

Nervous System

- Acute intoxication (This will be manifest in decision making, loss of inhibition, a sedative/depressive effect on the system, i.e. loss of coordination in body function – slurred speech, staggering, impaired ability to

* Thanks to "The Stauros Foundation" for their input on this section.

judge in the physical, moral and intellectual realms e.g. not fit to drive, promiscuous or other immoral/illegal behaviour, inability to reason effectively, therefore often irrational and inappropriate comments in discussion)

- ✿ 'black-outs' (AI &LT) The result of the anesthetic effect of alcohol on brain cell tissue or in longer term abuse the irreparable loss of brain cell tissue

Persistent brain damage

- ✧ Wernicke's encephalopathy (LT) This form of brain damage is extremely rare and usually the alcoholic has collapsed physically before this takes place
- ✧ Korsakoff's syndrome (LT) As above, thankfully not too common. This is brain damage resulting in a condition that diagnostically is similar to Alzheimer's disease, a form of dementia
- ✧ cerebral degeneration (LT) often after consistent abuse the brain can shrink. Korsakoff's syndrome and Wernicke's are the result of this. At a lesser degree of damage, there can be evidence of impaired reasoning, memory and motor skills, general loss of efficiency in a number of previously good performance areas
- ✧ dementia (LT) See above
- ✧ Hallucination (AI & LT)
- ✧ Cerebrovascular disease: For example strokes (AI &LT) especially in young people. Subarachnoid haemorrhage, this is only long term bleeding between the brain and its lining, usually as a result of brain shrinkage. Subdural haemotoma occurs often after head injury

Withdrawal symptoms

- ✿ Tremour. This is often colloquially known as 'the shakes'
- ✿ Hallucinations. Usually associated with delirium tremens (LT) occurring usually between 4th and 6th day of withdrawal and may be accompanied by fitting
- ✿ Fits. Usually associated with delirium tremens as above (LT)
- ✿ Palpitations (AI & LT)
- ✿ Swings of body temperature (AI & LT) Sometimes called "the sweats"
- ✿ Diarrhoea (AI & LT)
- ✿ Nausea (AI & LT)
- ✿ Loss of appetite (AI & LT)
- ✿ Insomnia (AI & LT)

❋   **Irritability/anxiety (AI & LT)**

Possible death. If fitting occurs, as in delirium tremens, there can be a risk of death. This is a result of unassisted withdrawal causing a severe shock to the **Central Nervous System**. If there is any history of fitting, medical advice should be sought immediately (LT). There is also the risk of death due to excess ingestion of alcohol causing alcoholic poisoning (AI & LT). There may be pneumonia as a result of inhalation of vomit, but there is also the risk of death as a result of choking on vomit (AI & LT)

Dehydration

A home remedy for withdrawal, glucose dissolved in lukewarm water. This is easy to take and if vomited up is easily replaced. The purpose is to rehydrate and augment sugar levels. This can also be given with travel sickness pills, which can assist in relieving nausea. Longer term Thiamine, Vitamin B can be administered safely and all these are able to be purchased at any chemist over the counter.

Nerve and muscle damage:

- **Weakness (LT)**
- **Paralysis (LT)**
- **Burning sensation in hands and feet.** This is called peripheral neuritis and is sometimes characterised by numbness or a feeling of pins and needles as well as the burning sensation described (LT)

Liver

❋   **Infiltration of liver with fat (LT)**
❋   **Alcoholic hepatitis (LT)**
❋   **Cirrhosis and eventual liver failure (LT)**
❋   **Liver cancer (LT)**

Gastrointestinal System

- **Reflux of acid into the oesophagus (AI &LT)**
- **Tearing and occasionally rupture of the oesophagus (AI &LT)** This is usually associated with the retching of severe vomiting
- **Cancer of the oesophagus (LT)**
- **Gastritis (AI &LT)**
- **Aggravation and impaired healing of peptic ulcers (LT)**
- **Diarrhoea and impaired absorption of food (AI &LT)**
- **Chronic inflammation of the pancreas leading in some to diabetes and malabsorption of food (LT)**

Nutrition

- Malnutrition from reduced intake of food, toxic effects of alcohol on intestine, and impaired metabolism, leading to weight loss (LT)
- Obesity, particularly in early stages of heavy drinking (LT)

Heart and Circulatory System

- Abnormal rhythms (AI &LT)
- High blood pressure (AI &LT)
- Chronic heart muscle damage leading to heart failure (LT)

Respiratory System

- Fractured rib (AI &LT). Obviously injury most likely sustained under the influence
- Pneumonia from inhalation of vomit (AI &LT)

The four bullet points below are to do with the interference, which the abuse of alcohol causes in the endocrine system. This manages the control of the release of certain chemicals within the body, such as cortisol, insulin, sugars, adrenalin etc. and are generally, with the exception of the diabetic, (LT) results of abuse.

- Overproduction of cortisol leading to obesity, acne, increased facial hair, and high blood pressure
- Condition mimicking over-activity of the thyroid with loss of weight, anxiety, palpitations, sweating, and tremor
- Severe fall in blood sugar, sometimes leading to coma
- Intense facial flushing in many diabetics taking the anti-diabetic drug chlorpropamide.

Reproductive System

- In men, loss of libido, reduced potency, shrinkage in size of testes and penis, reduced or absent sperm formation and so infertility, and loss of sexual hair (LT)
- In women, sexual difficulties, menstrual irregularities, and shrinkage of breasts and external genitalia (LT)

Occupation and Accidents

- Impaired work performance and decision making (AI &LT)
- Increased risk and severity of accidents (AI &LT)

The Foetus, the Child and the Family

- Damage to the foetus and the foetal alcohol syndrome (LT)
- Acute intoxication in young children produces hypothermia, low blood sugar levels, depressed respiration. (AI &LT)
- Effect on physical development and behaviour of child through heavy drinking by parents (LT)
- Interaction of alcohol with medicinal substances (AI &LT)
- Increased likelihood of unwanted effects of drugs (AI &LT)
- Reduced effectiveness of medicines. (AI &LT)

(SOURCE: © ROYAL COLLEGE OF PHYSICIANS: *A GREAT AND GROWING EVIL – THE MEDICAL CONSEQUENCES OF ALCOHOL ABUSE*. 1987)

Assessment

The following are some of the most up-to-date statistics in relation to the problem (Please see appendix A) and figures about alcohol. Some experts estimate the following:

- Between 25,000 and 40,000 people die every year in the UK as a result of their alcohol consumption.
- Alcohol is a factor in: 30% of murders, 30% of child abuse, 30% of drownings, 33% of accidents in the home, 44% of theft charges, 45% of woundings and assaults, 88% of criminal damage arrests.
- Every year up to 14 million working days are lost due to drinking.
- Every year alcohol costs the National Health Service over £160 million in treatment.
- Each year, about 1000 young people under the age of 15 are admitted to hospital as a result of alcohol poisoning, and all require emergency treatment.
- Every year industry loses £1.6 billion through lost productivity, unemployment and absenteeism, due to drinking alcohol.
- Every year material damage and criminal activities linked to drinking, cost over £142 million.
- Each year between 10,000 and 40,000 people die in the UK as a result of drinking alcohol.

By the age of 11, the majority of children will have drunk some alcohol. Different research studies have shown that:

- In Wales, 89.9% of boys and 88.3% of girls aged 11–16 have tasted alcohol

- ❋ In Northern Ireland 92% of boys and 87% of girls have tasted alcohol by the age of 18
- ❋ In England 90% of young people have tried alcohol by the age of 15 and in Scotland about 64% of young people aged 12–15 will have drunk alcohol

ADDRESSING

The following is a list of practical suggestions that may enable churches and organizations to take action that will alleviate the problem of alcohol abuse in their locality.

Indentifying the problem in the early stages

- ✧ Unexplained financial problems
- ✧ Loss of family/social priorities
- ✧ Family rows and tension
- ✧ Social/business life centred on alcohol
- ✧ Stomach trouble
- ✧ Establishment of drinking patterns
- ✧ Law breaking

Identifying the problem in its later stages

Social and Business
- ❋ Absenteeism from work, college or school
- ❋ Degeneration in company
- ❋ Cheaper types of alcohol
- ❋ Drinking alone

Physical Aspects
- ❋ Blackouts (alcoholic amnesia)
- ❋ Tremour, shakes, nausea, sweats, dehydration
- ❋ Fits (sometimes rather like epilepsy)
- ❋ Morning drinking

Moral Aspects
- ❋ Deceit and secrecy
- ❋ Decline in moral standards
- ❋ Increasing guilt
- ❋ More serious trouble with the law

Psychological/Psychiatric Aspects

- Depression, anxiety, tension and fear
- Delirium tremens, hallucination
- Evidence of change of personality
- Aggressive behaviour
- Irrational complaint and fault finding
- Growing awareness of need for drinking
- Unsuccessful attempts to cut out or cut down drinking
- Repeated requirement for medical attention

Alcoholics and Dextoxification

Detoxification literally means to get rid of the poison out of the body. The body cleanses itself and rids itself of all traces of alcohol after the person stops drinking.

If the body has accommodated and adapted to function despite the continuous presence of large quantities of alcohol, its sudden withdrawal can come as a shock. A person may exhibit "withdrawal symptoms" and may need medication to help relieve these. The process of withdrawal and readjustment normally takes a week to ten days (in our experience it is not as long as this, usually 5 to 7 days). Withdrawal symptoms are: severe anxiety, the shakes, heavy sweating at night, tingling in the fingers or toes. Severe symptoms can be visual or auditory hallucinations, fitting or delirium tremens.

Many alcoholics will scream for a Detox course, but the percentage that attend a program are back into binge drinking within five weeks of coming off the course.

It is extremely easy to Detox someone who desires change but to **REHABILITATE** becomes the problem. Four weeks in a Detox environment on blockers (these are drugs that purport to assist the normalization of the brain chemistry for the chronically dependent and are usually suggested as best effective in conjunction with counselling and other support. Sometimes Antabuse, a drug which creates a severe adverse physical reaction in one who would take even a small amount of alcohol, while using this medication. Years ago this was used in what was called aversion therapy. Again it can help to permit the chronic abuser an opportunity of time to make the psychological, emotional and social adjustments, but is not a long term solution usually) and constant supervision can stop the access to alcohol. Now what happens when the Detox Unit allows the referred alcoholic back into society at the end of the course? There are very few Rehab Centres to take on the work of the Detox and with regret the relapse of detoxified alcoholics is a very high percentage. Those who have failed in the main had no further support after the initial four weeks. By week five, with no support or counselling in a 24-hour period returned to their "best friend, the bottle".

Note that detoxification does not need to be done in a direct medically controlled environment, unless there is a perceived risk of complication. It can be done at home, supported by family and or community nurse, under the direction of the GP. The medication most frequently used in the UK for this is chlordiazepoxide or often better known as Librium.

Churches and their members could work with local organizations who seek to support alcoholics in rehabilitation. Many areas have such Detox and clinics but are under pressure for rehabilitation. Often all these specialist organizations require are people willing to sit along side those in need or to be on call to offer practical support.

Church buildings that are empty from Monday to Saturday could be open to alcohol abusers' support groups.

AFFIRMATION

The following is a list of churches, organizations or individuals who are taking action to alleviate alcohol/drug abuse. They will, we believe, be able to offer practical and professional advice to assist you in your efforts to take action against alcohol abuse. (Please see appendix B.)

HOPE UK
25F COPPERFIELD STREET
LONDON
SE1 0EN
TEL: 0207 928 0848
FAX: 0171 401 3477
WEBSITE: WWW.HOPEUK.ORG.UK
EMAIL: ENQUIRES@HOPEUK.ORG

THE STAUROS FOUNDATION
N. IRELAND
BALLYARDS CASTLE 123
KEADY ROAD ARMAGH
BT60 3AD
TEL: 02837 527124
EMAIL: ARTHUR.G.WILLIAMS@BTINTERNET.COM

SCOTLAND
25 KEYSTONE QUADRANT
MILNGAVIE
GLASGOW
G62 6LW
TEL: 0141 956 5966

ENGLAND
1 MALVERN CLOSE
FARNWORTH
BOLTON
BL4 0NA
TEL: 01204 794587

ALANON FAMILY GROUPS UK AND EIRE AND ALATEEN. AL-ANON OFFERS UNDERSTANDING AND SUPPORT FOR FAMILIES AND FRIENDS OF PROBLEM DRINKERS. ALATEEN, A PART OF AL-ANON, IS FOR YOUNG PEOPLE AGED 12–20 WHO HAVE BEEN AFFECTED BY SOMEONE ELSE'S DRINKING. OR YOUNG PEOPLE WITH FRIENDS OR FAMILY WHO ARE PROBLEM DRINKERS.
61 GREAT DOVER STREET
LONDON
SE1 4YF
TEL: 0207 403 0888 (24-HOUR)
WEBSITE: HTTP://WWW.HEXNET.CO.UK/ALANON

ALCOHOL CONCERN
OFFERS GENERAL INFORMATION ABOUT ALCOHOL. CALL TO FIND YOUR NEAREST ALCOHOL ADVISORY SERVICE
WATERBRIDGE HOUSE
32–36 LOMAN STREET
LONDON
SE1 0EE
TEL: 0207 928 7723
WEBSITE: HTTP://WWW.ALCOHOLCONCERN.ORG.UK

DRINKLINE
GIVES CONFIDENTIAL INFORMATION AND ADVICE
AND CAN PUT YOU IN TOUCH WITH YOUR LOCAL
ALCOHOL ADVICE CENTRE FOR ONE-TO-ONE HELP.
AVAILABLE IN BOTH ENGLISH AND WELSH.
TEL: 0800 917 8282 (FREEPHONE, MON–FRI
9AM–11PM, SAT–SUN 6PM–11PM)

WEBSITE WWW.WRECKED.CO.UK

HEALTH PROMOTION WALES
FFYNON-LAS
TY GLAS AVENUE
LLANISHEN
CARDIFF CF4 5DZ
TEL: 01222 752222
WEBSITE: HTTP://WWW.HPW.ORG.UK

SCOTTISH COUNCIL ON ALCOHOL
137–145 SAUCHIEHALL STREET
GLASGOW
G3 3EW
TEL: 0141 572 6700

HELP LINES
ALCOHOLICS ANONYMOUS: 0115 941 7100

ALCOHOL PROBLEMS ADVISORY SERVICE
LINKLINE: 0345 626316

ALCOHOL COUNSELLING SERVICE: 01472 340001

ALCOHOL TREATMENT CLINIC: 01200 445999

Books dealing with the issue of alcohol abuse

0551031832, *Under the Influence*, Fisher, MPH

0830718656, *Freedom from Addiction*, Anderson, REGAL

0801097371, *Addictive behaviour*, Welch & Shogren, Baker, £10.50

0802432840, *God is for the Alcoholic*, Dunn & Palmer, Moody, £7.75

HIV & AIDS

AWARENESS

The following information is included to raise the social awareness and understanding of ministers in relation to the contemporary issue of HIV & AIDS.*

Aids stands for **Acquired Immune Deficiency Syndrome** and is caused by a virus called **Human Immunodeficiency Virus**, this can damage the body's defence system so that it cannot fight certain infections. Breaking the words down gives a better understanding of what Aids and HIV are.

Human This is important. Only human beings are affected by this infection. Similar viruses do exist in other animals i.e. monkeys but they are not thought to be able to exist in humans.

Immunodeficiency This is made up of two words: immuno, meaning immunity or immune, which relates to the body's natural resistance to infection and deficiency which, describes a lack or shortage of something. Therefore, immunodeficiency means a deficiency or breakdown of the body's immune system.

Virus. A virus is a minute infective agent that invades certain body cells in order to survive and reproduce. The cells that are particularly affected by HIV are a type of white blood cell, the T-helper lymphocyte.

Acquired This means something that you gain rather than something that is inherited.

Immune The body's natural defense system which helps fight infection or disease.

Deficiency A lack or shortage of something.

Syndrome A collection of signs and symptoms indicative of a particular disease or disorder, in the case of Aids, a collection of opportunistic infections and tumors. Opportunistic infections are a group of germs that can create health problems when certain conditions e.g. immune deficiency exist. They seize the opportunity, which does not exist in other healthy people with normal immunity.

- ➡ **Although Aids has possibly been around for many years it was first diagnosed in 1981 in New York and Los Angeles. Since then the disease has spread around the world and affects many people, particularly drug users.**

- ➡ **HIV is transmitted in four main ways.**
    - ➡ **Through unprotected sex (vaginal and anal)**
    - ➡ **By injecting drug users sharing equipment, including syringes and needles.**
    - ➡ **From an infected mother to her unborn child.**

* Thanks to Lessly Bellerby for her contributions to this section

- Injection or transfusion of contaminated blood or blood products, donations of semen or skin grafts, organ transplant taken from some one who is infected.
- It is worth noting that any device that punctures the skin, including tattooing and acupuncture needles and equipment for ear piercing or removing hair by electrolysis, may be contaminated with blood and could in theory pass on the virus. Reliable practitioners will sterilize their equipment as will barbers their razors. Although risks are very small toothbrushes and razors should not be shared.
- The virus can enter the body through a wound, cut, sore or damaged skin. It can also enter through an injection using contaminated and un-sterilized injection equipment or through an invasive surgical procedure such as an organ transplant or a blood transfusion. It can also pass through particular interior sections of skin called mucous membrane, which are found in the rectum, vagina and urethra.
- HIV is a virus that is not easily caught and is not passed on through every day social contact such as coughing, sneezing, swimming, kissing or sharing household utensils.
- HIV survives for only a very short time outside the body, it is vulnerable to heat, ultraviolet light and many forms of disinfectant. This means the virus cannot be transmitted via toilet seats.
- Different body fluids present different degrees of risk. In some cases the virus is seen to be present in laboratory conditions rather than real life conditions. So, although HIV can be present in many body fluids, it dos not follow that this can present a risk as the virus may be in very low proportions.
- **HIV IS NOT PRESENT IN** urine, faeces, vomit or sweat.
- **HIV IS NOT PRESENT IN SUFFICIENT QUANTANTIES IN,** saliva, tears, and blister fluid.
- **HIV IS PRESENT IN SUFFICIENT QUANTITIES IN,** blood and blood products, semen and pre-semen, vaginal secretions, breast milk.
- The symptoms of HIV and AIDS are the symptoms of particular conditions caused by infections or tumours, which have developed as a result of a breaking down of the immune system. AIDS is not an illness in itself but a set of conditions which together lead to a diagnosis of AIDS. HIV is the Human Immunodeficiency Virus, which attacks the white blood cells in the immune system, thus making the body less able to fight off various infections and diseases.
- There are three phases of HIV infection:
    1. BECOMING HIV ANTIBODY POSITIVE. Most people who have become infected do not notice this has happened. Some people may experience a short illness soon after infection, such as a sore throat or a rash.

2. ASYMPTOMATIC HIV INFECTION. At this time, the person who has become infected feels no ill effects or shows no outward sign of HIV infection.

3. ASYMPTOMATIC HIV INFECTION. Germs and bacteria surround us all the time and our bodies will usually fight these off causing us no ill effects. In a person with symptomatic HIV infection, the body's immune system is not able to fight the germs and bacteria and can start to develop various conditions and infections. The immune system also controls how our cells multiply, but with a poorly functioning immune system, cells can multiply out of control resulting in tumors and sometimes cancers. HIV can also attack brain cells, which can cause the brain or nerves to function badly or poorly.

DIAGNOSIS OF AIDS varies around the world but a doctor would look for various conditions such as persistently swollen glands, pneumonia, tumours or other symptoms. In some countries a drop in CD4 cell count would be used as part of a diagnosis.

If a person is HIV positive, within three months their body produces antibodies to fight the HIV infection and these can be detected in a blood sample.

ASSESSMENT

The following are some of the most up-to-date statistics in relation to HIV & AIDS. (Please see appendix A.)

How HIV was Probably Acquired

	Infection only reported		Aids but not Death reported		Deaths in reported Aids Cases		Death without reported Aids		Total
	Male	Female	Male	Female	Male	Female	Male	Female	
Sex between men	11931		3021		8339		637		23928
Sex between men & women	2520	3580	722	715	860	752	135	100	9384
Drug use	1414	684	202	90	552	221	290	110	3563
Blood factor	452	4	64	2	594	5	230	1	1352
Blood tissue transfer	58	55	18	18	43	70	15	11	283
Mother to infant	130	125	96	106	78	69	4	4	612
Other/undetermined	675	186	36	8	119	13	141	27	1205
Total	17180	4634	4159	939	10585	1130	1452	253	40332

THE REPORT WAS COMPILED AT END OF DECEMBER 1999, BY
© PUBLIC HEALTH LABORATORY AIDS CENTER

HIV infected individuals* by year of first reported United Kingdom diagnosis: UK† data to end December 2000

* individuals with laboratory reports of infection, plus those with AIDS or death reports for whom no matching laboratory report has been received.
† includes 60 individuals first reported from the Channel Islands or the Isle of Man. Numbers, particularly for recent years, will increase as further reports are received.

Infections acquired through sex between men

How Infection was probably acquired	Year of diagnosis of HIV infection											Total
	1990	1991	1992	1993	1994	1995	1996	1997	1998	1999	2000	
Sex between men	11027	1704	1632	1495	1471	1460	1534	1370	1333	1286	1096	25408
Sex between men and women	1605	644	779	761	786	846	827	1002	1144	1368	1315	11077
Injecting drug use	2056	241	187	203	167	180	171	163	128	104	67	3667
Blood products, e.g. For haemophilia	1329	4	4	4	2	–	2	2	2	1	–	1350
Blood/tissue transfer	143	20	19	13	15	19	19	25	7	15	10	305
Mother to Infant	81	35	57	67	64	58	57	80	88	65	50	702
Other/undetermined	473	56	53	49	38	56	55	47	64	104	330	1325
Total	16714	2704	2731	2592	2543	2619	2665	2689	2766	2943	2868	43834

In the UK epidemic sex between men has remained the dominant route of infection, both in terms of the proportion of the total reports of diagnosed infection (58%) and the proportion of patient with diagnosed infections seen for care in 1999 (56%).[2] Table 1 shows the numbers of diagnoses each year by exposure category; for 2000 it gives a total of 1096 for those infected through sex between men. This number will increase as further reports are received and as follow-up of those currently in the undetermined category leads to their reassignment. Based on past patterns of reporting delay and of reassignment of those initially of undetermined exposure, the number is expected to rise in the future to above 1300. There is little evidence of any substantial change in recent years in the numbers diagnosed each year.

Infections acquired through sex between men and women

In contrast to the situation for men who have acquired HIV infection through sex between men, infections attributed to sex between men and women have shown a sustained upward trend and in 2000 there were more new diagnoses in this exposure category (1315) than there were for MSM (1096). This total, too, is expected to rise considerably as further reports are received. One thousand and sixty-seven of the 1315 heterosexually acquired infections diagnosed in 2000 have been further categorized (table 2). Of the 1067, 833 (78%) were categorized as infected in Africa and 128 (12%) as infected elsewhere abroad (table 2). Eighty-two (8%) infections were categorized as probably acquired within the UK from individuals themselves heterosexually infected. The numbers in this latter category are particularly likely to rise as follow-up is completed, as is the number of those infected through contact with a 'high risk' partner. Last year 65% of the diagnoses of HIV infections acquired in Africa, and 61% of all the heterosexually acquired infections diagnosed, were in women; over the whole surveillance period and over all sub-categories the proportion has been 56%. The higher proportion in 2000 partly reflects the promotion of antenatal testing, following the issuing of guidelines on reducing vertical transmission of HIV by the Department of Health in 1993.³ The only heterosexually infected sub-group where females do not predominate is those who acquired their infection abroad outside Africa; 86 of the 128 (67%) diagnoses in this group were in men.

© 2001 UNITED KINGDOM DATA FROM THE PHLS AIDS AND STD DIVISION,
SCOTTISH CENTRE FOR INFECTION AND ENVIRONMENTAL HEALTH,
INSTITUTE OF CHILD HEALTH, LONDON, AND OXFORD HAEMOPHILIA CENTRE

The following Web site offers a monthly update on HIV/Aids: www.phls.co.uk

Facts about HIV from the Terence Higgins Trust (THT)

Worldwide Facts

- HIV (Human Immunodeficiency Virus) is a virus which attacks part of the body's immune system
- 36million people are infected with HIV worldwide, that is 50% higher than was predicted in 1991
- This year there will be 5.3m new infections worldwide
- So far, 21.8m people have died with AIDS worldwide
- Russia currently has the biggest increase in new infections of any country, partly through intravenous drug use

UK facts

- The Public Health Laboratory Service (PHLS) estimate that there are over 30,000 people with HIV in the UK, up to one third of whom are unaware of their status
- There are approximately 2,500 new diagnoses of HIV in the UK every year – equivalent to seven new cases every day – and that figure has risen steadily in the last six years.
- The total figure of new UK HIV diagnoses for 1999 is 2846.
- The number of new HIV diagnoses is increasing. This can potentially be attributed to the fact that more people are now coming forward to be tested, including through the Government's new policy of offering universal antenatal screening to women
- According to the latest Government figures to March 2000 there have been 41,174 diagnoses of HIV in the UK and 16,995 AIDS cases. There have been 11,739 AIDS/HIV related deaths
- Since the widespread introduction of combination therapy in 1997, mortality rates have dropped dramatically. In 1998 there were 465 deaths in HIV infected individuals compared with 1679 in 1994

✝ **As more people are living with HIV, THT expects to help an additional 2000 more people this year compared with 1999**

© THT 2001

Addressing

The following is a list of practical suggestions that may enable churches and organizations to take action that will alleviate the problems HIV & AIDS.

- **The Christian church can be a place of healing and refuge for the person and their family who finds they are HIV positive or have AIDS by accepting them into their church family.**

- **Most people who have been infected with the virus HIV can remain healthy for a long time. Some people may have a less severe illness due to the virus whilst others are quite unwell. From what is known about the condition at the present moment most people infected with HIV will eventually go on to develop AIDS. Some people with HIV and Aids have been treated badly and discriminated against. Friendship and support are the most important things and the church can offer along with practical help in everyday living.**

- **Many infected with HIV are younger people who suddenly have to contemplate the fact they may die. The church can give spiritual guidance and help the person find God's love and eternal life.**

- **Confidentiality is of immense importance and only those who the sufferer wants to know must be told of their HIV status, personal details should not become public knowledge.**

- **Specialist counselors are available and particular help may be needed at the time of contemplating or seeking a HIV test.**

- **The telephone number of a church member willing to receive calls and give support in an emergency can be a great support. This person may also give support by accompanying them to the GP, Counselor or hospital.**

- **Training and education can be given regarding HIV and AIDS so that the congregation are well informed and aware of ungrounded prejudgments that can influence people to treat victims of HIV/AIDS negatively.**

Affirmation

The following is a list of churches, organizations or individuals who are taking action to alleviate the problems of HIV & AIDS.

They will, we believe, be able to offer practical and professional advice to assist you in your efforts to take action. (Please see appendix B.)

ACET – AIDS CARE EDUCATION AND TRAINING
PO BOX 3693
LONDON
SW15 2BQ
TEL: 0208 780 0400
WEBSITE: WWW.ACETUK.ORG

MILDMAY MISSION HOSPITAL
HACKNEY ROAD
SHOREDITCH
LONDON
E2 7NA
TEL: 0207613 6300
WEBSITE: WWW.MILDMAY.ORG.UK

PHONELINES IN OTHER LANGUAGES
PUNJAB, BENGALI, HINDI, URDU AND GJARATI.
0800 282 445.
CANTONESE 0800 282 446.
ARABIC 0800282 447

A MINICOM SERVICE IS AVAILABLE FOR PEOPLE
WITH HEARING DIFFICULTIES. 0800 521 361

FOR FREE COPIES OF LEAFLETS REGARDING AIDS
AND HIV 0800 555 777.

NATIONAL AIDS HELP LINE, 0800 567 123
PROVIDES INFORMATION ON AIDS OR TRAINED
ADVISORS ARE AVAILABLE TO TALK TO. THE CALLS
ARE FREE, CONFIDENTIAL AND AVAILABLE
24 HOURS A DAY, EVERY DAY.

Books that deal with the issue of HIV and Aids

071620472X, *Aids: a Christian hand book*, Colin Crowther, EPWPOR, £6.95

0880703091, *Aids Epidemic*, Wood Dietrich, MULTN, £5.84

A0860659836, *IDS And You*, Patrick Dixon, £2.99

0801043468, *AIDS Ministry Of An Epidemic*, Hoffmann & Grenz, £10.50

1852425210, *Scarlet Ribbons*, 9.99

0232521077, *Paths Through Pain*, 8.95

1841011967, *In the Palm of God's Hand*, 5.99 (cancer)

190155726X, *Praying for the Dawn – A Resource Book for the Ministry of Healing*, 10.99

0861043468, *Ministry in Midst Of an Epidemic*, Hoffman & Grenz, £10.50, Baker Books

0232520704, *Cry Love, cry Hope, Responding To Aids*, Bill Kirkpatrick, £6.95, Darton, Longman and Todd

BEREAVEMENT

Awareness

The following information is included to raise the social awareness and understanding of ministers in relation to the contemporary issue of bereavement.

When two have become 'one flesh' the death of a partner is like losing a limb.

'Just as man is destined to die once…' Heb 9: 27 Sooner or later most people will experience the death of someone they love. There are several feelings which are common to most people who are experiencing grief following the death of a loved one, whether it is a parent, a lifelong partner, child, stillbirth or miscarriage.

† **Feeling Grief**
For many people the initial reaction to a personal bereavement will be a feeling of Numbness toward the loss; Denial… being unable or unwilling to accept the person has died. Many people will find they are longing for, looking for and talking to the person they have lost.

Anger towards "doctors for not having done enough" is common, anger towards family and friends and even anger towards the person they have lost may be expressed.

A sense of Guilt that they never did enough or said what they would liked to have said or done differently for the one they have lost.

Bouts of Depression or an overwhelming sadness can be sparked off by people, places and songs, the constant media reminder of the perfect family or romantic couple is a continual reminder of their loss.

Periods of quiet Reminiscing can distress others but are helpful to the grieving person as they come to terms with their loss.

(There is no particular order to how a grieving person may experience the above feelings. Grief is very fluid and people frequently move in and out of the various stages of grief.)

† **The time period for most people to come to terms with bereavement is one to two years although life for them will never be the same again, some people on the other hand many never be able to cope without the one they have lost. When two have become "one flesh" the death of a partner is like losing a limb.**

There is no "standard" way or time period for a person to grieve, people are individuals and will react to bereavement in different ways.

† **Forgotten Grief**
Children who have been bereaved are sometimes forgotten amidst adult sympathy and the misconception that children don't feel the same way as adults.

Some children may appear to get over the bereavement quicker than adults, however, many young children and teenagers feel responsible for the death often can bottling up their feeling for fear of burdening adults. They may also try to take over the role of the absent adult.

† **Buried Grief**
Some people don't seem to show their grief and after the funeral and life appears to return to normal, they refuse to talk of their loss. This may be their way of dealing with the bereavement and it works for them.

Some people because of family and work commitments don't have the time to grieve.

Some don't grieve because their loss is not considered a "proper" bereavement, this often happens with women who have had a miscarriage, stillbirth and at times an abortion.

In cases like these frequent bouts of depression may occur at a later period.

Some people get stuck in their grief, finding it hard to accept the person has died, they sometimes can't stop thinking about the person or they turn their room into a shrine.

The depression of unresolved grief can sometimes lead to self-harm and even suicidal thoughts.

† **Different Reactions**
Reactions can be very different when a person dies after a long illness, as the bereaved may have already been grieving prior to the death, and also when the person who died had been very difficult to live with etc.

ASSESSMENT

The following are some of the most up-to-date statistics in relation to the issue of bereavement. (Please see appendix A.)

Deaths by Gender in the UK Thousands

Males		Females	
1991	314	1991	332
2001	299	2001	330
2011	298	2011	311
2021	327	2021	314

SOCIAL TREND 31 © CROWN COPYRIGHT 2001

Addressing

The following is a list of practical suggestions that may enable churches and organizations to minister effectively to the bereaved.

- ☆ **Often after a few weeks fewer and fewer people visit the bereaved person, this is perhaps when pastoral care is most required.**
- ☆ **Take note of the date of the person's death and offer comfort as the anniversary comes close.**
- ☆ **Remember it may be hard for a grieving person to return to a church building from where their loved one was buried.**
- ☆ **Don't say I know how you feel… You don't**
- ☆ **Don't say You'll get over it… You won't. Life carries on but it will never be the same. There will be a corner of your heart that may grieve for ever.**
- ☆ **Don't say, "You're young enough to try again, or have another, or there are other fish in the sea". The grieving person has lost a very special significant person who has left a vacuum in their life**
- ☆ **Don't sit quoting scripture… If the Lord drops something into your heart wait for the right moment, if not let the Lord bring scriptures to them in His own special way.**

Do Say

"I'm here"
"I do not really know what to say, but I'm here"
"I care"
"I will cry with you"
"I will laugh with you"
"I will listen to you"
"I will go away if you want to be alone"

God is the Great Comforter. He is the one who gave us feelings. Being told "we must offer a sacrifice of praise is scriptural," but maybe the grieving person needs to experience their pain and gain a little strength before they can exercise that scripture.

Affirmation

The following is a list of churches and organizations that minister to the bereaved. They will, we believe, be able to offer practical and professional advice to assist. (Please see appendix B.)

NATIONAL ASSOCIATION OF WIDOWS
48 QUEENS RD
COVENTRY
CV1 3EH
TEL: 024 7663 4848

THE COMPASSIONATE FRIENDS
53 NORTH ST
BRISTOL
BS3 1EN
TEL: 0117 953 9639

WAR WIDOWS ASSOCIATION
168 BROADWAY
DERBY
DE22 1BP
TEL: 01332 364272

CARDIAC RISK IN THE YOUNG (CRY)
UNIT 7 – EPSOM DOWNS METRO CENTRE
WATERFIELD
TADWORTH
SURREY
KT20 5LR
TEL: 01737 363 222 444
EMAIL: CRY@C-R-Y.ORG.UK
WEB SITE: WWW.C-R-Y.ORG.UK

SUDDEN DEATH SUPPORT ASSOCIATION
HELPLINE: 01189 790790 PROVIDES A 24-HOUR
TELEPHONE SUPPORT SERVICE FOR RELATIVES
AND FRIENDS

CHILD DEATH HELPLINE
HELPLINE: 0800 282 986 BEREAVEMENT
SERVICES DEPARTMENT

GREAT ORMOND STREET HOSPITAL FOR CHILDREN
NHS TRUST LONDON WC1N 3JH
TEL: 0207 813 8550/1

THE FOUNDATION FOR THE STUDY OF INFANT
DEATHS
ARTILLERY HOUSE
11–19 ARTILLERY ROW
TEL: GENERAL ENQUIRIES 0207 2228001
APPEALS: 0207 222 8003
TEL: 24 HOUR HELPLINE: 0207 233 2090
FAX: 0207 222 8002

COMPASSIONATE FRIENDS
53 NORTH STREET
BRISTOL
BS3 1EN
TEL: HELPLINE 0117 953 9639
ADMIN. 0117 966 5202
AN ORGANIZATION OF BEREAVED PARENTS WHO
OFFER SUPPORT AND UNDERSTANDING TO
FAMILIES WHOSE CHILD OF ANY AGE HAS DIED OF
ANY CAUSE.

CRUSE – BEREAVEMENT COUNSELLING
TEL: HELPLINE 0208 332 7227

OFFICE: 0208 940 4818

THE SAMARITANS TEL: 0345 909090

SUPPORT GROUPS

BRITISH CARDIAC PATIENTS ASSOCIATION
(ZIPPER CLUB)
BELMONT
30 PERNE ROAD
CAMBRIDGE
CB1 3RT
HELPLINE (01223 846845)
A PATIENT SUPPORT GROUP GIVING HELP AND
ADVICE TO PATIENTS AND RELATIVES

BRITISH HEART FEDERATION
14 FITZHARDING STREET
LONDON
W1H 4DH
TEL: 0207 935 0185

HYPERTROPHIC CARDIOMYOPATHY ASSOCIATION
40 THE METRO CENTRE
TOLPITS LANE
WATFORD
HERTS
TEL: 01923 249977
HELPLINE: 0800 0181024
WWW.CARDIOMYOPATHY.ORG
AN ORGANIZATION SUPPORTING SUFFERERS AND
THEIR FAMILIES FROM CARDIOMYOPATHY.

CHILDREN'S HEART FEDERATION
32 LITTLEHEATH
LONDON
SE7 8HU
TEL: 0207 820 8517
HELPLINE: 0808 808 5000 OFFERS HELP AND
SUPPORT FOR HEART CHILDREN AND THEIR
FAMILIES.

GROWN UP CONGENITAL HEART (GUCH)
HELPLINE: 01962 841635
PARENTS ASSOCIATION TO SUPPORT YOUNG
ADULT CONGENITAL HEART PATIENTS TO LIVE
FULL LIVES IN THE COMMUNITY. HELPLINE,
PRACTICAL ADVICE AND SUPPORT.

HEARTLINE ASSOCIATION
MISS PAMELA LAWRENCE
ROSSMORE HOUSE
26 PARK STREET
CAMBERLEY
SURREY
GU15 3PL
TEL: 01276 675 655
A SUPPORT GROUP FOR CHILDREN WITH HEART
CONDITIONS AND THEIR FAMILIES.

LEGAL HELP

ACTION FOR VICTIMS OF MEDICAL ACCIDENT
41 HIGH STREET
CROYDON
SURREY
CR0 1YB
TEL: 0208 686 8333
FAX: 0208 667 9065

Books that deal with the issue of bereavement

0-14-023608-2, *You'll Get Over It – The Rage of Bereavement*, Virginia Ironside, Penguin

A Special Scar – bereaved, Suicide Weirheimer

Miscarriage – Women's Experiences and Needs, C. Moulder

0-8070-2501-1, *Straight Talk about death for teenagers*, Grollman Beacon Press

When a Baby Dies, Nancy Kohner

SEXUAL EXPLOITATION

AWARENESS

The following information is included to raise the social awareness and understanding of ministers in relation to the contemporary issue of sexual exploitation.

Sexual exploitation includes the act of rape, sexual assault and child molestation, for the sexual gratification or gain of the offender. Sexual exploitation is always against the will of the victim, the victim of a rape/sexual assault is never to blame.

Often prostitution is a result of sexual exploitation. Because of poverty, drug or alcohol dependency, many desperate individuals find themselves turning to prostitution to support their drug habit and even on occasions to support their children. The Children's Society suggests that children trapped in prostitution should be considered the victim and not the criminal. Whatever the reasons an individual turns to prostitution they soon find themselves locked into a culture of sexual exploitation.

Victims of rape/sexual assault react in many different ways, the psychological and physical effects may change from day to day, and the process of recovery for some may be very slow.

After being sexually assaulted, some people are very afraid for a long time. Or they feel ashamed, anxious angry, guilty, powerless and depressed. For some victims it is difficult to sleep or eat properly, and their moods will go up and down. They might be irritable and short-tempered, and find it difficult to make decisions. Victims might also be very tearful at times, and it is possible that they will not feel like being close even to people they are extremely fond of. All of these feelings are usual for someone who has been through a bad experience.

Victims of rape/sexual assault may desperately want to talk to someone but find it extremely difficult to talk about their experience even to those closest to them. Talking to someone who understands all of this will help them to feel better. There are counselors who are trained to help victims sort out their emotions and listen to their problems. Those who are close to the victim may also need counselling to help them cope with the stress, and to help them to support and comfort the victim.

Victims of rape/sexual assault often don't want to report the crime to the police because they fear retribution from their attacker, or because they have feelings of shame. Rape/sexual assault is never the victim's fault, it an invasion of their privacy and victims should therefore be encouraged to report the crime to the police as soon as possible.

Police are well-trained and experienced in helping victims of rape/sexual assault. Many police services have a procedural policy for dealing with victims of rape/sexual assault similar to that of the Metropolitan Police Service.

Our promise to you

Whether you are male or female, if you are the victim of a serious sexual assault, we will:

- be kind, sensitive and courteous;
- speak to you in a way you can understand;
- make you as comfortable as possible;
- appoint an experienced detective who will do everything possible to catch your attacker;
- whenever possible, give you the choice of being examined by a female or a male doctor;
- tell you, with as much warning as possible, if you have to appear in court. We will also tell you if your court date is changed;
- try to make sure, before a defendant is sentenced, that the court is aware of the impact of the offence on you, your family and your life;
- talk to your employer if you want us to;
- whenever possible, give you back your property that was kept as evidence, if you want it.
- appoint a male or female officer, whichever you prefer, to 'chaperone' you. He or she will be sympathetic, discreet and tactful and will;
    - tell you, as far as possible, what is happening, and what will happen next;
    - contact a support group for you, if that is what you want;
    - make a hospital appointment for you, if you want one.
- We will also pass on to you information we receive from the Crown Prosecution Service:
    - about developments in your case;
    - when someone is to be prosecuted;
    - whether the person accused of assaulting you is to be released on bail and if any bail conditions apply. For example, that might be that the accused person must not contact you, or go to certain places.

© METROPOLITAN POLICE SERVICE, 1999

Victims of rape/sexual assault often fear sexually transmitted diseases; local GPs can offer victims advice and generally refer them to the local hospital's Genito-Urinary clinic, who will carry out tests for sexual transmitted diseases. If a victim is concerned about HIV then they can request this test at the same time. Is there any help for those who sexual assault or attack? Following the forgiveness principle of Jesus then we must say "Yes."

Like recovery from alcohol abuse, stopping the compulsion to assault others sexually involves much more than simply wanting to stop. For most addicted people, it also means reshaping their lives, learning to manage the stresses and strains that led them to rape or sexually assault someone in the first place.

Psychotherapy (including group therapy, individual therapy, and behaviour modification) has helped some people reorient their sexual drive toward a socially acceptable and consenting partner. Yet many sexual abusers, even with treatment, relapse and abuse again.

The National Association of work with Sexual Offenders (address below) can offer advice and support when dealing with those who sexually assault others

Assessment

The following are some of the most up-to-date statistics in relation to the issue of sexual exploitation. (Please see appendix A.)

Child prostitution figures double

The Children's Society says children should be treated as victims. The number of children convicted of child prostitution more than doubled in a year, according to Home Office figures. The statistics have prompted the Children's Society charity to call for a change in the law so that the children are treated as victims.

- Home Office figures show that 210 children aged 17 and under were convicted of offences relating to prostitution in 1996 compared to 101 children in 1995.
- The number of cautions also rose slightly from 263 to 287.
- Included in the figures is an 11-year-old girl who was cautioned for an offence relating to prostitution – the youngest person to be cautioned since 1992.
- The Children's Society chief executive Ian Sparks said: "The fact that an 11-year-old child has been cautioned is beyond belief.
- "We know that many police forces around the country have taken a more enlightened approach towards children on the streets, so the figures are a real shock to us."
- The Children's Society wants the law to target those who use child prostitutes rather than the children.

Annual Abstract of Statistics No 137, © Crown Copyright 2001

	England and Wales			Scotland			Northern Ireland		
	1981	1991	1998–9	1981	1991	1998–9	1981	1991	1998–9
Theft and handling stolen goods	1603	2761	2127	201	284	192	25	32	35
Of which; theft from vehicles	333	582	391	33	44	28	5	8	10
Theft from vehicles	380	913	681	—	—	50	7	7	6
Burglary	718	1220	952	96	116	57	20	17	15
Criminal damage	387	821	834	62	90	79	5	2	10
Violence against the person	100	190	231	8	16	16	3	4	7
Fraud and Forgery	107	175	174	21	26	24	3	5	5
Robbery	20	45	66	4	6	5	3	2	1
Sexual offences	19	29	35	2	3	5	—	1	1
Of which rape	1	4	8	—	1	1	—	—	—
Drug offences	—	11	21	2	12	31	—	—	—
Other notable offences	9	23	42	12	20	22	3	1	2
All notible offences	2964	5276	4482	408	573	432	62	63	77

2   Estimates of the number of offences under the old counting rules.
3   In N. Ireland excludes criminal damage valued at £200 or less.
4   In England and Wales trafficking was the only notifiable drugs offence counted under the old counting rules to 1 April 1998. In Scotland, trafficking was the only recorded drugs crime in 1981.
5   In Northern Ireland Includes 'possession of controlled drugs' and 'offences against the state'. In Scotland excludes 'offending while on ball' from 1991 onwards

SOURCE: HOME OFFICE; SCOTTISH EXECUTIVE; ROYAL ULSTER CONSTABULARY

ADDRESSING

The following is a list of practical suggestions that may enable churches and organizations to minister effectively to those trapped in sexual exploitation.

- **Pastors/church leaders should never counsel victims of rape/sexual assault with members of the opposite sex alone. Counselling those who have been raped/sexually assault may be beyond the ability of local pastors;**

- **Victim Support provide trained volunteers who will:**

    help victims cope with their feelings about the assault;
    give practical advice;
    arrange visits to the police station, clinics, doctors, etc.;
    tell victims about support agencies in their area;
    accompany them to court;
    help victims to apply for financial compensation to the Criminal Injuries Compensation Board and give victims any other help they may need.

- **Victims Support's national headquarters address is listed below and they will be able to tell you about your local victim support groups, or you could ask at the local police station.**

- **Local Churches could open their buildings up for Victim Support groups to**

- use, church leaders and members to work as voluntaries for Victim Support.
- Local Social Services can provide information of groups that are run to help and support those with a sexual addiction.

AFFIRMATION

The following is a list of churches, organizations or individuals who are ministering to those harmed by sexual exploitation. They will, we believe, be able to offer practical and professional advice to assist you. (Please see appendix B.)

VICTIM SUPPORT
CRANMER HOUSE
39 BRIXTON ROAD
LONDON
5W9 6DZ
TEL: 0207 735 9166
FAX: 0207 582 5712
AS A RANGE OF LEAFLETS ON VARIOUS TYPES OF SUPPORT OFFERED BY VICTIM SUPPORT.

WOMEN IN PRISON
22 HIGHBURY GROVE
LONDON
N5 2EA
TEL: 0207 226 5879
FAX: 0207 354 8005

CRIME CONCERN
BEAVER HOUSE
147–150 VICTORIA ROAD
SWINDON
SN1 3UY
TEL: 01793863500
FAX;. 01793 514654
WORKS WITH LOCAL PARTNERS TO PREVENT CRIME AND CREATE SAFER COMMUNITIES. PRODUCES A WIDE RANGE OF CRIME SURVEYS, REPORTS AND BRIEFINGS SPECIALIZING IN YOUTH CRIME.

BARNABUS
144 BROOMHALL ROAD
PENDLEBURY
SWINTON
MANCHESTER
M27 8XG
TEL: 0161 950 6936
BARNABUS OFFER PRACTICAL AND MEDICAL CARE FOR THOSE TRAPPED IN PROSTITUTION.

CADAR
512 BURY NEW ROAD
PRESTWICH
MANCHESTER
M25 3AN
TEL: 0161 773 9913
CADAR WORK WITH WOMEN TRAPPED IN PROSTITUTION, DRUG ADDICTION AND VICTIMS OF SEXUAL EXPLOITATION.

NATIONAL ASSOCIATION OF WORK WITH SEXUAL OFFENDERS (NOTA)
50 HAYBURN AVE
HULL
HU5 4NA
TEL: 01482 343625

LONDON RAPE CRISIS CENTRE
PO BOX 69
LONDON
WC1X 9JN
TEL: 020 7837 1600

Books that deal with the issue of sexual exploitation
0842304878, *Counselling Survivors of sexual abuse*, Diane Langberg, TYN, £17.50
0801038634, *Encountering shame and guilt*, Green and Lawrenz, Baker, £10.50
0814624421, *Recovering The Lost Self*, 8.99
0572930551, *Learning to Trust Again*, 9.99
0859698106, *Breaking Free*, 12.99

ADVICE ON LOBBYING

The UK political system is one where the members of parliament (MPs) represent the people that voted them into office. MPs are therefore, obligated to listen to the views of their constituents.

This obligation provides constituents with the opportunity to lobby their MP to take into account their views when representing them in parliament.

The simple motto "together we can do more than we can do on our own" is a powerful premise to work upon when it comes to lobbying.

Forms of lobbying

- Visit your MP at his local office.
- Telephone your MP and make your feelings known.
- Write to your MP at his local office or at the Houses of Parliament.
- Write direct to the Department dealing with the issue
- Write to your local government office
- Write to your Member of the European Parliament (MEP)
- Petition and survey your community and present your finding to your MP or MEP.

Guidelines to follow

- Always be polite, non-confrontational, when visiting or telephoning your MP
- Make sure you understand both sides of the issues that you are lobbying
- When you write, be brief, to the point and reasoned
- Avoid preaching a sermon
- Petitions must offer people the opportunity to disagree with you
- Keep to the issues avoid forcing your own opinion of the Government or your local MP
- Write as an individual
- Write to represent your family, church or members of your neighbourhood
- Write to the right person and address him or her according to their title e.g. "Lord," "Lady" or "Sir."

Addresses

HOUSE OF COMMONS
WESTMINSTER
LONDON
SW1A 0AA

HOUSE OF LORDS
WESTMINSTER
LONDON
SW1A 0PW

FURTHER ADVICE ON LOBBYING THE GOVERNMENT BOTH THE FOLLOWING ORGANIZATION RESEARCH AND CAMPAIGN TO BRING CHRISTIAN VALUES TO BEAR UPON PUBLIC POLICY.

THE CHRISTIAN INSTITUTE
(INFLUENCING PUBLIC POLICY)
26 JESMOND ROAD
NEWCASTLE UPON TYNE
ME2 4PQ
TEL: 0191 281 5664
EMAIL: INFO@CHRISTIAN.ORG.UK
WWW.CHRISTIAN.ORG.UK

JUBILEE CENTRE
JUBILEE HOUSE
3 HOOPER STREET
CAMBRIDGE
CB1 2NZ
TEL: 01223 566319
FAX: 01223 566359
EMAIL: JUBILEE.CENTRE@CLARA.NET

THE MEDIA OFTEN COMMUNICATES DIRECTLY OR INDIRECTLY IDEOLOGIES THAT UNDERMINE THE FAMILY AND GOD ORDAINED SEXUALITY. THE MEDIA ARE ALSO OBLIGATED TO LISTEN TO ANY COMPLAINTS THAT ARE PUT TO THEM.

NATIONAL VIEWERS' AND LISTENERS' ASSOCIATION (NVALA)
3 WILLOW HOUSE
KENNINGTON RD
ASHFORD
KENT
TN24 0NR
TEL: 01223 633936

ENCOURAGES VIEWERS AND LISTENERS TO REACT EFFECTIVELY TO PROGRAM CONTENT. TO SECURE EFFECTIVE LEGISLATION TO CONTROL OBSCENITY AND PORNOGRAPHY IN THE MEDIA.

THE NVALA PROVIDE AN EXCELLENT DIRECTORY CONTAINING THE NAMES ADDRESSES ETC, OF TELEVISION COMPANIES.

A RECOMMENDED QUALITY ASSURANCE POLICY

This document is only a guideline. Those setting up a Quality Assurance package should make these guidelines and others applicable to their own setting. Adopting a Quality Assurance Policy is a commitment to self-assessment in the hope of producing excellence in service.

A Quality Assurance Policy will:

1. Affirm that high quality of standards are met.
2. Give assurance that a service is provided.
3. Make Assessment to ensure standard are met and service provided.

1.1 Commitment to quality

What this standard covers

This standard underpins all others. It enables a Social Concern UK facility (SCF) to introduce and maintain quality management. By operating a system of quality management, the SCF is making a public commitment to provide services of the right quality to the users of SCF services.

As a member of the Social Concern UK network, every SCF is encouraged to use a quality assurance system and to undertake regular self-assessments. Meeting this standard demonstrates the SCF's commitment to quality.

A Quality Assurance policy ensures that a SCF:

- meets agreed standards for all areas of service delivery
- has policies, practices and procedures on key areas of work
- meets statutory and legal requirements
- meets the requirements of any other relevant professional body as applicable
- implements a cycle and culture of continuous improvement and learning
- encourages innovation in its service delivery.

1.2 Measuring performance

What this standard covers

Every SCF needs to know if it is achieving what it planned to achieve. The standard for measuring performance enables the SCF to do this by addressing these questions:

- What are you aiming to achieve?

- ✢ What information tells you if you have achieved it?
- ✢ What has your work produced?
- ✢ What are the positive outcomes of your work, especially for service users?

Examples only – Set your own.
Meeting this standard means doing two things:

- ✢ having mechanisms and methods in place for collecting information about performance, for example service user satisfaction surveys.
- ✢ identifying and collecting information that can be used to review and evaluate the effectiveness of the SCF.

The information could range from testimonials and case histories through to performance figures and statistics. The aim is to collect the same type of information for long enough to be able to recognize and understand changes and developments.

1.3 Governance (Leadership, Trustees, Management)

What this standard covers

Governance is how an organization's governing body ensures that the organization carries out its responsibilities correctly and legally and meets the requirements of its governing document, i.e. its constitution.

1.4 Planning and policy development

What this standard covers

To achieve its purpose and mission, an SCF has to decide in advance on, the objectives and activities it needs to pursue in order to implement the values it is committed to. Planning is the means of doing this. To be successful, a planning process has to include procedures for reviewing progress towards the agreed goals.

This standard covers how the SCF plans what it does, how it reviews past activities and performance in order to measure progress and how it involves trustees and workers in the process. Planning describes a number of activities:

- ✢ short term operational planning
- ✢ longer term strategic planning
- ✢ business planning
- ✢ target and objective setting
- ✢ maintaining and reviewing policies
- ✢ keeping track of progress

1.5 Financial management and systems

What these standards cover
Good financial management in an SCF depends on effective financial controls being in place. These include systems for monitoring and controlling the organization's finances, for budgeting and for reporting. These standards set out key elements for the effective management of financial resources, taking into account the legal responsibilities of the SCF and its trustees as well as accountability to funders.

Note: quality in this area is dependent on meeting legal requirements.

1.6 People management

What these standards cover
These standards concern the management of people in SCFs. They apply to all categories of people who work in the SCF, whether they are paid, unpaid, full-time, part-time or sessional workers.

The standards on people management set out what the SCF needs to do in order to ensure that it has sufficient skilled people to achieve its aims and objectives. The standards cover:

- recruitment
- induction
- supervision, support and appraisal
- training and development
- performance management
- communications and internal relations
- health and safety

Note: Quality in the area of health and safety is linked to the meeting of various legal requirements.

1.7 Information

What these standards cover

- the receiving, recording, storage, maintenance and distribution of information used by SCFs in the course of their work
- the use of information and communications technology (ICT). ICT includes computers, telephones, faxes, email and the internet

Note: The standards for information are closely linked to the standards for financial management, planning and policy development and measuring performance.

1.8 Equality and diversity

What these standards cover
These standards enable SCFs to promote equality and diversity, meeting them will ensure that the SCF:

- reflects and responds to the diversity of the communities in which it works
- provides and delivers accessible services
- practises equal opportunities in all areas

1.9 Networking and partnerships

What the standards cover

These standards relate to the networking and partnership activities carried out by SCFs, they also address relationships with current and potential funders as well as networking and partnership activities with other relevant organizations.

Networking and partnership activities include service development, provision and co-ordination; sharing good practice and knowledge; strategy development; campaigning and lobbying; research and information collection; performance monitoring; funding development; and referral and access to other services.

2.0 Standards for all services

What these standards cover

SCFs need to deliver services that are well planned and organized, appropriate to the service user and consistent with the values of the supporting church. They should also support the workers who deliver them.

These standards apply to all direct support and care services provided by the SCF. They cover all the quality areas that are essential to ensure safe and respectful practice for all service users, whether in a formal, structured setting or in a more informal one.

2.1 Advice and information services

What these standards cover and apply to:

- SCFs that provide people with information, either on a self-access basis or with the assistance of an information worker. Contact with the service user may be in person or over the telephone. Information may be in the form of leaflets and other published materials, directories, websites and other computer based systems, or information given verbally
- SCFs that seek to provide people with advice to help them recognize problems and determine possible options. These SCFs have workers who give information and offer basic assistance; they may also have advice workers who provide a casework service, taking action on behalf of service users

2.2 Advocacy services

What this standard covers

SCFs providing advocacy services do so in order to support service users and enable them to:

- have their voice heard
- express their views and concerns
- improve their access to services and information
- defend and promote their rights and responsibilities
- explore choices and options

This standard applies to the various models of advocacy available. These include:

- **Self-advocacy,** when service users are supported to express their own needs and concerns and take a more active role in their community.
- **Peer advocacy,** describing advocacy services offered by other service users.
- **Citizen advocacy,** in which trained and supported volunteers, known as citizen advocates, offer a long-term advocacy service to service users.
- **Collective advocacy,** consisting of a group of service users working together to speak up for what they want.
- **Professional advocacy,** where trained and supported advocates provide advocacy on a direct access or referral basis to service users.

Note: professional advocates in this context may be either paid or unpaid workers.

2.3 Befriending/Mentoring services

What this standard covers

Befriending services aim to reduce the isolation of service users. Befriending services are designed to enable service users to develop more confidence, rebuild relationships and establish new ones and develop their personal resources.

The SCF's befriending service will facilitate confidential and supportive relationships between befrienders. The befriending relationship is initiated, supported and monitored by the SCF.

Befriending is non-judgmental, mutual and purposeful, with a commitment over time from the befriender. Befriending has boundaries and is not the same as personal friendship.

The SCF's befriending service may provide:

- long-term support that enables people to become more involved in their local community
- short term befriending, providing a bridge between acute services and networks in the community
- one-to-one time-limited befriending
- group befriending, where a number of befrienders meet with a number of befriendees in a social setting

2.4 Community support services

What this standard covers

SCF community support services give practical and social support to people experiencing mental distress. The services aim to be flexible and imaginative in their use of community resources to meet service user needs and to promote social inclusion. Service users may self-refer and work in partnership with the SCF to develop a service based on their self-defined needs.

Community support services share a common philosophy and aims. But they can have very different forms of management, service structure, staffing and funding arrangements. They also vary in the amount and intensity of support they offer.

2.5 Counselling services

What this standard covers

SCF counselling services aim to give the service user an opportunity to explore, discover and clarify ways of living more resourcefully and to develop a greater sense of well-being through talking to a counsellor in an agreed set of counselling sessions. Only when both the user and counsellor explicitly agree to enter into a counselling relationship does it become 'counselling'. This standard specifies the level of training required for counsellors to enable the SCF to provide counselling services of an appropriate quality.

2.6 Crisis services

What this standard covers

SCFs providing crisis services do so in order to support people experiencing a crisis. The services are designed to ensure ease of access for users, a rapid and timely response by the SCF, a brief intervention or involvement with the user, a focus on the current situation, non-coercive support and, if appropriate, planning to prevent future crises. They are a variety of models, employ a range of interventions and often use different terminology.

Crisis services cover a wide range of activities, including for example:

- ✛ **rapid response team**
- ✛ **crisis team**
- ✛ **home support team**
- ✛ **crisis sanctuary**
- ✛ **advance directive scheme**
- ✛ **crisis telephone line**
- ✛ **crisis card scheme**
- ✛ **crisis (counselling) centre**

- overnight drop-in service
- crisis house
- crisis befriending service
- crisis response team

2.7 Day services

What this standard covers

Day services provide social interaction and personal development to service users through a variety of enjoyable and meaningful activities in community settings. These can take place not only during the day, but also in the evenings and at weekends, in safe and supportive environments.

Day services covered by these standards may follow one of the following models:

- recreational, encouraging individuals to develop a range of interests and activities
- social care, supporting normal living and personal development for family and community living
- resource, providing access to a wide range of facilities beyond health and social care services

Day services covered by these standards may offer a daily structured timetable, an open drop-in programme, open access to service users or access to the day services through a referral process.

2.8 Employment services

What this standard covers

This standard is for employment services. Employment services provide activities relating to employment, paid and unpaid work, training and education.

These services aim to support service users to achieve their work aspirations and goals. Employment services may also work with employers, the benefits agency and other key groups to promote access to meaningful occupation for people experiencing mental distress.

Employment services covered by this standard may follow the following models:

- **Employment training**
  A variety of work preparation courses, such as job clubs, CV writing, job search skills
- **Supported employment**
  Supporting a person in choosing a job in the open market, getting such a job, and then keeping it, and developing their career. It includes reasonable adjustments to the working environment. Good

practice will involve a personal adviser for each mental health service user, and making on-going support available as and when required.

This has not been a comprehensive list of standards and services. SCF's managements are encouraged to examine their service and apply a Quality Assurance Policy.

CLONING

AWARENESS

The following information is included to raise the social awareness and understanding of ministers in relation to the contemporary issue of cloning.

As created beings we are accountable for the use of this power not only to global humanity, but also to every realm of created life that God has entrusted to our stewardship. Ultimately we are accountable to the Maker of the universe who holds us responsible for the care of each other and of the earth.

When creation came forth from the Creator's hand it was "very good." (Gen. 1: 31) The genetic endowment which Adam and Eve received from their Creator was without defects. The genetic diseases from which humans now suffer are not the result of normal variation. They have developed through harmful mutation. In restoring the human genome to a healthier condition, modern health sciences may attempt to recover more of creation's original condition. To the extent that helpful genetic interventions can be conducted in harmony with Christian principles, they are to be welcomed as cooperation with the divine intention of alleviating the painful results of sin.

Genetic engineering has directly benefited human medicine. It has made possible, for example, the production of human insulin and human growth factor, neither of which was previously obtainable in sufficient quantities. Genetic engineering also makes it possible to treat diseases through genetic alteration. With this type of treatment, a patient whose cells have missing or defective genes receives needed genetic material. No one knows how many genetic diseases may eventually be treated in this way, but initial successes with diseases such as cystic fibrosis give hope that other genetic disorders may be treatable.

A Matter of Life and Death

Why shouldn't we use our embryos and genes to make our lives better? The world awaits a Christian answer.

Humanity will spend much of the twenty-first century attempting to speak that language. A fast-developing biotech vocabulary-genetic therapy, stem cells, reproductive cloning, and so on strains the ability of even the most thoughtful to keep up. Human life may soon be changed dramatically, and Christians must participate in the international conversation about these changes before they become irreversible.

The Christian faith has the potential to serve not just the church but the world by penetrating the fog of current events to discern their deeper meaning – and to offer clear-headed analysis amid growing confusion.

Opposing Forces

Long-established forces threaten to crowd out the voice of faith:

Market forces. The sprawling biotech industry, already doing $80 billion in business in the United States alone, would not be awash in money were there not a demand for its innovations. These products and services include stem cells, gene therapies and enhancements, and, one day, perhaps soon, clones. Biotech firms promise what people want – health, pain relief, reproduction, longevity, success.

Moral fragmentation. A morally fragmented nation may lack the basic requisites for a conversation – a shared framework of meaning, a minimal level of trust, and an agreed vocabulary. But by failing to converse and arrive at a national (much less international) decision about the biotech revolution, we default to existing powers and interests and likely stumble into disaster.

"Our society currently lives from moral fragments and community fragments only, both of which are being destroyed faster than they are being replenished," writes ethicist Larry L. Rasmussen.

Worldview dynamics. This leads us to a still deeper reality: beneath both economic practice and moral fragmentation lies the foundation of worldview. Among those who press most aggressively for unrestrained development of biotech advances – including non-scientists – worldviews and philosophies such as naturalism, atheism, utilitarianism, and scientific utopianism reign. Much of our culture's élite lives without a working hypothesis of God. Assuming we dwell alone in the universe, they believe we must simply keep improving life until the next comet hits.

Libertarian ideology – which stresses individualism, privacy, moral relativism, unlimited choice-making, and autonomy – folds neatly into these godless worldviews. It holds that no one should deny himself anything that will bring self-realization and is not immediately harmful to another.

Hence a powerful contingent argues for the largely unrestrained pursuit of biotechnology as a matter of personal (including reproductive) liberty. This quest is driven by a Utopian dream: overcoming our species' limits through human power and scientific progress.

Leaving the limits of nature and the past behind, we will remake ourselves. Still, as bioethicist Audrey Chapman has written, the nations are not sure they ought to heed this siren song. They seem to be pausing at the brink, waiting to hear from the church or any other voice on why they should not plunge into the remaking of humanity.

The Challenge to Christians

Tell us why we should not proceed to remake humanity now that we are developing the power to do so – this is the challenge presented to Christians.

To offer answers, we must consider some difficult theological conundrums. After we identify a few of them, we will sketch an initial response – exhaustive neither in scope nor argument – to specific biotech challenges.

Is God responsible for these technological advances? A vibrant theology of divine sovereignty would have to answer "yes," at least in some sense. If so, then why worry? Because our affirmation of God's sovereignty comes with the equally biblical assertion that human beings have the freedom to make good or bad decisions.

God did indeed make us with the intelligence to develop these technologies, but we are responsible for what we do with that intelligence. We may stumble into areas beyond our appropriate range; this was the primordial sin, after all. But it is also possible that God is at work in some of these biotechnological advances.

Are suffering, finitude, and death revocable by human effort? Human sin introduced suffering and death into a previously unmarred creation. The reversal of sin's effects marked the kingdom-inaugurating ministry of Jesus Christ, but until he returns the creation will continue to "groan" (Rom. 8: 18ff) – illness, death, and finitude will remain a reality.

Indeed, both Scripture and history show that Utopian visions of the elimination of suffering tend toward disaster, either through tyranny or as the unforeseen consequence of well-intended schemes. One of the best things biblical faith contributes to the biotech discussion is a well-considered understanding of human weakness, finitude, and sin, and the double-edged potential of many human endeavours.

The Dominion Mandate

And yet does God not mandate human efforts to mitigate the effects of sin? Along with Christ's kingdom mandate to heal and restore, in creation God called humanity to exercise dominion over (Gen. 1: 28) and preserve/protect (Gen. 2: 15) the Earth. After the Fall, the dominion/protection (stewardship) mandate was not removed, but extended to more difficult conditions.

God calls us to "sustain, restore, and improve" our fallen world, according to ethicist James C. Peterson. While the term "created co-creators" overstates our status, we are called to mitigate the Fall's effects and thus improve human and planetary life. It would be disobedient to resist human progress toward these ends, but the issue becomes complex when innovations risk bringing more harm than benefit-and when they risk transgressing divinely established boundaries.

To what extent does God intend to "fix the world," as opposed to redeeming a people for eternity from within a broken world? Lutheran theologian Philip Hefner has argued that a dubious "fix-it" mentality lies behind much of the biotech revolution. And yet a healthy theology of God's sovereignty as Creator and Redeemer drives us to reclaim "every square inch" of creation, as Dutch

Calvinist Abraham Kuyper (1837–1920) once famously said. Likewise, a kingdom approach emphasizes Jesus' mission as reclaiming a rebellious and suffering world for its rightful King.

More pessimistic theologies allow for much less actual transformation before Christ returns. Our bioethical dilemmas underscore both the possibilities and the limits of transformation in this world, and perhaps keeping both in tension is the best way forward.

Are genetic anomalies, and the diseases they cause, God's will? Some argue that interventions such as gene therapies constitute an attempt to thwart God's will. Yet, only if we think of cancer, crib death, car accidents, tornadoes, and nearsightedness as God's will in some nonbiblical, fatalistic sense, ought we also understand genetic anomalies such as cystic fibrosis or spina bifida this way. We should instead see these inherited diseases as legacies of the Fall and hence worthy subjects of our best efforts to safely mitigate them.

What is normatively human? Has God established a fixed human nature (the *imago dei*) that we are not permitted to alter or transcend? While humanity is made in the image of God, strikingly diverse Christian interpretations of the *imago dei* abound. It may be that Christians can ascribe no single meaning to it, but at minimum the *imago dei* means that humans were designed to resemble God in ways that other creatures do not – this includes our intelligence, moral agency, and our ability to form interdependent relationships in community.

Human life merits a special imputed respect, even sacred value, on the basis of this design as well as God's unique declaration of our status. Also, by sharing this status, all humans partake of a fundamental equality. But given that much about us is far from Godlike, in the biotech era we must find the balance between reaching our potential and respecting our limits – both of which are fundamental to human life.

To what extent does God work through the agency of government to restrain sin and prevent disaster? Reflection on the biotech challenge helps to settle the question of whether Christians should remain politically engaged despite the many disappointments we have with government. God created the State to advance the common good (Rom. 13: 1–7), and at times it is the only human power capable of restraining threatening forces.

We cannot withdraw from political engagement, especially in times like these.

At least three pressing issues demand an immediate Christian response: stem-cell research, human cloning, and genetic therapy.

Stemming Life

The effort to use stem cells obtained from adult neural cells, bone marrow, live-birth umbilical cord and placental blood, and other sources raises no moral problems. The potential health benefits of stem cells remain unclear (despite dramatic claims in the media), but there is no reason to limit research as long as the source of such cells is morally licit. Indeed, Christians should support initiatives such as Rep. Chris Smith's (R–N.J.) proposal to establish a national stem-cell donor bank involving only these nonembryonic cell sources. Such a donor bank would make stem-cell research a public initiative with near-universal support, and would greatly expand the availability of such cells.

The use of embryonic stem cells from elective abortion, or, more importantly, from the "leftovers" from *in vitro* fertilization (IVF), has heated up the debate. Both concern the moral status of embryonic life, and thus this issue intertwines with the moral struggle over abortion. The biotech community and its allies have pressed hard for the right to use embryonic stem cells freely, and for an end to the ban on federal funding of such research.

In one sense, the moral issues are similar whether we are considering aborted foetuses or "surplus" IVF embryos. Both are (or were) among that class of human beings rightly called the unborn, or those in the process of being born – human beings valued by God whose lives began at conception.

Research using aborted foetuses entangles the researcher in a prior wrong. A researcher can be guilty of complicity even if he had no role in the original wrong and his own motives were beyond reproach. Complicity can be avoided. For example, the medical community rightly rejected any use of knowledge gained from the Nazis' horrific experiments on concentration camp prisoners.

Of all potential sources of stem cells, producing embryos for experimentation and research via cloning techniques – known as therapeutic cloning – is the most troubling. Yet private research firms have begun doing precisely this. Therapeutic cloning is odious because (a) it could surreptitiously lead to morally dubious reproductive cloning, and (b) it intentionally manufactures human life with the certainty of its destruction.

Many leaders here and abroad are pressing for therapeutic cloning; the Christian community must reject it. As a matter of public policy, Christians and others who value embryonic and foetal life have a right and obligation to press for the exemption of embryonic stem cells from research efforts.

This is especially true in light of the apparent promise of other sources of stem cells and other paths to the goals of regenerative medicine. Discovery of treatments for such diseases as Parkinsons and Alzheimers would be a tremendous accomplishment, but deeper biblical values proscribe us from pursuing those ends at the expense of developing human life – especially when alternative sources are viable.

Drawing the Line at Dolly

A fascinating thing happened during the debate that broke out after Dolly the cloned sheep made her appearance – large sectors of society said, "This crosses a line; this must not happen."

This does not mean that powerful voices are not continuing to make their best case for cloning (extracting the nucleus of an adult cell and inserting it into an egg cell that has been stripped of its own nucleus, then stimulating it to begin cell division). Nor does it mean that research has halted; no one knows how many private laboratories have ignored the moral, physiological, and legal risks in attempts to clone humans. But it may mean that the human family will rouse itself to actually draw a line before cloning becomes a *fait accompli*.

University of Chicago medical ethics professor Leon Kass, summarizes the overwhelming case against cloning in four points: unethical experimentation; threat to human identity and individuality; turning procreation into manufacturing; and despotism over children in the perversion of parenthood.

1. **Cloning is a form of experimentation on a nonconsenting subject.** Attempts on animals reveal extremely high failure rates, resulting in many disabilities and deformities. No ethical scientist would attempt human cloning at current odds.

2. **Cloning threatens human identity and individuality by permitting the intentional genetic replication of a person whose life is already in process.** The clone, says Kass, "will not be fully a surprise to the world; people are always likely to compare his doings in life with those of his alter ego."

3. **Cloning turns procreating into manufacturing by enabling the advance selection of a total genetic blueprint.** Things are made, but people are begotten. In cloning, that boundary line is erased (although a form of baby manufacturing has been underway since *in vitro* fertilization began, Kass rightly notes).

4. **Cloning is an act of despotism that perverts parenthood by turning children into genetically engineered possessions intended to fulfil parental wants.** Some argue that many children are already brought into the world for reasons other than the sheer desire to welcome new life. But we must reject treating children, however they are born, as commodities or as instruments to other ends.

A number of other arguments have emerged: cloning would mark the first instance of humans reproducing through asexual replication, radically altering the nature of procreation and eliminating dual genetic origin in the cloned. Notre Dame law professor Kathleen Kaveny has shown how dramatically cloning would confuse family lines and relations.

If made available solely by the market based on ability to pay, cloning would contribute to distributive injustice. It would weaken marriage and the relationships between men and women by further eroding the link connecting marriage, sex, and childbearing – likely extending the practice of assisted reproduction among homosexuals. Kass has made the point that it could deepen the misery of children after divorce – if, for example, Mom had to look at the clone of the now-despised Dad all day long.

Cloning would contribute to our epidemic narcissism by enabling self-creation without any involvement of another person. The potential for multiple self-cloning could create a household freak show. It could bring more children into the world who lack the benefit of two parents. The sly might try to clone others without their consent; or, conversely, famous people and corporate interests might market highly desired genotypes to those seeking (in vain) to guarantee successful offspring.

Finally, cloning does not meet any legitimate human need. Many kinds of reproductive technology exist for the infertile. Misguided efforts to bring back a dead child through cloning would mark a sad attempt to salve a grief that cannot be salved, and at the cost of exploiting another human being through her very creation.

Tinkering with Genes

Genetic therapy may be the most morally difficult of the three areas considered here. A distinction between somatic interventions (repairing a defect in the genes of a living person) and germline interventions (altering reproductive DNA inheritable by future generations) has been recognized in this field since the 1980s, with ethicists saying yes to the first and no to the second. But recently questions have been raised about this distinction's scientific accuracy and moral relevance.

An American Association for the Advancement of Science (AAAS) study group has suggested abandoning the terminology and instead distinguishing only between inheritable and nonheritable genetic modifications.

In *Genetic Turning Points: The Ethics of Human Genetic Intervention*, geneticist/ethicist Peterson argues that all genetic intervention should be evaluated based on four criteria: safety; improvement for the recipient; maintaining an open, and not foreclosed, future for the recipient; and just resource allocation. While the stakes of germline intervention (or inheritable modifications) are certainly higher than for somatic intervention, Peterson argues that either could meet these criteria if the science develops adequately. He further asserts that we might have a moral obligation to pass on to progeny the healthiest possible genetic legacy.

Several points argue in favour of germline therapy: some maladies might be cured, it may be the only way to attack some diseases, and prevention costs less than cures. If, for example, the gene for Tay-Sachs or Huntington's disease could be eliminated from the reproductive DNA of all those who carry it, the disease itself could presumably be wiped out. Why just offer somatic interventions to millions of sufferers if we can eliminate the disease altogether?

Among concerns, one is simply scientific. If, as Francis Collins (director of the National Human Genome Research Institute) argues, the role of genes is complicated and undeterministic-genes interact unpredictably with each other, with other cellular actors, environment, and free will – then the supposed promise of some germline interventions may be vastly overstated. At present, at least, we may simply be in over our heads and end up doing more harm than good.

The AAAS report states flatly that inheritable modifications cannot now be carried out safely on human beings.

Furthermore, germline intervention would affect not just one person but all offspring; more broadly, it would affect the gene pool of the human race. Another concern is distributive justice – unless everyone gets access to germline therapies, such exclusivity could worsen our already unjust allocation of health-care resources.

Some fear, further, that the effort to eradicate genetic diseases will contribute to the social stigmatization of those who have them.

Finally, we will not be able to draw a firm line against *morally odious genetic enhancements* if we permit germline therapy. Genetic enhancement suggests outrageous possibilities. We rightly scorn the prospect of a society in which people with means purchase prepackaged genetic endowments of athletic, artistic, intellectual, or physical prowess for themselves or their children (if this ever really proves possible).

It is easy to envision a split between what Princeton University molecular biologist Lee M. Silver creatively labels the GenRich and the Naturals – those who would be able to buy genetic excellence and those who would not.

A tragically ironic misunderstanding of human satisfaction lies behind such a possibility; not giftedness alone, but a blend of natural endowment, discovery, and hard work makes excellence satisfying. Undoubtedly, however, a market would grow instead for engineered excellence, even if it were a black market. Recently *Sports Illustrated* suggested the drive for athletic success will make genetically engineered athletes inevitable.

The implications of genetic enhancement for human reproduction, family life, childhood, and society as a whole are indeed chilling. Ethicists address this issue in various ways. In *From Chance to Choice: Genetics and Justice* (Cambridge, 2000), by Allen Buchanan, *et al.*, the authors flatly propose that the purchase of what I am calling "excellence enhancements" should be prohibited by law.

They argue, however, for a consensus on a small core of very basic human capabilities, and for access by all citizens in all health plans to the genetic therapies that could help obtain them. In a sense, this is the model that already prevails in health care (though it is deeply corrupted by unequal access). It would simply be extended to genetic medicine.

At a theological level, John Feinberg argues for drawing a distinction between conditions traceable to the Fall of humanity and its consequences, and those that are not; genetic interventions would be permissible for the former, and only for the latter if motives were morally correct. But who will decide that?

While the current state of science on inheritable modifications demands at least a moratorium on any application of them, research should continue. Making fundamental distinctions between narcissistic excellence enhancements and genuine health care, perhaps one day we will be able to eliminate genetic maladies through rigorously tested therapies available to all.

A Bioethical Decalogue

I have argued that the world, especially the biotech industry, presents this challenge to the church: **Tell us why we should not proceed to remake humanity now that we are developing the power to do so.**

Our answer should be this: You rightly perceive a mandate to understand and alleviate illness and the suffering it brings. We will support this effort, but within the boundaries of human well-being under the sovereignty of God. These boundaries include limits on the means we may use to achieve the goals.

Human beings may not be manufactured, engineered, or destroyed; we may not experiment on or otherwise use the vulnerable without their consent; we may not set aside the essential structures of the created physical and social order; we may not casually alter or enhance the nature of the person (and other forms of life); we may not restrict the legitimate benefits of innovations to the privileged but instead must serve the common good; and the biotech community may not make decisions without the participation and consent of society.

In turn, we will pledge to protect biotech efforts from the attacks of those who do not understand them, and will do everything we can to nurture a culture in which innovations will honour human dignity.

Bioethicist Chapman asks, "Will society have the wisdom, the powers of discernment, and the appropriate commitments to apply its new knowledge and capabilities for ethical ends?" May God graciously guide our steps, that the answer to that question will reflect wise exercise of our dominion.

David P. Gushee is Graves Associate Professor of Moral Philosophy and Senior Fellow of the Center for Christian Leadership, Union University, Jackson, Tennessee.

COPYRIGHT © 2001 BY THE AUTHOR OR CHRISTIANITY TODAY INTERNATIONAL
CHRISTIANITY TODAY MAGAZINE.
OCTOBER 1, 2001, VOL. 45, NO. 12, PAGE 34

GLOSSARY

Base pairs. Pairs of complementary bases forming the DNA structure; the units used to measure the length of DNA. Base pairs consist of adenine (A), which must always pair with thymine (T), and guanine (G), which must always pair with cytosine (C).

Chromosome. The condensed rod made up of a linear thread of DNA interwoven with protein that is the gene-bearing structure of living cells. Human beings have twenty-three pairs of chromosomes.

DNA (deoxyribonucleic acid). The double helix molecule that encodes genetic information and is the primary hereditary molecule in most species.

Enzyme. A protein that facilitates a specific chemical reaction without changing its direction or nature.

Eugenics. Strategies for attempting to improve the gene pool of a species either by halting the transmission of unwanted characteristics or increasing the transmission of desired characteristics.

Gene. The basic unit of heredity; a section of DNA that contains information for the production of specific protein molecules.

Gene mapping. The process of ascertaining the genetic sequence of a species.

Gene therapy. The medical replacement or repair of defective genes in living cells.

Genetic engineering. The process of altering the genetic makeup of cells or individual organisms by deliberately inserting, removing, or changing specific genes.

Genetic testing. The examination of individuals' genetic makeup for the purpose of identifying possible hereditary traits, including defects or abnormalities.

Germ cell. Reproductive cell.

Genome. All of the genetic material in the chromosomes of a particular organism or individual.

Genotype. An individual's genetic makeup.

Human Genome Project. The international, scientific effort to construct a detailed map of human genes, identifying their structure and function.

Implantation. The attachment of an embryo to the wall of the uterus.

Mutation. A permanent alteration of DNA that can be inherited.

Negative eugenics. Strategies for preventing the transmission of genetic traits which are deemed undesirable.

Phenotype. The observable characteristics resulting from a particular genotype as influenced by environmental factors.

Positive eugenics. Strategies for promoting the transmission of genetic traits which are deemed desirable.

Pre-embryo. A fertilized ovum (or conceptus) prior to implantation and the beginning of pregnancy.

Recombinant DNA. A novel sequence of DNA that is artificially produced by joining segments of DNA.

Assessment

The following are some of the most up-to-date statistics in relation to the issue of cloning. (Please see appendix A.)

- *The Independent* reported in March 1999 that it is possible by 2020 that 95% of human body parts could be replaceable by laboratory-grown organs.

- Dolly the cloned sheep is one out of 156 sheep. According to *Compassion in World Faming* 155 embryos either died or were killed on the way to cloning one sheep.

Addressing

The following is a list of practical suggestions that may enable churches and organizations to minister effectively to those concerned about the issues of cloning.

- Cloning is of course a major ethical concern for many people. It would be wise for Church leaders/workers to understand the arguments for and against cloning. The "Society, Religion and Technology Project" www.srtp.org.uk offer the "pros and cons" of cloning from a Christian point of view.

- What's wrong with proposed cloning laws

    1. Embryos could be produced here in the UK and exported for implantation abroad or in a portakabin on a ship anchored offshore – the woman could then return to have her baby in the UK.

    2. Cloned babies could still be born here if they are both produced and implanted abroad.

    3. Cloned embryos could be grown in a lab past 14 days (and if the technology becomes available to the foetal stage or even 'to birth') because, as has already been established by the recent High Court ruling, cloned embryos are not governed by the HFE Act. The HFE Act prohibits embryos being allowed to live beyond 14 days.

    4. Cloned embryos could conceivably be placed in the womb of a female of another species or in a man (theoretical possibilities but not beyond technological advance).

    5. It might be successfully argued that cloned embryos are not embryos at all (and thus not covered under the new Bill) but simply 'cellular life' – this is what Dr West from Advanced Cell Technology has already argued in this morning's *Independent*. This would mean that the new Bill may not apply to cloned embryos because they are not embryos (the Bill doesn't even define embryo!).

    6. The law will be impossible to police – this is because no-one will announce illegal cloned humans until after they are born – when it will be impossible to prove that they are cloned without producing the

human beings from whom the genetic material in the embryo (both nuclear and mitochondial) was derived. Lawyers will simply deny that the child is a clone and the burden of proof will be on the government to prove it with all the hassle and taxpayer's money that that involves. And suppose one of the DNA donors has since emigrated, or eluded detection or even worse died? Will the police then be left to hunt down the 'suspects'?

☆ What's wrong with cloning

1. Cloning embryos is unethical because it uses human embryos as a means to an end. This runs counter to the Judaeo-Christian ethic, enshrined in our legal system and in international codes such as the Declaration of Geneva (1948) which affirms unequivocally that human life – at every stage of its development – deserves the utmost respect.

2. Therapeutic cloning will lead inevitably to reproductive cloning. Once cloned embryos exist, theoretically all that is needed to produce human clones would be to implant them in a womb – a technique that is simple to perform and impossible to police.

3. There is a viable alternative to embryonic cloning in adult stem cell technology. The latest research suggests that adult stem cells, e.g. from the bone marrow, have much more flexibility than was previously thought and are therefore more effective in replacing damaged cells.

4. "It took 277 attempts to produce Dolly the sheep and early indications are that human cloning will be much more difficult. The ACT clone was only grown to the 6 cell stage and then failed to progress further. Foetuses produced by nuclear transfer are ten times more likely to die in utero than foetuses produced by normal sexual means, while cloned offspring are three times more likely to die after birth.

5. Cloning humans would lead to high foetal loss and deformities in the newborn – and will always be wrong for these reasons alone – not to mention the social and psychological squeals for the clones, their families and society at large.

☆ Church leaders/workers should bear in mind that cloning is promising answers to infirmities for which there is no known cure. Those people will of course cling to this promise and so their desperate plight should be handled sensitively when seeking to discuss cloning with them.

AFFIRMATION

The following is a list of churches, organizations or individuals who are dealing with the issue of Cloning. They will, we believe, be able to offer practical and professional advice to assist you in your efforts to minister. (Please see appendix B.)

ANIMAL AID
THE OLD CHAPEL
BRADFORD STREET
TONBRIDGE
TN9 1AW
TEL: 01732 364546
FAX: 01732 366533
EMAIL: INFO@ANIMALAID.ORG.UK
WEBSITE: WWW.ANIMALAID.ORG.UK
ANIMAL AID AIMS TO EXPOSE AND CAMPAIGN PEACEFULLY AGAINST THE ABUSE OF ANIMALS IN ALL ITS FORMS AND TO PROMOTE A CRUELTY-FREE LIFESTYLE. PRODUCES INFORMATION INCLUDING THEIR QUARTERLY MAGAZINE OUTRAGE. TO RECEIVE INFORMATION ON AN ISSUE OR FOR A LIST OF EDUCATIONAL AND INFORMATION RESOURCES, PLEASE SEND A LARGE SAE TO THE ADDRESS ABOVE.

BIOINDUSTRY ASSOCIATION
14–15 BELGRAVE SQUARE
LONDON
SW1X 8PS
TEL: 0207 565 7190
FAX: 0207 565 7191
EMAIL: ADMIN@BIOINDUSTRY.ORG
WEBSITE: WWW.BIOINDUSTRY.ORG
AIMS TO FOSTER GREATER PUBLIC AWARENESS AND UNDERSTANDING OF BIOTECHNOLOGY AND TO ENCOURAGE INFORMED PUBLIC DEBATE ABOUT ITS DEVELOPMENT. IF YOU HAVE ANY QUESTIONS OR COMMENTS ON THE WORK OF THE BIA OR THEIR WEB SITE, CONTACT THEM AT THE ABOVE ADDRESS.

COMPASSION IN WORLD FARMING TRUST (CIWF)
5A CHARLES STREET
PETERSFIELD
HAMPSHIRE
GU32 3EH
TEL: 01730 268070
FAX: 01730 260791
EMAIL: CIWFTRUST@CIWF.CO.UK
WEBSITE: WWW.CIWF.CO.UK
CIWF TRUST IS THE EDUCATIONAL WING OF BRITAIN'S LEADING FARM ANIMAL WELFARE ORGANIZATION, COMPASSION IN WORLD FARMING (CIWF), WHICH HAS BEEN CAMPAIGNING FOR IMPROVEMENTS IN THE WELFARE OF FARM ANIMALS FOR THE LAST THIRTY YEARS. PRODUCES A GENETIC ENGINEERING & FARM ANIMALS VIDEO. SEE THE EDUCATIONAL RESOURCES SECTION ON THEIR WEB SITE, OR CONTACT THEM DIRECTLY AT THE ABOVE ADDRESS FOR DETAILS.

GENETICS FORUM
94 WHITE LION STREET
LONDON
N1 9PF
TEL: 0207 837 9229
FAX: 0207 837 1141
EMAIL: GENETICSFORUM@GN.APC.ORG
WEBSITE: WWW.GENETICSFORUM.ORG.UK
THE GENETICS FORUM WORKS TO EDUCATE AND INFORM INTERESTED PARTIES ABOUT THE IMPLICATIONS OF GENETIC ENGINEERING. RESEARCHES THE USES AND IMPLICATIONS OF GENETIC TECHNOLOGIES ON HUMAN HEALTH, THE ENVIRONMENT AND ANIMAL WELFARE. IT ACTS AS AN INDEPENDENTLY FUNDED SOURCE OF INFORMATION FOR SCIENTISTS, GOVERNMENT, EDUCATION AND THE GENERAL PUBLIC. THEY PUBLISH SPLICE MAGAZINE. ASK FOR THEIR PUBLICATIONS LIST.

HUMAN GENETICS ADVISORY COMMISSION (HGAC)
OFFICE OF SCIENCE AND TECHNOLOGY
ALBANY HOUSE
94–98 PETTY FRANCE
LONDON
SW1H 9ST
TEL: 0207 271 2131
FAX: 0207 271 2028
WEBSITE: WWW.DTI.GOV.UK/HGAC
THE HGAC WAS ESTABLISHED IN DECEMBER 1996 TO OFFER GOVERNMENT INDEPENDENT ADVICE ON ISSUES ARISING FROM DEVELOPMENTS IN HUMAN GENETICS. AMONGST OTHERS, ONE OF THE TOPICS THAT THE COMMISSION HAS ADDRESSED AS A PRIORITY IS CLONING.

SOCIETY, RELIGION AND TECHNOLOGY PROJECT (SRT)
CHURCH OF SCOTLAND JOHN KNOX HOUSE
45 HIGH STREET
EDINBURGH
EH1 1SR
TEL: 0131 556 2953
FAX: 0131 556 7478
EMAIL: SRTP@SRTP.ORG.UK
WEBSITE: WWW.SRTP.ORG.UK

SRT is a project of the Church of Scotland set up in 1970 to examine ethical issues emerging from modern technology and to engage with key scientists and policy makers. It seeks to provide balanced and informed insights on major current issues. Its work includes genetic engineering, cloning, patenting, risk, environment, energy and 'God and Science' issues. It produces information sheets on a wide variety of issues which are available from the above address.

THE WELLCOME TRUST
THE WELLCOME BUILDING
183 EUSTON ROAD
LONDON
NW1 2BE
TEL: 0207 611 8888
FAX: 0207 611 8545
EMAIL: RECEPTION@WELLCOME.AC.UK
WEBSITE: WWW.WELLCOME.AC.UK/

The Wellcome Trust runs many innovative activities for teachers and students, and offers a number of teaching resources. The teaching resources also help teachers stay up to date with the latest research in biomedical science, and detail practical activities that help to bring scientific subjects to life in the classroom.

WORLD WIDE WEB INFORMATION GROUPS
SOCIETY, RELIGION AND TECHNOLOGY PROJECT
WWW.SRTP.ORG.UK

This site aims to bring professional expertise by providing informed and penetrating comment for technologists, educators, media, the church, the public – in fact anyone with an interest in how technology is affecting our lives, and the issues it raises. For their views on cloning, scroll down the home page to the click on a heading section. Click on subject heading. This takes you to their main index. Under the heading of biotechnology is a link called cloning. Click on this for a wide range of articles about human and animal cloning issues. Well worth a visit.

HUMAN CLONING FOUNDATION
WWW.HUMANCLONING.ORG

The Human Cloning Foundation (TM) promotes education about human cloning and other forms of biotechnology with an emphasis on the positive aspects of new technologies. A huge site with articles on a wide range of cloning issues including the benefits of human cloning and the reasons why we should clone human beings.

ROSLIN INSTITUTE
WWW.2.RI.BBSRC.AC.UK

Click on special topic: cloning. Then click on background notes on nuclear transfer and cloning. This site includes all the background material produced by the institute on cloning and nuclear transfer. And unfortunately many sites contain inaccurate, misleading or heavily biased information. Our researchers have therefore undertaken an extensive analysis to bring you a selection of quality web site addresses.

THE GENETICS FORUM
WWW.GENETICSFORUM.ORG.UK

The Genetics Forum is the only independent organization in the UK concerned with the use of new genetic technologies and their public policy implications. It was founded in 1989 by a group of scientists, lawyers and advocates from the animal welfare, environmental and consumer movements concerned about the long-term impact of rapid developments in the genetic sciences. Since its inception, the Genetics Forum has been instrumental in raising the issues of genetic engineering to a prominent position on the public policy agenda.

MATCH
WWW.MATCH.INWEB.CO.UK

Match is the first Scottish pressure group dedicated to campaigning against the cloning of human beings. Go to the match cloning reference page and click on the link articles on cloning to read the first of their articles on cloning.

INTERNATIONAL CLONING SOCIETY
WWW.SURESITE.COM/WA/I/ICS

THE INTERNATIONAL CLONING SOCIETY (ICS) IS ESSENTIALLY A BODY OF PEOPLE WHO HAVE EXPRESSED AN INTEREST IN BEING CLONED AT SOME POINT IN THE FUTURE. THE SOCIETY IS CURRENTLY MAKING ARRANGEMENTS TO COLLECT, STORE AND PRESERVE THE CELL/DNA SPECIMENS OF THOSE MEMBERS WHO ELECT TO MAKE THEMSELVES AVAILABLE TO BE CLONED, UNDER SPECIFIC AND STATED CIRCUMSTANCES, IN THE FUTURE.

A FEW MORE HELPFUL SITES.

HTTP://WWW.LIFEUK.ORG/CLONING/HUMAN-CLONINGANDABUSEOFPOWER.HTML

HTTP://WWW.LIFEUK.ORG/MAIN.HTML TYPE IN CLONING

HTTP://WWW.PROLIFE.ORG.UK/ TYPE IN CLONING

NATURE PUBLISHING GROUP

NATURE REVIEWS, AN EXCITING NEW SERIES OF REVIEW JOURNALS FROM THE NATURE PUBLISHING GROUP (NPG) DUE TO BE LAUNCHED IN OCTOBER 2000.

Books that deal with the issue of cloning.

1563583179, *Beyond Cloning: Religion and the Remaking of Humanity*, Trin ity Press International, Ronald Cole-Turner
0664257712, *Human Cloning Religious Responses Westminster*, John Knox, Ron Cole Turner
0800756681, *Human Cloning: Playing God or Scientific Process?*, Baker/Revell, Lane P. Lester James C. Hefley

ALTERNATIVE MEDICINE

AWARENESS

The following information is included to raise the social awareness and understanding of ministers in relation to the contemporary issue of Complementary Medicine.

How should we respond to alternative medicine? Peter Saunders, CMF Student Secretary, gives an overview of the field and suggests some principles to apply in assessing individual modalities.

Alternative medicine is rising rapidly up the healthcare agenda. One in four people in the UK use at least one form of alternative medicine and three out of four people are in favour of alternative therapies being available on the NHS.

One study cited by a recent BMA report suggested that there may be up to 15 million consultations to non-conventional therapists each year in the UK, with about 1.5 million people (2.5% of the population) each year receiving treatment.

The British Register of Complementary Practitioners has 1,000 members and the number is rising by 10% per year. A 1980 UK survey suggested that there were 12.1 non-medically qualified practitioners per 100,000 population – 27% of the number of general practitioners. In addition, 35% of UK GPs have received some training in alternative medicine.

In most member states of the European Union (e.g. Belgium, France, Spain, Italy and Greece) the practice of medicine by non-recognized health professionals is illegal. In Germany and Scandinavia there is some regulation but in the United Kingdom and Ireland there is virtually no regulation at all.[1]

When one considers the tight controls on the training and practice of orthodox medical practitioners there is clearly a double standard operating. If there are no proper controls for alternative medicine practitioners, then the way is open for charlatans, profiteers and tricksters to operate alongside those who are genuinely providing service of proven value.

WHAT IS ALTERNATIVE MEDICINE?

Problems of definition

The report of the BMA's Board of Science and Education's working party, *Complementary Medicine, New Approaches to Good Practice*[2] defines non-conventional therapies as 'those which are not widely used by orthodox medical professionals nor widely taught at undergraduate level in medical and paramedical courses' – but some therapies regarded as alternative in the UK are taught formally in medical schools elsewhere.

The three terms complementary, alternative and holistic are used almost interchangeably — but convey different messages. 'Alternative' implies an either/or relationship with orthodox medicine; 'complementary' a both/and relationship while 'holistic' implies that non-orthodox therapies treat the 'whole person'. All these assumptions are controversial.

The Diversity of Therapies

The BMA report says that as many as 160 different forms of non-conventional therapy have been identified. An A to Z of some of the most common includes: Acupuncture, Acupressure, Alexander Technique, Aromatherapy, Auricular Therapy, Bach Flower Remedies, Chiropractic, Crystal Therapy, Herbs, Homeopathy, Hypnosis, Iridology, Macrobiotics, Massage, Naturopathy, Osteopathy, Reflexology, Shiatsu, Therapeutic Touch, Transcendental Meditation (TM), Yoga, Zen and Zone Therapy.

On first glance there seems to be very little similarity between one form of alternative medicine and another; but what unifies most of them is the idea of a 'life force' or 'vital energy' which ensures health, becomes disrupted in disease and can be manipulated by various means.

For example, underlying acupuncture is the belief that there is a vital force or energy called 'Chi' which flows freely through the body in twelve meridians or channels. The flow of this energy depends on the balance between two opposite forces; an active, 'male' force called 'yin' and a passive, 'female' force called 'yang'. When the flow of the Chi energy is free and uninterrupted health is ensured but if the balance between yin and yang is disturbed or if there is any blockage to energy flow then disease results.

These ideas have their roots in the ancient Chinese religion of Taoism which has Chi, yin and yang as fundamental concepts.

Ideologies which underlie other forms of medicine use different words for the same general concept of 'life force'. Shiatsu is based on Shintoism and calls the energy 'Ki'. Yoga and TM are based on Hinduism and call the force 'prana'. Homeopathy uses the term 'vital energy', chiropractic 'innate intelligence' and Maori medicine terms the life force 'mana'.

The common theme of 'correcting imbalance'

In most alternative therapies health is believed to be restored by relieving blockage and restoring flow in the 'life force', but the means whereby this is achieved vary widely as listed below:

- Method
- Modality
- Needling
- Acupuncture
- Homeopathy
- Minute doses of diluted medicine
- Reflexology

Foot massage
Aromatherapy
Aromatic Oils
Yoga
Adopting Body Postures
Transcendental Meditation
Meditation
Therapeutic Touch
Hovering hands
Macrobiotics
Diet

Why is Alternative Medicine so popular?

There are seven main factors accounting for the rise in popularity of alternative medicine in the Western World.

1. Changes in the Western worldview

Two hundred years ago in Britain most people had a Christian worldview; they believed in a creator God who made us, intervened in our world and to whom we were accountable. But with the publication of Darwin's *Origin of the Species* and the rise of biblical criticism, this theistic world view gave way to an atheistic one.

People began to doubt the existence of God and life after death. Man came to be seen simply as a clever monkey, the product of matter, chance and time in a directionless and purposeless universe. Morality became relative ('what's right for me') rather than absolute.

Now we are seeing another worldview shift from atheism into pantheism. Pantheism is the ideology which lies behind Eastern religions like Hinduism and also the New Age Movement. God is an impersonal force of which we are all simply a part. Death leads to reincarnation, and morality simply means being in harmony with nature. All is one and all is God. This has meant an increasing openness to all sorts of non-Christian spiritual belief along with a scepticism and suspicion about science.

The change of worldview from theism, to atheism and then pantheism has had profound effects on the way that medicine is practised. While Christian doctors see human beings as a tri-unity of spirit, soul (or mind) and body (1 Thes 5: 23), atheistic doctors see them as consisting of just body and mind. By contrast, New Age or alternative medicine practitioners see human beings as an integrated whole; but from a pantheistic rather than a theistic perspective.

Much of alternative medicine has its roots in the New Age Movement which in turn is rooted in Astrology. Exponents believe that for the last 2,000 years we have been in the age of Pisces (the fishes), but that now we are moving into the age of Aquarius (the water-carrier). The Age of Pisces was characterised by rationality, logic, objectivity and black and white analytical 'left brain' thinking. By contrast the Age of Aquarius is characterised by intuitional, subjective, grey 'right brain' thinking.

Sociologically the New Age Movement spawned the counterculture of the 1960s with 'flower-power', peace protests, drug experimentation and the Hippie movement. Spiritually it paved the way for a wide acceptance of Eastern religious ideology, Astrology and the Occult. Medically the New Age Movement has meant an increasing disillusionment with and scepticism about scientific medicine.

As Christians we reject both the atheistic and pantheistic worldviews. They are quite simply not the way the world is. God does exist. We are made in his image, yet fallen; and death leads to judgement. We embrace the scientific method as a gift of God, but we also see human beings as being more than simply the sum of their parts.

2. Failings of orthodox medicine

There have been great advances in orthodox medicine over the last two centuries which have led to the eradication and alleviation of many diseases which were previously neither preventable nor curable: immunisations for smallpox, antibiotics for infection, anti-psychotics for schizophrenia, chemotherapy for cancer, drugs for heart failure and surgery for a whole host of structural and anatomical problems.

But medicine also has its limits. With many illnesses we have a long way to go. Solid tumours (e.g. lung, breast and bowel) are in general difficult to treat if surgery fails. There is still much progress to be made in chronic diseases like multiple sclerosis and rheumatoid arthritis, and there is still no orthodox cure for musculoskeletal back pain and the common cold. If we also consider that 75% of people seeing their doctor do not have any defined organic illness, it is easy to see why people may decide to consult alternative practitioners. Patients may also become impatient or disillusioned with the NHS system of referrals and waiting lists.

With some diseases alternative medicine fares no worse than orthodox medicine and it is in these areas that alternative medicine thrives.

3. Medical arrogance

Doctors have not always been ready to admit failure; and on occasions may go on using treatments of doubtful value, or with potential side-effects rather than being honest that nothing else can be done. The inappropriate use of some chemotherapeutic agents or radical surgery for advanced cancer, for instance, may cultivate distrust in patients who then seek other solutions.

4. The side effects of orthodox medicine

Orthodox medicines and surgery can produce side effects and complications which are sometimes fatal. Examples are often widely publicised by an unforgiving press. By contrast most alternative medicine has little in the way of side-effects.

5. Loss of a whole person perspective

Advances in the science of medicine may be at the expense of the art of medicine. Doctors have less time for the patient, touch patients less often, and are tempted much more now to treat their patients simply as anatomical structures or biochemical machines. There is much less in medicine now of the ritual handshake, pulse-taking, hand on the shoulder etc. Too often the doctor is now ensconced behind his PC and perhaps a formidable desk; while many alternative therapies involve plenty of 'hands-on' diagnosis and treatment.

Alternative medical practitioners generally are able to give much more in terms of time and touch, thereby engendering more trust. Homeopaths, for example, may spend up to 90 minutes in a first consultation and 45 minutes on follow up. Patients naturally assume, 'He must know what he is doing because he spends so much time with me'.

6. Costs of high-tech medicine
High-tech medicine is expensive, while often the only cost of alternative medicine is the therapist's time. This is one feature making alternative therapies increasingly attractive to NHS managers looking to cut costs.

7. Consumer demand
Patients are prepared to pay for therapies which promise what orthodox medicine has failed to deliver; especially for incurable cancer or chronic pain. This demand means that there is plenty of room in the market place for more practitioners.

Why does alternative medicine seem to work?

Why is it that so many people are seeking alternative medicine therapies when so many of them have been shown not to work in clinical trials? There are at least eight reasons why.

1. Genuine therapeutic effects
Some alternative medicines genuinely work. Over half of prescription and over-the-counter drugs originate as natural compounds or are based on them (e.g. aspirin, digitalis, morphine, adrenaline, curare, all antibiotics except the quinolones etc); and the natural world may hold many more therapeutic treasures.[3]

It is quite conceivable that some alternative medicine practitioners are using useful compounds or techniques which are not yet known to orthodox medicine. But if this is the case then we need to discover what they are so that they can be isolated and given in the correct dose!

2. The placebo effect
If we strongly believe that something (or someone) has the power to help us, then we are much more likely to experience benefit. It is a fact that one third of people given an inert compound to relieve a particular symptom will report relief of that symptom. This is called the placebo effect. In the same way patients who share the therapist's belief in New Age pantheism or the existence of 'life force' will be more likely to benefit from their therapy.

3. Concurrent use of therapies
Belief in an alternative therapy's effectiveness may develop when it is used concurrently with another more effective orthodox therapy. The effect is then wrongly ascribed to the alternative therapy.

4. Psychosomatic illness

Many illnesses are psychosomatic; in other words a patient's stress level or mental state can aggravate the symptoms. Asthma, eczema, peptic ulcer and rheumatoid arthritis fall in this category. Alternative therapies which induce relaxation may then improve the symptoms.

5. Spontaneous remissions

Many diseases get better by themselves. Viral infections (e.g. warts, common cold) and some tumours (e.g. malignant melanoma) are examples of conditions which may spontaneously regress. In such cases people may well then attribute therapeutic effect to the remedy they were trying at the time of recovery, when it fact their improvement at that time may just have been coincidence. This is called the 'post hoc ergo propter hoc' fallacy; in other words 'because B followed A, then A must have caused B'.

6. Dietary influences

There is a strong link between diet and health, and many alternative therapists recommend that patients drink less coffee or alcohol, eat less fat or more fibre or take vitamins. The resulting improvement may then be due to the change in diet, rather that the alternative therapy being used concurrently.

7. Imagined improvement

Some patients, especially if open to suggestion from others that they 'look better', may simply imagine that they 'feel better'; especially if the symptoms were of a vague nature in the first place. Alternatively they may simply get better at tolerating symptoms, and imagine that the symptoms themselves have diminished.

8. Demonic involvement

There may be real spiritual forces operating to bring healing through demonic power. Such healings may be the bait that Satan then uses to draw a person more deeply into the occult, or into accepting a pantheistic worldview.

How do we assess individual modalities?

It is not possible in this brief review to comment on each and every alternative therapy; but here are some principles which can be generally applied.

1. Do the claims fit the facts?

Any new orthodox medicine has to undergo extensive pharmacological testing to assess its therapeutic potential, side-effects and interactions with other drugs. Tests are first carried out in animals, then in human volunteers and only then are short and long term studies carried out on real patients.

In the UK if a drug passes these tests it must then be approved by the Licensing Authority. This ensures that drugs reaching the public are both safe and effective.

In the same way medical practitioners must undergo a five-year undergraduate training and then work for a further year before they are registered and able to practice independently of a NHS institution.

Similar safeguards for alternative medicines and practitioners are largely absent. There is simply no comparison between the double-blind, randomised, placebo-controlled cross-over trials which many orthodox drugs undergo and the subjective anecdotal 'evidence' supporting much alternative medicine. Furthermore, when proper trials are employed the results are often unconvincing.

A Department of Complementary Medicine has recently been set up at the University of Exeter to review trials on alternative and complementary therapies. The contents pages of their quarterly journal FACT (*Focus on Alternative and Complementary Therapies*) are available on the internet[4] and make interesting reading. Many of the published studies give inconclusive results.

A 1990 French review of 40 controlled trials on homeopathy concluded that the majority were flawed by small sample size and subjective measures of improvement.[5] A 1991 review of 107 trials was similarly inconclusive.[6]

By contrast there is evidence that patients with low back pain treated with chiropractic derive more benefit and long-term satisfaction than those treated by hospitals;[7] and that, according to a consensus panel of the US National Institutes of Health, acupuncture is an effective treatment for nausea and vomiting induced by anaesthesia, pregnancy or chemotherapy.[8]

The biblical injunction to 'enquire, probe and investigate thoroughly' (Dt 13: 14ff) must surely be relevant here. We should always ask, 'What is the evidence that this therapy really works?'

2. Is there a rational scientific basis?

We know how most orthodox drugs work. They may stimulate receptors (e.g. b agonists in asthma), modify cell transport (e.g. probenecid), block enzymes (e.g. allopurinol), replace missing compounds (e.g. vitamin B12) or chelate toxins (e.g. penicillamine). The action of any given drug is determined by its concentration at the site of action; and the actions are understandable in view of their known biochemical and physiological effects. By contrast the majority of alternative medicines have no rational scientific basis.

Homeopathy involves diluting an active compound to such a degree that the resulting 'potency' contains not even a molecule of the original active ingredient.

Iridology claims to link each area of the iris with a separate part of the body when it is known that no such anatomical links exist. Reflexology is based on the belief that there are connections between the sole of the foot and internal organs; again in the absence of any scientific evidence.

There is similarly no evidence for the existence of the 'meridians' (energy channels) of acupuncture or the 'chakras' (psychic spinal centres) of yoga.

In some cases an alternative therapy may be working because of some scientific reason unknown to the therapist. It has been suggested, for instance that the therapeutic effects of acupuncture could be explained by the release of endogenous (naturally produced) pain-killers called endorphins. If this is indeed confirmed, then acupuncture will be shown to have a scientific basis, but this will not, by any means prove that Taoist ideology is true or that Chi energy exists.

3. Is it the improvement due to the therapy or some other factor?

Transcendental Meditation lowers blood pressure, but why? Is it because it enables the Goddess Kundalini to migrate up the spine and unite with Brahman in the head (as Hindus believe); or is it simply that meditation induces relaxation and reduces the sympathetic output that raises blood pressure?

Similarly, chiropractic has been shown to help low back pain, but is this because manipulation of the spine alters the flow of 'innate intelligence' or because it helps to alleviate musculoskeletal trigger points?

In each of these cases it seems to be the methodology rather than the principle of prana or innate intelligence that brings the therapeutic effect.

There is thus a world of difference between the GP who makes a diagnosis by taking a history and doing an examination and the alternative medicine practitioner who does it by examining an iris or swinging a pendulum. There is also a huge gulf between the GP who uses acupuncture on the basis of its proven effectiveness in clinical trials and the practitioner who uses it because he believes it alters the balance of yin and yang.

4. What is the worldview behind it?

What is the worldview behind the therapy? As mentioned acupuncture has its roots in Taoism, yoga in Hinduism and therapeutic touch in New Age ideology. This alone should make us suspicious.

What was the motivation of the therapist who developed the treatment? Hahnemann, the German physician who developed homeopathy, was a freemason. Kreger, the New York Nursing Professor who invented therapeutic touch, is a Buddhist; and her collaborator Kunz was Vice President of the Theosophical Society and an occultist and psychic. Edward Bach (of 'flower remedy' fame) was a doctor who trusted his 'spirit self' for knowledge and guidance.

It might be objected here that much orthodox medicine has been developed by atheists with an atheistic worldview and yet that does not stop us benefiting from their insights. This is true. We are not saying that pantheists are unable to discover beneficial treatments which are God-given; but simply that their worldview should make us wary in assessing their therapies.

5. Does it involve the occult?

Are occult means of divination used in deciding on diagnosis or treatment? We should heed the biblical warnings about Mediums and Spiritists (Lev 9: 31, 20: 6; Acts 16: 16-21), Astrology (Is 47: 13-15), Magic Charms (Ezk 13: 20-23), Diviner's Wands (Ho 4: 12),Sorcery (Acts 19: 19), Witchcraft (Gal 5: 20), Magic Arts (Rev 9: 21, 21: 8, 22: 15) and the Occult (Dut 18: 10-12) generally.

6. Is it medically safe?

Most alternative therapies have little in the way of side effects, but there are exceptions. Acupuncture, for example, may cause pneumothaorax or transmit infection. Chiropractic neck manipulation has been associated with vertebral artery obstruction and some herbal therapies result in toxicity or even death. But perhaps the greatest danger is that alternative therapies can create a false sense of security which leads to delay in diagnosis or in implementation of effective orthodox medicine.

7. Has it stood the test of time?
This is not a guarantee, as clearly many occult devices stand the test of time, but we can be equally sure that something which genuinely works or is of God will stand the test of time.

Applying the tests

As an example of applying the tests above let us consider homeopathy. First, there is no clear evidence that it actually works. Second, it has no rational scientific basis; there is no reason known to science why a solution containing not a single molecule of a given active substance should have any therapeutic effect. Third, it is based on a pantheistic worldview with the concept of 'vital energy' playing a prominent role Fourth, practitioners will often use occult means (such as pendulums) in diagnosis. While it does appear to be safe and to have stood the test of time, these other considerations should make us very wary indeed.

Difficult Questions

Finally let us finish by considering some of the objections which Christians might raise to the kind of critique I have just given.

1. Weren't many medical treatments initially 'natural' anyway?
This is correct (e.g. aspirin [willow bark], digitalis [foxglove], Morphine [poppies]) but the natural ingredient needs to be clearly identified and given in the right dose. Many useful natural drugs are toxic if given in too high a dose (e.g. digitalis, opium).

Decisions about which compound to give must also not be based on occult practices (e.g. rituals, spells, charms, astrology, clairvoyance, pendulums, spirit guides etc) as previously mentioned.

2. How can something be wrong if it actually works?
First, we need to be sure that the given therapy does actually work. Have there been properly controlled clinical trials carried out showing that it is better than placebo, or is it supported simply by anecdotal testimony?

Second we need to ask why it works. Is it working as a result of occult power? (Dut 13: 1-6; Ex 7: 11,22, 8: 7, 18,19; Mt 24: 24). If so it may be leading to the bondage, rather than to the liberation, of the patient. We must be ready to test everything (1 Thes 5: 21).

3. Isn't there some good in it?
It's often objected that we should not throw out the baby with the bath water; and there is some truth in this ... but is the baby and bath water really a good analogy? It is very easy to see the difference between baby and bath water but often extremely difficult to separate out the good and bad in alternative medicine.

A better analogy is the poison mushroom.[9] While poison mushrooms contain plenty of good fat, carbohydrate and protein we recommend that people don't eat them because it is impossible to separate out the good and the bad.

Everything that does not proceed from faith is sin; so if we have doubts it may well be better to abstain (Rom 14: 23).

4. How can it be wrong if good Christians I know use it?

Good Christians may be ignorant or deceived or simply have their consciences blunted from habitual sin. There is no-one with perfect discernment who is right in all their words, let alone all their beliefs (Jas 3: 1). Good Christians may also have a lot personally invested in a therapy if a friend or relative is practising in it or has benefited from it and their objectivity may be accordingly clouded.

Summary

We have reviewed the rapid rise in popularity in alternative medicine, and seen that while therapies are diverse, there is a pantheistic ideology behind many of them.

Alternative medicine is popular because of changes in the Western worldview, the perceived failings, arrogance, costs and side effects of orthodox medicine, and because it appears to bring a 'whole person' perspective.

While some therapies may genuinely work, apparent improvements are often due to other reasons such as spontaneous remissions, the use of concurrent orthodox medicine or the placebo effect.

Each branch of alternative medicine needs to be assessed individually to determine its effectiveness, scientific basis, mode of action, safety, underlying worldview and links with the occult.

We should be wary, but we must be careful also that we do not miss genuine gifts which God has given. The biblical injunction to 'test everything… hold on to the good… avoid every kind of evil' (1 Thess 5: 21,22) is surely as relevant here as in any other area of the Christian life.

PETER SAUNDERS

References

1. Two exceptions to this state of affairs are osteopathy and homeopathy.
2. *Complementary Medicine – Controls needed*, says BMA. BMJ 1993; 306: 1713 (26 June)
3. BMJ 1998;316: 1266 (25 April)
4. http://www.exeter.ac.uk/FACT/
5. Hill C. and Doyon F., *Review of randomised trials of homeopathy*. Rev Epidemiol Sante Publique 1990 38: 139–147
6. Kleijnen J. et al. *Clinical Trials of Homeopathy*. BMJ 1991; 302: 316–323
7. Meade TW et al. *Randomised Comparison of chiropractic and hospital outpatient management for low back pain*. BMJ 1995; 311: 349–351 (5 August)
8. BMJ 1997; 315: 1252 (15 November)
9. I am indebted to Jock McGregor of L'Abri Christian Fellowship for this analogy

Assessment

The following are some of the most up-to-date statistics in relation to the issue of Complementary Medicine. (Please see appendix A.)

It is almost impossible to assess the numbers of people using complementary medicine and how many complementary therapists there are in the UK because not all therapists are registered. *Which?* Magazine however points out the following;

> Complementary therapies are becoming increasingly popular, according to the British Complementary Medicine Association, there are now around 40,000 registered complementary therapists in the UK. Indeed they now out number the 36,000 GPs

Which? October 1999

Addressing

The following is a list of practical suggestions that may enable churches and organizations to minister effectively to those concerned about Complementary Medicine.

Church leaders/workers dealing with those people who turn to alternative medicines are doing so because they believe that conventional medicine is not working for them. Compassion and understanding should be at the heart of any advice that is given. Also it would be wise to bear in mind that natural remedies are not the same as many of the alternative therapies/medicines that are from a religious basis.

Affirmation

The following is a list of churches, organizations or individuals who are ministering to those concerned about Complementary Medicine. They will, we believe, be able to offer practical and professional advice to assist you in your efforts to minister. (Please see appendix B.)

CHRISTIAN MEDICAL FELLOWSHIP (CMF)
157 WATERLOO ROAD
LONDON
SE1 8XN
TEL: 020 7928 4694
FAX: 020 7620 2453
EMAIL: INFO@CMF.ORG.UK
WEBSITE: WWW.CMF.ORG.UK

A NETWORK OF OVER 4,500 DOCTORS IN ALL BRANCHES OF MEDICINE, AND OVER 1,000 MEDICAL STUDENTS, THROUGHOUT THE UK AND REPUBLIC OF IRELAND. IT PUBLISHES A RANGE OF BOOKLETS AND LEAFLETS.

THE DR EDWARD BACH CENTRE
MOUNT VERNON
BAKERS LANE
SOTWELL
OXON
OX10 0PZ
TEL: 01491 834678
FAX: 01491 825022
WEBSITE: WWW.BACHCENTRE.COM
THIS WAS THE HOME AND WORKPLACE OF DR BACH IN THE LAST YEARS OF HIS LIFE, WHEN HE COMPLETED HIS RESEARCH INTO THE FLOWER REMEDIES THAT STILL BEAR HIS NAME.

GENERAL OSTEOPATHIC COUNCIL
OSTEOPATHY HOUSE
176 TOWER BRIDGE STREET
LONDON
SE1 3LU
TEL: 020 7357 6655
FAX: 020 7357 0011
EMAIL: INFO@OSTEOPATHY.ORG.UK
WEBSITE: WWW.OSTEOPATHY.ORG.UK
THE GENERAL OSTEOPATHIC COUNCIL OFFERS AN INFORMATION SERVICE WHERE YOU CAN OBTAIN FACT SHEETS, HAVE YOUR QUESTIONS ANSWERED AND FIND ADDRESSES OF REGISTERED OSTEOPATHS.

NATIONAL INSTITUTE OF MEDICAL HERBALISTS (NIMH)
56 LONGBROOK STREET
EXETER
EX4 6AH
TEL: 01392 426022
FAX: 01392 498963
WEBSITE: WWW.BTINTERNET.COM/-NIMH/
THE NIMH IS THE UK'S LEADING PROFESSIONAL ORGANIZATION OF PRACTITIONERS OF HERBAL MEDICINE.

THE NATURAL MEDICINES SOCIETY (NMS)
PO BOX 232
EAST MOLESEY
KT8 1YF
TEL: 020 8974 1166
FAX: 020 8974 1166
EMAIL: NMS@CHARITY.VFREE.COM
WEBSITE: WWW.THENMS.DEMON.CO.UK
THE ONLY UK CONSUMER BODY THAT DEFENDS YOUR FREEDOM TO USE ALTERNATIVE AND COMPLEMENTARY MEDICINES AND THERAPIES.

WORLD WIDE WEB LINKS THAT WILL BE HELPFUL IN UNDERSTANDING ALTERNATIVE MEDICINE.

NATIONAL INSTITUTE OF MEDICAL HERBALISTS
WWW.BTINTERNET.COM/~NIMH/
FROM THE HOME PAGE YOU CAN ACCESS INFORMATION ABOUT HERBS, RESEARCH, EDUCATION OR POLITICS. YOU CAN ALSO FIND YOUR NEAREST PRACTITIONER IN THEIR ONLINE REGISTER OF FULLY-QUALIFIED THERAPISTS.

GENERAL OSTEOPATHS COUNCIL
WWW.OSTEOPATHY.ORG.UK
ON THE OSTEOPATHIC INFORMATION SERVICE WEB SITE YOU CAN FIND FACT SHEETS INCLUDING LOOKING AFTER YOURSELF IN YOUR TEENS AND TWENTIES.

BRITISH HOMEOPATHIC ASSOCIATION (BHA)
WWW.TRUSTHOMEOPATHY.ORG/FACULTY
FROM THIS HOME PAGE YOU HAVE THREE OPTIONS: FACULTY OF HOMEOPATHY, BRITISH HOMEOPATHIC ASSOCIATION OR THE CASE FOR HOMEOPATHY. FROM EACH OF THESE CHOICES YOU CAN FIND OUT INFORMATION ON HOMEOPATHY, TREATMENTS AND EDUCATION AND TRAINING RESPECTIVELY. AND UNFORTUNATELY MANY SITES CONTAIN INACCURATE, MISLEADING OR HEAVILY BIASED INFORMATION. OUR RESEARCHERS HAVE THEREFORE UNDERTAKEN AN EXTENSIVE ANALYSIS TO BRING YOU A SELECTION OF QUALITY WEB SITE ADDRESSES.

NEW YORK ONLINE ACCESS TO HEALTH (NOAH)
WWW.NOAH-HEALTH.ORG
AT THE HOME PAGE, CLICK ON HEALTH TOPICS WHICH TAKES YOU TO A LONG LIST INCLUDING ALTERNATIVE MEDICINE. WITHIN THIS LINK THERE ARE HUNDREDS OR ARTICLES ON COMPLEMENTARY MEDICINE. WELL WORTH A VISIT.

BRITISH ACUPUNCTURE COUNCIL
WWW.ACUPUNETURE.ORG.UK
THIS SITE IS WHERE YOU WILL FIND HELPFUL AND REPRESENTATIVE INFORMATION ABOUT ALL ASPECTS OF ACUPUNCTURE AND PARTICULARLY TRADITIONAL ACUPUNCTURE AS PRACTISED IN THE UNITED KINGDOM.

THE DR EDWARD BACH CENTRE
WWW.BACHCENTRE.COM
FROM THIS HOME PAGE YOU CAN VISIT EITHER THE DR EDWARD BACH CENTRE, THE DR EDWARD BACH FOUNDATION OR THE DR EDWARD BACH HEALING TRUST. AT THE CENTRE YOU CAN FIND OUT ALL ABOUT BACH FLOWER REMEDIES.

Books that deal with the issue of complementary medicine

0830822755, *Examining Alternative Medicine: An Inside Look at the Benefits & Risks*, Inter-varsity Press, P. Reisser, D. Mabe, R. Valarde

0825430712, *Basic Questions on Alternative Medicine,* Kregel Publications, P. Cunningham

Bio Basics – Alternative Medicine

Kregel, Coker R., *Alternative Medicine – Helpful or Harmful?* Great Britain: Monarch and CMF, 1995.

Fergusson A., *Alternative Medicine – A Review.*, Journal of the CMF 1988;26-29 (April)

Pfeiffer S., *Healing at any Price*, Word Books, 1988.

Smith G., *A Christian Perspective on Alternative Medicine*, Christians in Caring Professions, 1997.

GENETIC MODIFICATION

Awareness

The following information is included to raise the social awareness and understanding of ministers in relation to the contemporary issue of genetic modification.

The following is an article by Pastor Joe Hayes

Few people read what the contents label says when they do their weekly or monthly food shopping, simply because, for the majority of us, what is listed on those labels is a maze of "Es," "Numbers" and "Flavourings."

The mass production of foods for our modern Western world has deemed it necessary that chemical additives are combined with human and animal foodstuffs. Cases of BSE and CJD have put fear and uncertainty into people's minds about what they consume and on a lesser scale, parents wonder if their children's behaviour is affected by the "Es," "Numbers" and "Flavourings" in their sweets and drinks.

The media has become the "educator" of the masses of our generation and hardly a week seems to go by without the populace's "educator" telling us that biotechnology is either creating "Frankenstein foods" or making yet another "fantastic breakthrough."

It becomes more and more wondrous what bio-technicians claim they are able to do by modifying the DNA or deoxyribonucleic acid of an organism;

Fruit and vegetables can now, because of genetic modification be made resistant to weeds, insects, diseases and viruses that once would have destroyed vast crops. The nutritional value of foods can be vastly increased by genetically reducing fats and increasing vitamin contents.

Bio-technicians also believe they have discovered the genes that cause some forms of breast cancer, diabetes and kidney failure and with continued research will soon be able to offer cures. The genetic engineering of animals to provide human hearts, liver and kidneys is offering hope to many people who face imminent death without a transplant.

The recent cloning of "Dolly the Sheep" in Scotland revealed the amazing prospect that scientists could be able to clone a human being. The cloning of human embryos is illegal and continues to be a moral taboo, however, the potential of cloning human blood and nerve cells could find cures for Parkinson's disease, Alzheimer's disease and leukaemia.

While the governments of the world continue fighting off, on moral grounds, the pressure from scientists to be allowed to carry out experiments on human beings that could clone people or create "designer babies."

For many people suffering from Parkinson's, Alzheimer's or leukaemia, biotechnology would seem to be their saviour and only hope of a better future.

With the prospect of the world's population doubling in the next fifty years, the promises of genetically modified foods seem to be the solitary answer to avoiding a reoccurrence of major famines.

The church of today is undoubtedly facing difficult issues that it did not encounter only a few decades ago, issues that the Bible would seem to say very little about.

Is biotechnology our "friend or foe"?

Is biotechnology simply an advance on Jacob's selective breeding methods in Genesis or are scientists playing "God" by tampering with the ontological order of His creation?

Should we be inconsistent and take one law of Moses that says "You shall not breed together two kinds of your animal;" and disregard the rest that say "you shall not sow your field with two kinds of seed, nor wear a garment upon you of two kinds of material mixed together." Leviticus 19: 19

Perhaps we should thank God for the scientific talents He has given to mankind so that we can care more effectively for this earth that the Lord has entrusted to Adam and his descendants!

As Christian's we must be careful that because of a lack of understanding of modern scientific technology we don't "throw the baby out with the bath water!" Any God given talent can be used for good or for evil, we often thank God for the skills, knowledge and discoveries of medical surgeons when they save lives. Biotechnology can be used for evil but also for the good of the human race.

Christian opinions and arguments over the ethics and morals of biotechnology will no doubt vary greatly and the debating will go on for a long time. However, I believe we should be careful not to get bogged down in endless humanistic arguments. The Churches commission is to win souls not arguments.

The Utopia and the fears, the hype and hope created in society by media representations of biotechnology sets before the Christian Church an opportunity to speak about God as our Creator and the one who continues to sustain the whole of creation. King David said; "I praise you because I am fearfully and wonderfully made; your works are wonderful, I know that full well." Psalm 139: 14

Bio-technicians can only copy or reproduce God's perfect creation, they can of course play at being God but scientists will never be God.

Joe Hayes (Joy, 2000)

ASSESSMENT

The following are some of the most up-to-date statistics in relation to the issue of genetic modification. (Please see appendix A.)

The Soil Association report that 90% of foods are already genetically modified in some way. 61% of the British public are opposed to the growing of GM foods, 71% want produces to stop genetic modification of food stuff and 58% believe that supermarkets should stop stocking GM foods.

ADDRESSING

The following is a list of practical suggestions that may enable churches and organizations to minister effectively to those concerned about genetic modification.

As with cloning this is an ethical issue that is of great concern to many people and church leaders/workers should seek to be understanding and aware of the issue.

AFFIRMATION

The following is a list of churches, organizations or individuals who are ministering to those concerned about genetic modification. They will, we believe, be able to offer practical and professional advice to assist you in your efforts to minister. (Please see appendix B.)

WORLD WIDE WEB SITES THAT WILL BE HELP IN UNDERSTANDING GENETIC MODIFICATION.

BIOINDUSTRY ASSOCIATION
WWW.BIOINDUSTRY.ORG

FRIENDS OF THE EARTH
WWW.FOE.CO.UK

GREENPEACE
WWW.GREENPEACE.ORG.UK

THE SOIL ASSOCIATION
WWW.SOILASSOCIATION.ORG

SOCIETY, RELIGION AND TECHNOLOGY PROJECT
WWW.SRTP.ORG.UK

FOOD AND DRINK FEDERATION
WWW.FOODFUTURE.ORG.UK

MONSANTO PLC
WWW.MONSANTO.CO.UK

THE CAMPAIGN FOR FOOD SAFETY
WWW.PUREFOOD.ORG

SOCIETY, RELIGION AND TECHNOLOGY PROJECT
WWW.SRTP.ORG.UK
THIS SITE AIMS TO BRING PROFESSIONAL EXPERTISE BY PROVIDING INFORMED AND PENETRATING COMMENT FOR TECHNOLOGISTS, EDUCATORS, MEDIA, THE CHURCH, THE PUBLIC – IN FACT ANYONE WITH AN INTEREST IN HOW TECHNOLOGY IS AFFECTING OUR LIVES, AND THE ISSUES IT RAISES. FOR THEIR VIEWS ON CLONING, SCROLL DOWN THE HOME PAGE TO THE CLICK ON A HEADING SECTION. CLICK ON SUBJECT HEADING. THIS TAKES YOU TO THEIR MAIN INDEX. UNDER THE HEADING OF BIOTECHNOLOGY IS A LINK CALLED CLONING. CLICK ON THIS FOR A WIDE RANGE OF ARTICLES ABOUT HUMAN AND ANIMAL CLONING ISSUES. WELL WORTH A VISIT.

HUMAN CLONING FOUNDATION
WWW.HUMANCLONING.ORG
THE HUMAN CLONING FOUNDATION PROMOTES EDUCATION ABOUT HUMAN CLONING AND OTHER FORMS OF BIOTECHNOLOGY WITH AN EMPHASIS ON THE POSITIVE ASPECTS OF NEW TECHNOLOGIES. A HUGE SITE WITH ARTICLES ON A WIDE RANGE OF CLONING ISSUES INCLUDING THE BENEFITS OF HUMAN CLONING AND THE REASONS WHY WE SHOULD CLONE HUMAN BEINGS.

ROSLIN INSTITUTE
WWW.2.RI.BBSRC.AC.UK
CLICK ON SPECIAL TOPIC: CLONING. THEN CLICK ON BACKGROUND NOTES ON NUCLEAR TRANSFER AND CLONING. THIS SITE INCLUDES ALL THE BACKGROUND MATERIAL PRODUCED BY THE INSTITUTE ON CLONING AND NUCLEAR TRANSFER.

UNFORTUNATELY MANY SITES CONTAIN INACCURATE, MISLEADING OR HEAVILY BIASED information. Our researchers have therefore undertaken an extensive analysis to bring you a selection of quality web site addresses.

THE GENETICS FORUM
WWW.GENETICSFORUM.ORG.UK
The Genetics Forum™ is the only independent organization in the UK concerned with the use of new genetic technologies and their public policy implications. It was founded in 1989 by a group of scientists, lawyers and advocates from the animal welfare, environmental and consumer movements concerned about the long-term impact of rapid developments in the genetic sciences. Since its inception, the Genetics Forum has been instrumental in raising the issues of genetic engineering to a prominent position on the public policy – Blueridge Institute News and Views on Genetic Modification

Corporate Watch produce some excellent briefing papers on genetic engineering and the people behind it.

Dig it Up! Launched on the 24th May 2000, the Dig it Up! campaign website provides campaign news and ideas for action.

5 Year Freeze Moratorium on the growing and importing of GMO food

FOOD COMMISSION
The Food Commission is the UK's leading independent watchdog on food issues. It has been campaigning for safer, healthier food for over ten years.

Friends of the Earth link to their Food and Biotechnology home page.

Genetic Engineering Network GE in the UK. An effective conduit of information through which a network of individuals, groups and other genewatch subscribe to genewatch for briefing papers on genetic engineering developments.

GREENPEACE TRUE FOOD CAMPAIGN
Opposing GM foods and promoting organic food

IFOAM
Represents the worldwide movement of organic agriculture and provides a platform for global exchange and cooperation.

ORGANIC CONSUMERS ASSOCIATION (USA)
The OCA is a grassroots non-profit public interest organization which deals with crucial issues of food safety, industrial agriculture, genetic engineering, corporate accountability, and environmental sustainability.

POSITIVE NEWS
SUSTAIN
The alliance for better food and farming.
The GMO campaign, Oxford
The risks and hazards of GM foods and animal feed explored.

THE INTERNATIONAL SOCIETY FOR ECOLOGY AND CULTURE (ISEC)
ISEC is a non-profit organization concerned with the protection of both biological and cultural diversity. Our emphasis is on education for action: moving beyond single issues to look at the more fundamental influences that shape our lives.

INDUSTRY ORGANIZATIONS

CROPGEN
New, industry funded, initiative giving "independent" information to the media and public.

FOOD & DRINK FEDERATION
The Future of Food: Proponents of the benefits of GM express their views.

MONSANTO

TRANSNATIONAL COMPANY. HEAVILY INVOLVED IN DEVELOPING AND MARKETING GM CROPS.

NOVARTIS
TRANSNATIONAL COMPANY INVOLVED IN BIOTECHNOLOGICAL PRODUCTS.

GOVERNMENT ORGANIZATIONS

EUROPEAN HEALTH AND CONSUMER PROTECTION DIRECTORATE

FIND OUT WHAT IS HAPPENING ABOUT GMOS IN EUROPEAN LEGISLATION

MAFF
NATURE PUBLISHING GROUP
NATURE REVIEWS, AN EXCITING NEW SERIES OF REVIEW JOURNALS FROM THE NATURE PUBLISHING GROUP (NPG) DUE TO BE LAUNCHED IN OCTOBER 2000.

Books that deal with the issue of concerned about genetic modification

0520224418, *From Genesis to Genetics, University of California*, John A Moore

0829812512, *Genetics: Issues of Social Justice, Pilgrim Press*, Ted Peters

0664500250, *In Whose Image: Science, Faith, & the New Genetics*, Westminster/John Knox, John P. Burgess

0814651046, *The Problem of Evil in the Western Tradition: From the Book of Job to Modern Genetics*, Liturgical Press, Joseph F. Kelly

REFUGEES AND ASYLUM SEEKERS

Awareness

Under international law, the word 'refugee' has a very precise meaning, as set out in the 1951 *United Nations Convention Relating to Refugees* www.refugee council.org.uk/downloads/1951supportersbriefing.doc. In the 1951 *United Nations Convention Relating to Refugees*, a refugee is defined as someone who:

- has a well-founded fear of persecution for reasons of race, religion, nationality, membership of a particular social group, or political opinion;
- is outside the country they belong to or normally reside in
- unable or unwilling to return home for fear of persecution

The plight of refugees and asylum seekers is something that many churches are now having to face in the twenty-first century. Many of these people are also beginning to enquire about Christianity, for some this will be their first opportunity to hear the Gospel This of course is encouraging as churches find that people from the ends of the earth are coming to seek help and social care in the form of refugees and asylum seekers.

The Church of course needs to become informed and equipped to respond to these people who come from another culture and are often in ignorance of God's loving care through Jesus Christ.

Many have fled for their lives from cruel regimes where religious fanaticism presents a god who is neither loving nor caring.

Others come in poverty hoping to find a better life.

Many come damaged both physically and emotionally. A recent report in the *Nursing Standard* pointed out that 40% of refugees have been tortured and between 20,000 and 50,000 women from the former Yugoslavia have been raped.[1]

Often compassion for these desperate people is poured out in media appeals, however, that same compassion is hard to find when these same people arrive on our shores.

Whatever their reasons for coming the Church is compelled to respond as Jesus did when He said, "Come to me all you who are weary and I will give you rest."

Assessment

The European Monitoring Centre on Racism and Xenophobia in Vienna published a report on Racism and Cultural Diversity in the Mass Media www.eumc.at/publications/media-report/index.htm. www.eumc.at/publications

/media-report/index.htm. The report found the British to have some of the most hostile attitudes towards asylum seekers compared to their European counterparts and criticised the British media for their xenophobic and intolerant coverage of asylum issues. Whilst the media might lead us to believe that this is now a massive problem, in fact in the year 2000, the UK received 76,000 applications for asylum which is 0.04% of the total world refugee population. So we have a "drop" not a flood coming to British shores. On the 1st January 2000 an estimated 7 million people from 24 countries were in the process of fleeing from wars, oppression and other persecution in fear of their lives, seeking the protection of the international community.

As church leaders it's important to protect vulnerable people from the evil of racism.

Racial harassment is a serious criminal offence. It can take many forms such as:

- **Verbal: offensive remarks; comments; jokes or threats; name calling or swearing;**
- **Molestation: abusive or obscene telephone calls or letters; dumping of rubbish outside your home or through your letterbox; creating persistent noise; malicious complaints about you especially to those in authority;**
- **Physical violence: actual grievous bodily harm or threat of such;**
- **damaging your home or property by, for example, smashing windows or doors;**
- **Racist graffiti: written or drawn slogans.**

Racial harassment is illegal. People who do these sorts of things can be prosecuted in the courts. Everyone has the right to live without the fear of attack against themselves or their home and property. Authorities like the police, the local authority and children's schools have a duty to protect people from racial harassment and to take action against the attackers. People who attack others because of their race can be evicted from their homes, fined or put in prison.

The Home Office figures show that 88,000 asylum seekers and their dependents arrived in the UK in the 10 months until February 2001, and the government has set a new target of 24,000 failed asylum seekers to be deported, as well as 6,000 dependents, in the year to the end of March 2002. However, as time goes on it will be easy for governments to become hardened to this problem and in the national interest become less hospitable to the refugees and asylum seekers who approach our shores.

What the Papers Say

> These immigrants are not escaping from persecution. No-one from France is persecuting them, so they could apply for asylum there.
>
> THE YORKSHIRE POST, 10/09/01.

> Bogus refugees treated better than UK citizens
>
> THE SUN, 18/02/02

> Broken promises on asylum cheats...only 2,450 were deported in the final 3 months of last year
>
> DAILY STAR, 01/03/02

> Refugees are flooding into UK 'like ants'
>
> DAILY EXPRESS, 7/11/01

> Britain is top asylum haven
>
> DAILY MAIL, 2/2/02

> Asylum cheats are a threat to our future
>
> FROM THE MAIL ON SUNDAY, 4/3/01

> Our town's too nice for refugees...they will try to escape, rapists and thieves will terrorise us
>
> DAILY EXPRESS, 23/3/02

> ...illegals flooding into UK...
>
> DAILY STAR, 31/10/01

> ...we resent the scroungers, beggars and crooks who are prepared to cross every country in Europe to reach our generous benefits system.
>
> THE SUN, 7/3/01

Of course none of us believes all of what we read in the newspapers.

Many of these people have particular needs whilst here in our country which we should seek to understand and then show the compassion of Christ through practical support.

ASSISTANCE

In addressing this challenging opportunity it is very important that we have an understanding for their plight.

Many feel lost, alone, isolated and fearful in a strange country that speaks a foreign language and has a different culture.

- Social Services departments arrange accommodation for asylum seekers whilst they await Home Office decisions as to whether they can stay. Only when they are accepted as genuine refugees and granted permission to stay are they legally able to claim benefits, get work and find their own housing.
- Accepted refugees have two weeks to find themselves somewhere to live once they have received their Home Office "leave to remain."
- However, it can take four to five weeks to get a National Insurance number

- without which they cannot claim any benefits to help with housing, or income support to buy food.

- Therefore, the Church needs to be aware of the genuine asylum seeker plight and be proactive in helping them when they come to our towns and cities. What did Jesus say about offering a cup of cold water in His name to a stranger? Maybe today's equivalent is food and shelter.

- Despite the fact some asylum seekers arrive here by illegal means for fear of their lives, and others simply because they can enjoy a more prosperous lifestyle, we still need to show them the love of Christ rather than find ourselves categorized with the racial bigots that say they should all be sent home!

- In supporting their rights we will show a love that is compelling and Christ-like. Isn't the Gospel about acceptance rather than rejection?

- Some of these people are coming from countries such as Iran, Iraq, Afghanistan, Somalia, and former Yugoslavia, and don't they have the right to hear the good news of Jesus Christ and experience his love and compassion from Christian church communities?

- God is bringing a harvest to our doorstep and we need to see it and sow into it so that we can reap what God wants to give.

- Sadly these vulnerable people are open to exploitation when they find themselves helpless in a social system and culture they are not familiar with.

- In Leviticus 19: 33 we read…
  "Do not exploit the foreigners who live in your land, they should be treated like everyone else and you must love them as you love yourself."

- The Church needs to affirm these people as those who are just as in need of the love of the gospel as any British citizen.

- We must not allow the barrier of language or culture to become an excuse for neither accepting nor affirming them. Many of these people are gentle and kind when you get to know them, and are so grateful for the love and care that they are offered.

- Often in the countries that they have come from, showing hospitality by being invited into someone's home is the highest honor that can be offered to someone. Therefore one of the greatest ways we can honor and affirm them is by inviting them into our homes for a meal and show genuine care and concern.

- We need to be open hearted and inclusive of those who come to our land by practically showing them the love of Christ, helping them allay their fears and giving them the welcome that comes with the Gospel.

AFFIRMATION

The following organizations are able to advise on matters relating to asylum seekers and refugees;

The following Web site will provide all the information you need, it also provides the information for refugees in several different languages; www.refugee council.org.uk
www.refugeecouncil.org.uk
REFUGEE COUNCIL
3 BONDWAY
LONDON
SW8 1SJ
TEL: 020 758 6922

ASYLUM AID
28 COMMERCIAL STREET
LONDON
E1 6LS
TEL: 020 7377 5123
ASYLUM AID IS AN INDEPENDENT ORGANIZATION PROVIDING FREE ADVICE AND SUPPORT FOR REFUGEES AND ASYLUM SEEKERS IN THE UK. THEY HELP PEOPLE TO PRESENT THEIR ASYLUM APPLICATIONS.

BAIL FOR IMMIGRATION DETAINEES (BID)
28 COMMERCIAL STREET
LONDON
E1 6LS
TEL: 020 7247 3590

BRITISH RED CROSS SOCIETY (BRCS)
FAMILY REUNION SECTION
9 GROSVENOR CRESCENT
LONDON
SW1 X 7EJ
TEL: 020 7235 5454
BRCS PROVIDES AN INTERNATIONAL TRACING SERVICE FOR FAMILIES SEPARATED BY CONFLICT AND A MESSAGE SERVICE WHERE COMMUNICATIONS HAVE BROKEN DOWN DUE TO WAR OR DISASTER. IT CO-ORDINATES TRAVEL ASSISTANCE APPLICATIONS ON BEHALF OF UNHCR FOR FAMILY REUNION AND RESETTLEMENT OF RECOGNIZED REFUGEES FROM A FIRST COUNTRY TO THE UK.

COMMUNITY LEGAL SERVICES (CLS)
CLS IS A NEW SERVICES (REPLACING OLD LEGAL AID BOARD) THAT WORKS TO BUILD NETWORKS OF LEGAL REPRESENTATIVES AND ADVICE ORGANIZATIONS. PUBLISHES THE CLS DIRECTORY — A LIST OF LEGAL ADVISERS IN YOUR AREA. PHONE THE HELPLINE OR SEE THE WEBSITE FOR THE WEBSITE FOR THE NEAREST LEGAL REPRESENTATIVE IN YOUR AREA.

ENGLAND AND WALES:
HELPLINE: 0845 608 1122 (OPEN 7.00 A.M. – 11.00P.M., MONDAY–FRIDAY)
(WWW.JUSTASK.ORG.UK)
SCOTTISH LEGAL AID BOARD
TEL: 0131 2267061

LAW SOCIETY OF NORTHERN IRELAND
TEL: 028 9024 6441

DETENTION ADVICE SERVICE (DAS)
308 SEVEN SISTERS ROAD
LONDON
N4 2AG
TEL: 020 8802 3422
DAS OFFERS ADVICE, IN FORMATION AND SUPPORT TO ANYONE DETAINED OR THREATENED WITH DETENTION UNDER IMMIGRATION ACT POWERS.

HOME OFFICE
IMMIGRATION & NATIONALITY DIRECTORATE (IND)
ASYLUM GROUP
LUNAR HOUSE
40 WELLESLEY ROAD
CROYDON
CR9 2BY
TEL: 0870 606 7766
THE IND IS THE GOVERNMENT DEPARTMENT WHICH PROCESSES ASYLUM CLAIMS.

IMMIGRATION ADVISORY SERVICE (IAS)
COUNTY HOUSE
190 GREAT DOVER STREET
LONDON
SE1 3XF
TEL: 020 7357 6917
24-HOUR HELPLINE. 020 7318 9191
PROVIDES LEGAL ADVICE. OFFICES ALSO IN:
BIRMINGHAM: TEL: 0121 742 1 221
CARDIFF: TEL: 029 2049 6662
GLASGOW TEL: 0141 248 2956
HOUNSLOW: TEL: 020 8814 1115
LEEDS: TEL: 0113 244 2460
LIVERPOOL: TEL: 0151 475 1628
MANCHESTER: TEL: 0161 8349942
NORWICH: TEL: 01603 496 623

AKINGTON: TEL: 01954 783 300

JOINT COUNCIL FOR THE WELFARE OF
IMMIGRANTS (JCWI)
115 OLD STREET
LONDON
EC1V 9JR
TEL: 020 7251 8708
ADVICE LINE: TEL 020 7251 8706
JCWI ADVISES ON IMMIGRATION AND
NATIONALITY LAW.

REFUGEE LEGAL CENTRE (RLC)
NELSON HOUE
153–157 COMMERCIAL ROAD
LONDON
E1 2EB
ADVICE LINE: TEL: 020 7780 3220

RAGU
(REFUGEE ASSESSMENT AND GUIDANCE UNIT)
UNIVERSITY OF NORTH LONDON
236–250 HOLLOWAY ROAD
LONDON
N7 6PP
TEL: 020 7753 5044
ADVICE ON EDUCATION, TRAINING AND
EMPLOYMENT OPPORTUNITIES.

REFUGEE COUNCIL TRAINING AND EMPLOYMENT
SECTION (TES)
240–250 FERNDALE ROAD
LONDON
SW9 8BB
TEL: 020 7346 6700
TES GIVES ADVICE TO ASYLUM SEEKERS AND
REFUGEES ON THE EDUCATIONAL, TRAINING AND
EMPLOYMENT OPTIONS AVAILABLE TO THEM.

CAMBRIDGESHIRE REFUGEE SUPPORT GROUP
LLANDAFF CHAMBERS
2 REGENT STREET
CAMBRIDGE
CB2 1AX
TEL: 01223 575 489
OFFERS COUNSELLING AND ENABLES ACCESS TO
NHS.

MEDICAL FOUNDATION FOR THE CARE OF VICTIMS
OF TORTURE
96–98 GRAFTON ROAD
LONDON NW5 3EJ
TEL: 020 7813 7777
THE MEDICAL FOUNDATION PROVIDES
SURVIVORS OF TORTURE WITH MEDICAL
TREATMENT. YOU MUST BE REFERRED BY
ANOTHER AGENCY SUCH AS YOUR GP OR AN
ADVICE AGENCY.

MIDLANDS REFUGEE COUNCIL
FIFTH FLOOR
SMITHFIELD HOUSE
DIGBETH
BIRMINGHAM
B5 6BS
TEL: 0121 2422200
HELP PROVIDED WITH ACCESSING THE NHS.

REFUGEE SUPPORT CENTRE (RSC)
47 SOUTH LAMBETH ROAD
LONDON
SW8 1RH
TEL: 020 7820 3606
RSC OFFERS A COUNSELLING SERVICE TO
REFUGEES AND ASYLUM SEEKERS WHO ARE
EXPERIENCING EMOTIONAL DIFFICULTY OR
PSYCHOLOGICAL SUFFERING. YOU WILL NEED TO
BE REFERRED BY A GP OR AN ADVICE AGENCY.

REFUGEE THERAPY CENTRE
MANOR GARDENS CENTRE
6–9 MANOR GARDENS
LONDON
N7 6LA
TEL: 020 7272 4231
THE REFUGEE THERAPY CENTRE PROVIDES
COUNSELLING AND PSYCHOTHERAPY.

ONE STOP SERVICES (ONS)
REFUGEE AGENCIES RUN THESE IN DIFFERENT UK
REGIONS. ONE STOP SERVICES PROVIDE GENERAL
ADVICE. SOME HAVE SPECIALIST WORKERS
PROVIDING ADVICE ON HEALTH, MENTAL HEALTH,
EDUCATION AND TRAINING.
(ONS) MIGRANT HELPLINE (KENT, SUSSEX)
ROOM 65
NO 1 CONTROL BUILDING
EASTERN DOCKS
DOVER
CT1 6 1DP
TEL: 01304 203 977

17 HIGH STREET
DOVER
KENT
CT1 6 1 DP
TEL: 01304 226 830

48 HAVELOCK ROAD
HASTINGS
TN34 1 BE
TEL: (1)01424 717 011

1 CECIL STREET MARGATE
KENT
CT9 1 NX
TEL: (1)01843 292 921

7A CHURCH STREET
BRIGHTON
BN1 1US
TEL: 01273 671 711

(ONS) NORTH OF ENGLAND REFUGEE SERVICE (NORTHUMBERLAND, TYNE & WEAR, DURHAM, CLEVELAND)

19 THE BIGG MARKET
NEWCASTLE
ME1 1UN
TEL: (1) 0191 2220406

THIRD FLOOR
FORUM HOUSE
THE FORUM
WALLSEND
TYNE & WEAR
ME28 8LX
TEL: (1)01912001109

27 BOROUGH ROAD
MIDDLESBROUGH
TS1 4AD
TEL: 01642 217 447

GROUND FLOOR
MARITIME BUILDING
ST THOMAS STREET
SUNDERLAND
TYNE & WEAR
SR1 1 BL
TEL: 0191 5108685

(ONS) NORTHERN IRELAND COUNCIL FOR ETHNIC MINORITIES (NORTHERN IRELAND)

THIRD FLOOR
ASCOTT HOUSE
24/3 1 SHAFTESBURY SQUARE
BELFAST
BT2 7DB
TEL: (1) 028 9023 8645

(ONS) REFUGEE ACTION (EAST MIDLANDS, NORTH WEST, SOUTH CENTRAL, SOUTH WEST)

50 OXFORD STREET
SOUTHAMPTON
SQL 4 3PP
TEL: 023 8024 8130

(ONS) REFUGEE ARRIVALS PROJECT (HEATHROW, GATWICK, CITY, STANSTED AND LUTON AIRPORTS)

41B CROSS LANCES ROAD
HOUNSLOW
MIDDLESEX
TW3 0ES
TEL: 020 8607 6888

1 THE KINGSWAY
YMCA
SWANSEA
SAL 5JQ
TEL: 01792 301 729

(ONS) REFUGEE COUNCIL (LONDON, WEST MIDLANDS, EASTERN REGION, YORKSHIRE AND HUMBERSIDE)

240–250 FERNDALE ROAD
BRIXTON
LONDON
SW9 8BB
TEL: 020 7346 6770

FIRST FLOOR
SMITHFIELD HOUSE
DIGBETH
BIRMINGHAM
B5 6BS
TEL: 0121 622 1515

FIRST FLOOR
4–8 MUSEUM STREET
IPSWICH
LPL 1 HT
TEL: 01473 221 560

FIRST FLOOR
WADE HOUSE
THE MERRION CENTRE
LEEDS
LS2 8NG
TEL: 0113 244 9404

(ONS) SCOTTISH REFUGEE COUNCIL (SCOTLAND)

82 GORDON STREET
GLASGOW
G2 6QA
TEL: 0141 248 9799/0800 085 6087

(ONS) WELSH REFUGEE COUNCIL (WALES)

UNIT 8
WILLIAMS COURT TRADE STREET
CARDIFF
CF10 5DQ
TEL: 029 2066 6250

REFUGEE SUPPORT CENTRE
47 SOUTH LAMBETH ROAD
LONDON
SW8 1RH
TEL: 020 7820 3606

1 *Nursing Standard* march13/vol16/no26/2002, page 9.

Thanks to the Refugee Council for their help and information.

SUICIDE

AWARENESS

The following information is included to raise the social awareness and understanding of ministers in relation to the contemporary issue of suicide.

Will Jesus welcome home a believer who died at her own hands? I believe he will, tenderly and lovingly.

The hope-giving promise of Romans 8: 32, that neither life nor death can separate the believer from the love of God in Jesus Christ.

How can I trust in this promise and then deny its comfort to people who doubly grieve for brothers, sisters, fathers, and mothers who in horrible moments of despair decided to end their lives? I believe that Jesus died not only for the sins of us all but for all of our sins, including the forgotten ones, including suicide – if indeed he reckons it always as sin.

The Bible does not seem to condemn suicide. There are, I think, six accounts of suicide in the Bible, the most notorious being those of King Saul (1 Sam. 31: 2–5) and Judas (Matt. 27: 3–5). Others are Abimelech (Judg. 9: 50–54), Samson (Judg. 16: 23–31), Ahithophel (2 Sam. 17: 23), and Zimri (1 Kings 16: 15–20). As far as I can tell, none of the six is explicitly condemned for taking his life.

It has often been debated that suicide cannot be forgiven because the person who did it could not have repented of doing it. But all of us commit sins that we are too spiritually cloddish to recognize for the sins they are. And we all die with sins not named and repented of.

As Christians, we should worry less about whether Christians who have killed themselves go to heaven, and worry more about how we can help people like them find hope and joy in living. Our most urgent problem is not the morality of suicide but the spiritual and mental despair that drags people down to it.

The following is an article by Pastor Joe Hayes

While greeting people one Sunday morning a person came to me and quietly said; "I tried to commit suicide yesterday, please pray for me." Of course I took this cry for help seriously. Unlike a preacher who told the true story of a member in his congregation who rang him in the night to tell him he was going to commit suicide, the preacher replied, "Ring me back in the morning if you are still here." The reason behind his indifferent and flippant advice was; 'those who tell you they are going to do it, never actually do it.'

Research reveals that two out of every three people who successfully take their own life have spoken to someone about their suicidal feelings at least two weeks prior to killing themselves.

It is estimated that over 150,000 people every year in the UK and Ireland attempt suicide. Over one million people world wide committed suicide in the year 2000. A Government white paper on public health estimates that one person in the UK dies every two hours as a result of suicide. MIND point out that we can never be sure of the true figure as coroners are reluctant to state suicide as the cause of death for the sake of family left behind.

Despite *She* magazine reporting that half of the women they surveyed stated "they had considered suicide" the majority of those who commit suicide are men particularly young men between the ages of 14 and 19 years old.

When it comes to suicide men definitely behave badly. It is most likely that the one in three who committed suicide and did not talk to anyone was a man. Male reluctance to express their feelings is a result of Western society's stereotyping men as "Strong, serious and silent." This is where I believe the Church can break down damaging social stereotypes by continuing to cultivate the atmosphere of sharing and supporting one another particularly among men. "Promise Keepers International" a ministry aimed at men only asks its members to make seven commitments, the second reads: A Promise Keeper is committed to pursuing vital relationships with a few other men, understanding that he needs brothers to help him keep his promises."

A young man or woman contemplating suicide is more likely to talk to the youth leader or pastor than their parent or teacher. A "quick fix prayer"" is not necessarily the best solution, what they are crying out for is someone who will take the time to listen to them.

"Befrienders" state on their World Wide Web page, "those who attempt suicide want someone whom they can trust, someone who will care and someone whom they can talk to."

Should someone approach you as a leader or simply as their friend revealing their suicidal feelings, I would encourage you not to panic and send them off to see their GP or a psychiatrist nor should you try to be their psychiatrists! Listen to them, pray with them but most of all be there for them. If you know you are out of your depth seek the help of medical professionals.

When listening and talking don't fear putting the idea of suicide in a person's head by talking to them about the consequences of suicide, they need to hear that you, Jesus and the Church care if they live or die.

The mother of a young man who took his own life said the following;

> The things I regret so bitterly are not saying things more directly. Like "Don't commit suicide." I never said; "Don't kill yourself." I felt it, but I should have said; "Look if you kill yourself it will be terrible for us." I never said any thing that might give him the idea that I cared enough.[1]

The simple reason why so many people attempt suicide is because it is a quick and permanent solution to their temporary troubles. "Without hope and without God"[2] one person every two hours ends their life on this earth.

As well as being there for the desperate of our society we can communicate the Gospel of Hope and pray that the "God of hope fill them with all joy and peace as they trust in him, so that they may overflow with hope by the power of the Holy Spirit"³

1. Teenage Suicide & Self Harm, Trust for the study of Adolescence.
2. Eph 2: 12
3. Romans 15: 13

Assessment

The following are some of the most up-to-date statistics in relation to the issue of suicide. (Please see appendix A.)

Suicide Statistics

Background
The World Health Organization estimates that in the year 2000 approximately one million people will die from suicide. A global mortality rate of 16 per 100,000. One death every 40 seconds.

The WHO further reports that:

❖ **In the last 45 years suicide rates have increased by 60% worldwide. Suicide is now among the three leading causes of death among those aged 15–44 (both sexes). Suicide attempts are up to 20 times more frequent than completed suicides.**

❖ **Although suicide rates have traditionally been highest among elderly males, rates among young people have been increasing to such an extent that they are now the group at highest risk in a third of all countries.**

❖ **Mental disorders (particularly depression and substance abuse) are associated with more than 90% of all cases of suicide. However, suicide results from many complex sociocultural factors and is more likely to occur during periods of socioeconomic, family and individual crisis (e.g. loss of a loved one, employment, honour).**

In the US, the Centers for Disease Control reports that:

❖ **More people die from suicide than from homicide. In 1997, there were 1.5 times as many suicides as homicides.**

❖ **Overall, suicide is the eighth leading cause of death for all Americans, and is the third leading cause of death for young people aged 15–24.**

❖ **Males are four times more likely to die from suicide than are females. However, females are more likely to attempt suicide than are males.**

Statistics about suicide
Statistics about suicide are difficult to collate, and may be inaccurate because of the sensitivity of the issue, particularly in countries where suicide is an absolute taboo. You can find suicide statistics in the following English language sites:

* **International Statistics:** World Health Organization – for international suicide statistics, including the most recent global stats by country.
- **USA Statistics:** American Association of Suicidology – for USA suicide statistics.
- **New Zealand Statistics:** New Zealand Health Information Service – for NZ Statistics. There is also specific information about NZ youth suicide statistics.
- **Canada Statistics:** Canada Statistics Agency – for Canadian suicide statistics.
- **UK Statistics:** UK Samaritans provide statistics for the United Kingdom and the Republic of Ireland.

UK & Republic of Ireland (combined)

- 6,216* suicides in the UK, 439* suicides in the Republic of Ireland in 1999.
- One suicide every 79 minutes in UK and Republic of Ireland.
- 36% increase in suicide in the Republic of Ireland.
- 76% of suicides are by males.
- 813* suicides by young people in UK and Republic of Ireland – more than 2 per day.
- Rising trend in self-harm – in 1998 an estimated 160,000 people in England and Wales self-harmed**
- 24,000 of those that self-harmed in 1998 were aged 15–19 years
- Every hour 3 young people self-harm
- Suicide was decriminalised in the UK in 1961 and in the Republic of Ireland in 1993

England 1999

- 4858 suicides in 1999 – 3637 males and 1221 females
- The English suicide rate was 12 per 100,000 population in 1999
- For males, the suicide rate was 18, for females it was 6 per 100,000
- There has been an 8% decrease in the suicide rate since 1990 in England

Northern Ireland 1999

- 154 suicides in 1999 – 127 males and 27 females
- Northern Ireland's suicide rate was 12 per 100,000 population in 1999
- For males, the suicide rate was 20, for females it was 4 per 100,00 population
- There has been a 9% increase in the suicide rate since 1989 in Northern Ireland

Republic of Ireland 2000

- The 413 suicides in 2000 – 341 males and 72 females
- The Republic of Ireland's suicide rate was 14 per 100,000 population in 2000
- For males, the suicide rate was 23, for females it was 5 per 100,000 population
- The highest male suicide rate was 30 per 100,000. This was in the 25–34 year old age group
- The highest female suicide rate was 6 per 100,000. This was within the 35–45 year old and 55–64-year-old age group
- There has been a 8% increase in the suicide rate since 1990 in the Republic of Ireland
- Within 15–24-year-old males, there has been a 73% increase in the suicide rate since 1990

Note Bene: Suicide statistics are based on ICD codes E950–9 from the Central Statistics Office, Cork.

Scotland 2000

- 880 suicides in 2000 – 676 males and 204 females
- The Scottish suicide rate was 21 per 100,000 population in 2000
- For males, the suicide rate was 36, for females it was 9 per 100,000 population
- The highest male suicide rate was 42 per 100,000. This was in the 25–34 year old age group
- The highest female suicide rate was 12 per 100,000. This was in the 35–45 year old and 45–54-year-old age group
- There has been a 17% increase in the suicide rate since 1990 in Scotland
- Within 15–24-year-old males there has been a 57% increase in the suicide rate since 1990

Wales 1999

- 330 suicides in 1999 – 267 males and 63 females
- The Welsh suicide rate was 14 per 100,000 population in 1999
- For males, the suicide rate was 23, for females it was 5 per 100,000 population
- The suicide rate has remained constant in Wales since 1990

Addressing

The following is a list of practical suggestions that may enable churches and organizations to minister effectively to those considering suicide or supporting friends or family bereaved as a result of suicide.

Suicide and the Silence of Scripture

Though the church has come to opposing conclusions about the fate of victims, we have a mandate to minister to those left behind.

Suicide is confusing for Christians. Although the general thrust of scripture is clearly opposed to the taking of one's own life, it provides no clear disapproval of the few cases of apparent suicide it recounts. Suicide also confuses us because some of those we believe to be strong in the faith have considered it as a "way out."

Samson and St Augustine

Must we believe that those who have taken their own lives suffer the eternal punishment of God? Nothing in scripture drives us to that conclusion.

Of the seven or so suicides reported in Scripture, most familiar are Saul, Samson, and Judas. Saul apparently committed suicide to avoid dishonour and suffering at the hands of the Philistines. He is rewarded by the Israelites with a war hero's burial, there being no apparent disapproval of his suicide (1 Sam. 31: 1–6). And while there is no hero's burial for Judas Iscariot (Matt. 27: 5–7), Scripture is once more silent on the morality of this suicide of remorse.

The suicide of Samson has posed a greater problem for Christian theologians. Both Saint Augustine and Saint Thomas Aquinas wrestled with the case and concluded that Samson's suicide was justified as an act of obedience to a direct command of God.

Objections to suicide have a long history in the church. But the idea that suicide is an unforgivable sin is less easily traced. Among the church fathers, Saint Augustine was the most prominent and influential opponent of suicide. And early church synods declared that bequests from those who committed suicide (as well as the offering of those who attempted suicide) ought not to be accepted; and throughout the medieval period, proper Christian burial was refused those who committed suicide.

Saint Thomas Aquinas believed that suicide, by excluding a final repentance, was a mortal sin. Dante is likely to have influenced Christian thought at least as much as Saint Thomas, placing those who committed suicide in the seventh circle of the inferno. Luther and Calvin, despite their abhorrence of suicide do not suggest that it is an unpardonable sin. John Calvin is perhaps the most helpful on the issue, concluding that blaspheming against the Holy Spirit is the only unpardonable sin (Matt.12: 31), and suicide need not be viewed as blasphemy. The pedigree of the view that suicide is unforgivable seems to lie in the medieval church and its distinction between mortal and venial sins.

Freely Chosen

We must understand suicide as free and uncoerced actions engaged in for the purpose of bringing about one's own death. Once we define it this way, it is easy to grasp the church's clear teaching throughout the centuries that suicide is morally wrong and ought never to be considered by the Christian. Life is a gift from God. To take one's own life is to show insufficient gratitude. Our lives belong to God; we are but stewards. To end my own life is to usurp that the prerogative that is God's alone. Suicide, the church has taught, is ordinarily a rejection of the goodness of God, and it can never be right to reject God's goodness.

If we define suicide as consisting of only free and uncoerced actions, we must ask a series of questions as we try to understand any particular suicide: to what extent do we know the suicide in question was genuinely free? Could pain (either physical or emotional) have coerced the individual to do what he otherwise might not have done? But even if we could know that an act of suicide was genuinely free, can we know that the aim of the act was indeed one's own death rather than a misguided cry for help? Can we know that the suicide believed this action would really kill?

These questions lead us to withhold judgment in many cases; but more telling yet is this question: Did the individual aim at removing himself from God's goodness by suicide? Was this an act of suicide directly aimed at saying no to God? Or was it rather a tragically misguided attempt at saying yes to God? Eternal punishment is reserved, Christians believe, for those who directly reject God and reject God as a consistent pattern in life, not merely in a solitary final act. Every suicide is not a rejection of God's goodness. Indeed, in many cases suicide is mistakenly chosen to bring one nearer to God. We cannot say that such a motive for suicide is correct. Nor can we say that a person who makes this tragic mistake has removed herself forever from the grace of God.

The Church's Task

When I comes to dealing with suicide, the church must do more than teach about it, for the church's primary task is to be the people of God.

First of all, the church must commit itself to being a community of truth, a community in which believers tell the truth about their own lives. A church must hear the stories of pain, suffering, and failure in the lives of its members; and those who tell the stories must receive from the church both lamentation and the healing balm of Christ. When the church is open and honest about pain and suffering, it can then confront in love even the most difficult of human crises and failures – suicide.

Second, the church must commit itself to being a community of love, not quick to judge. Since suicide often brings with it the stigma of "unpardonable sin" and feelings of shame and guilt for the surviving family members, those currently free of pain must welcome those who suffer in the name of Christ; and with the aid of the Holy Spirit, they must place themselves at one another's disposal. A church might well have a team ministry to contact and inquire daily about those who are troubled. A church might also designate certain gifted individuals to whom one might turn in distress. A community of love bears patiently with those who contemplate suicide and those who grieve and feel guilty as a result of suicide.

Third, the church must commit itself to being a community of joy, a community in which the new life of Christ is celebrated, a community that calls others to celebrate in the new life of Christ. By living as a community of joy, by regularly celebrating God's goodness to us in Jesus Christ, the church ministers to those who are saddened, joyfully acquainting them with the One who has known their sorrows.

This article originally appeared in the 20 March 1987, issue of *Christianity Today*. At the time, Thomas D. Kennedy was visiting assistant professor of religion at Hope College in Holland, Michigan. He is now associate professor of philosophy at Valparaiso University in Valparaiso, Indiana.

SUGGESTIONS FOR HELPING YOURSELF SURVIVE

In addition to the help of relatives, friends, and possibly a counsellor, the survivor must make efforts to help him/herself. You are the one who sets the pace and limits of your grief. To some extent, you can shorten or lengthen the process of grief depending on your willingness to work through the grief.

1. Lean into the grief. You can't go around it, over it, or under it. You have to go through it to survive. It is important to face the full force of the pain. Be careful not to get stuck at some phase. Keep working on your grief.

2. As soon as you are able, begin to deal with the facts of suicide. The longer that the facts are avoided or denied, the more difficult the recovery could be. Get the facts straight about the suicide – whats, whys, and hows. To know the facts relieves the survivor's doubts and allows them to face the truth. It is important to be honest with oneself and face the reality that the death was a suicide.

3. It may be helpful to make reference to the suicide at the funeral.

4. The emotions of a survivor are often raw. It is important to let these feelings out. If you don't let your feelings out now, they will come out some other time, some other way. That is certain. You won't suffer nearly as much from "getting too upset" as you will from being brave and keeping your honest emotions all locked up inside. Share your "falling to pieces" with supportive loved ones, as often as you feel the need.

5. You may have psychosomatic complaints which are physical problems brought on by an emotional reaction. The physical problems are real. Take steps to remedy them.

6. Don't be afraid to ask for help from those close to you when you need it. So much hurt and pain go unheeded during grief because we don't want to bother anyone else with our problems. Wouldn't you want someone close to you to ask for help if they needed it? Some relatives and friends will not be able to handle your grief. Find someone with whom to talk. Seek out an understanding friend, survivor, or support group member.

7. Most survivors feel it is important to see their dead loved one at the time of the death and funeral. Otherwise there can always be that nagging doubt "Is my loved one really dead?" Grief may take longer because the reality of the death isn't faced. Survivors often stay longer in denial when they have not seen with their own eyes.

8. Keep a daily diary of your thoughts and feelings.

9. Don't be afraid to say the word suicide. It may take months to be able to say it, but keep trying.

10. For some survivors there is a tendency to withdraw to their room, isolate themselves from friends and family, and constantly dwell on their feelings. This may be helpful initially, but not when carried to an extreme.

11. Some survivors throw themselves into their work or take flight in activity. This prevents the person from dealing with the grief. Save time to face your grief.

12. Thinking that you are going crazy is very normal. Most grieving people experience this. Remind yourself that you are not losing your mind but are reacting to a devastating blow.

13. Don't assume that everyone is blaming you or thinking ill of you. They probably are hurt for you but don't know what to say or how to say it.

14. Be prepared that relatives may say seemingly cruel or thoughtless things because of their own pain, frustration, or anger.

15. Do not be afraid to tell those around you exactly how you feel. You may need to remind another that you are not quite yourself. Tell them how much you appreciate their patience and understanding.

16. Some feel that the less said the better and that everyone should try to forget. Studies show this to be the least effective and usually the most damaging approach. Survivors need to release their feelings and resolve their questions, not lock their troubles deep inside.

17. Work on guilt. Something beyond your control has happened. Blaming oneself for the actions of another is illogical and dangerously self-damaging.

18. Read recommended literature on suicide and grief. The reading will not solve all of your pain and questions, but it does offer understanding and suggestions for coping.

19. If grief is intense and prolonged, it may harm your physical and mental well-being. If it is necessary, seek out a competent counsellor. Check to see if your health insurance covers the charges. It is important to take care of yourself. Then you can be of help to your family also.

20. In a time of severe grief be extremely careful in the use of either alcohol or prescription drugs. Tranquillizers don't end the pain; they only mask it. This may lead to further withdrawal, loneliness, and even addiction. Grief work is best done when you are awake, not drugged into sleepiness.

21. It helps to admit our mistakes. We are human. There is so much that we tried to do. There are things we did not do. Accepting our imperfections aids us in working out our grief.

22. If you feel guilt, ask yourself what things specifically are bothering you the most. Talk over your feelings of guilt with a trusted friend or professional, or confess your guilt to God. Telling the truth about why you feel guilty will help. Forgive yourself, ask the forgiveness of your loved one, and of God. Then try to realize what happened is past. There is nothing that you can do about it now. Become determined to live life to the best of your ability now. God's forgiveness should help us to begin to forgive ourselves.

23. You can learn from your guilt and adopt a new lifestyle for the future. From past mistakes you may be able to change for the better.

24. Depression is common to those in grief. Be aware of withdrawing from others and isolating yourself. You may even consider suicide yourself. Be sure to get counselling help if you feel this way.

25. Some survivors find it helpful to give the clothes to the needy and to rearrange furniture. Be cautious about moving. Later, after the pain subsides, you may regret moving from the happy memories.

26. It may be beneficial to concentrate on helping other family members and friends, but don't ignore problems that may be building inside you.

27. Take an empty chair and put a picture of your loved one in it. Tell all your feelings about what happened, remember the good times, and tell of your guilt. It is a way of articulating those confusing thoughts and finishing unfinished business.

28. It is easy and understandable to feel sorry for yourself, but, unchecked, self-pity can lead to anger, bitterness, and depression.

29. Some survivors build a wall around themselves because they are afraid of being hurt again. They miss so much of life this way. It is important to love and enjoy the people in your life instead of distancing from them.

30. Become involved in the needs of other people. Doing things for others builds one's self confidence and self-worth.

31. Don't become discouraged that you are alone in your grief. Sometimes it is helpful to contact other survivors of a suicide. When you read about a suicide in the paper you may want to write a short note to the survivors and give them your phone number.

32. If appropriate, encourage community education on what it is like to survive the suicide of a loved one. Many people truly care but they don't know what to do or say.

33. Your anger may be directed at the deceased, yourself, others, God, or you may just feel angry. It is

extremely important to get the anger out. This may be done by going to a remote spot and screaming, chopping wood, hitting a punching bag, playing tennis, swimming, pounding a pillow, etc. Anger that is not recognized and directed outward may turn back on you. Such anger unleashed at ourselves is very harmful.

34. It is best to be honest with your close friends about the suicide. If you aren't honest with them, then you will always wonder if and how much they know. You won't be able to lean on your friends, and this leads to isolation and loneliness.

35. It is helpful to consider that usually the victim wanted to stay and to live. Yet, at the same time, he or she couldn't live, so, in confusion, gave in to suicide.

36. At the anniversary of the suicide, birthday, and special holidays get together with a few understanding friends or relatives, or somehow find a way to escape the full brunt of the occasion. It is important to plan the day. It won't be great, but it can be less painful if you don't expect too much of yourself or others.

37. It is not helpful to compare yourself to another survivor of suicide. It may not seem that you are adjusting as well as they are. Remember that no two people go through grief alike.

38. Remember the commandment "Love Your Neighbour as Yourself." Of all the times in your life this is one where you need to take gentle care of yourself as you would care for someone else trying to survive.

39. The best remedy for heartache is to lead as happy a life as possible. You and your genuine friends understand that you have done your best to work though your grief and now you are trying to reinvest in life. If others don't understand, don't worry about them. Surviving and rebuilding your life is what is important.

40. When you are ready, aim at regaining a healthy, balanced life by broadening your interests. As a survivor you should take time to think through which activities can bring you some degree of purpose. Remember to start slowly and move carefully in this direction – with friends who are supportive and understanding. Think about taking up something you've always wanted to do: going back to school; volunteering; joining church groups; community projects; or hobby clubs.

41. Practice taking one moment – one day – at a time. Say to yourself, "I have decided to live!" Recognize that you have been hit with a terrible tragedy and yet you have still survived.

42. You had no choice and no control over the suicide but you do have a choice to survive and live through it. It may be the hardest task that you will ever have to perform, but you will survive!

SUGGESTIONS FOR COPING AS A FAMILY

It is important to sit down together to talk, cry, rage, feel guilty and even to be silent. Communication is the key to survival in the aftermath of suicide. At the same time there should be respect for each person's individual way of handling grief. Some family members will grieve privately, others openly, and others a combination of these two styles. In many ways each family member must grieve alone. Here are some suggestions to help with family grief.

1. Pay attention to your family members when you're with them. Let them know that you love them.
2. Be sensitive to how other family members feel.
3. Listen to what is meant as well as what is being said.
4. Accept the other person and what they say.
5. Don't give each other the silent treatment. This has many negative effects.
6. Sit back and listen. Let other family members have an opportunity to talk.
7. Be sure to hug and touch each other at every opportunity.
8. If depression, grief, or problems in your family are getting out of control, seek the advice of a counsellor.
9. Recognize that anniversaries, birthdays and special holidays will be difficult for the family and each member of the family.
10. Remember you can't help anyone if you are falling apart. Do what you can do, get help for what you can't do, and trust in the help that God gives.
11. Studies show that a bereaved person's self-esteem is extremely low. Survivors should work on their image of themselves and help each family member to think and feel good about themselves.
12. If there is a suicide note, discuss as a family what to do with it. If you think it will only bring you pain, then have a private burning and commit its contents to God.

Suggestions for Helping Survivors

Bereaved people, especially suicide survivors, need the support, love, and concern of their relatives and friends. Often a survivor is like someone who has trouble standing by him or herself. It is up to us to reach out to help. Their basic needs are for kindness and caring. With time, understanding, and the concern of their friends, the survivor's feelings of grief will soften. The following suggestions would apply to both the time immediately after the suicide, including the funeral, and for as long as necessary afterwards.

1. Make an extra special effort to go to the funeral home. The shock, denial, and embarrassment are overwhelming for the survivors. They need all the support they can get. Due to the cause of death, in most cases the coffin is left closed.

2. When going to the funeral home, do as you would normally do at any other type of wake. It will not be easy, since you sincerely want to comfort the bereaved person, but really don't know what to say. Just a few words can be a help. "I am so very sorry, I just don't know what else to say to you as I have never been through what you are going through now." "Please accept my deepest and sincerest sympathies; my heart goes out to you." When the person is close, take their hand, by all means hug them and don't feel the need to say anything.

3. Don't be afraid to cry openly if you were closed to the deceased. Often the survivors find themselves comforting you but at the same time they understand your tears and don't feel so all alone in their grief.

4. Don't say "It was God's will" or "God called your loved one home because He needed some flowers in His Garden." Such explanations do not console.

5. Survivors can tend to become more paranoid than the average person. The guilt is so overwhelming that when people do not attend the funeral or send a card the guilt increases. A note or visit in the weeks and months to come is of great help to the survivors.

6. Don't try to comfort the survivor by saying "It was an accident, a terrible accident." The survivors need to start dealing with the fact of suicide.

7. Do not say "He or she was on drugs or drunk." You weren't there during the suicide, so how could you possibly know? It is not helpful or necessary to give reasons for the suicide.

8. Survivors may ask "Why?" It is best to say "I don't know why and maybe I'll never know."

9. Be aware that the survivor's grief is so painful that sometimes it is easier to deny that it ever happened. Be patient and understanding. Sometimes this denial gives them a breather before the reality comes crashing in again.

10. Come to the survivors as a friend who sets aside prejudice and judgment. Show genuine and sincere interest.

11. Don't say that the suicidal person was not in his or her right mind or was "crazy". The majority of people who complete suicide are ambivalent and tormented; they may have a character disorder or are neurotic, but they are not insane. Telling the survivors that the person was crazy may invoke worries of inheriting mental illness. Suicide is not inherited.

12. Be a good listener. Survivors have a tendency to repeat and ramble. They may have a tremendous sense of guilt. It is helpful to listen over and over and over again.

13. Be patient. Often the survivor is the first one to realize that they are not easy to get along with, but they need people to persevere with them until their grief eases.

14. Don't say "snap out of it." Often the survivor reacts to such a statement by pushing down his or her feelings and thoughts which slows the process of working through ones grief.

15. Be the type of friend with whom the survivor can talk and feel comfortable and accepted. Be available to spend time with the survivor. Most people find the best way to work through their emotions is to talk them out with someone they trust. When the survivor tells about their feelings often they are helped in understanding what is going on. Talking also releases some of their pressures. Often while talking the survivor comes up with his or her own solutions.

16. Survivors have every right to feel sensitive. Some people deliberately avoid the survivors. They will cross the street or pretend that they don't see the survivors. This adds to their guilt. Such actions are not done out

of malice, but rather out of confusion about what to say. It is not important to make every effort to befriend the survivor and to reach out.

17. Encourage the bereaved to talk. It is of no help to say "Don't talk about it." Let the person pour his heart out. It is helpful to share pleasant and unpleasant memories; to get in touch with what they are feeling; and to express what they think.

18. Vicious and cruel remarks are sometimes made. They hurt the survivor deeply. Don't repeat such remarks and try to help the originators of the remarks to realize the hurt that they are causing the survivor.

19. Don't start telling the survivors that your child or friend "almost" tried to commit suicide and you "know" how they feel. Your loved one is still alive and theirs is dead.

20. Never say "you'll get over it in time." Hopefully, the survivor will learn to deal with it and cope with it in time, but never will they "get over it."

21. Discussing the signs of suicide with a survivor is not helpful since the suicide is a fact. Telling them "there must have been signs indicating depression" only lays more guilt on the survivor.

22. Be sincere if you ask "How are you coming along?" and then really listen to what the survivor says. Don't prevent him from talking. Don't change the subject or walk away.

23. The anniversary of the suicide is a very painful time. Relatives and friends should make every effort to be available, to listen, to call, to visit, to send a note, to do little acts of thoughtfulness.

24. Accept the survivors feelings. Practice unconditional love. Feelings of rage, anger, and frustration are not pleasant to observe or listen to, but it is necessary for the survivor to recognize and work on these feelings in order to work through the grief rather than become stuck in one phase.

25. As time goes on, it is still appropriate to say that you are sorry or to reminisce about the loved one. It is comforting to survivors that their loved one hasn't been forgotten and that people are still concerned about them as survivors.

These suggestions were gleaned from *Suicide: Prevention, Intervention, Postvention* by Earl Grollman, Beacon Press, 1971; *Understanding Suicide* by William Coleman, David Cook Publishing Co., 1979; *After Suicide* by John Hewitt, Westminster Press, 1980, and from suggestions by Mickey Vorobel, a survivor.

Copyright © Hope for Bereaved. All Rights Reserved.
Hope for Bereaved, INC. 4500 Onondaga Blvd., Syracuse, NY 13219.

Affirmation

The following is a list of churches, organizations or individuals who are ministering to those considering suicide or supporting friends or family bereaved as a result of suicide. They will, we believe, be able to offer practical and professional advice to assist you in your efforts to minister. (Please see appendix B)

BEFRIENDERS INTERNATIONAL
26–27 MARKET PLACE
KINGSTON UPON THAMES
SURREY
KT1 1JH
TEL: 020 85414949
FAX: 0208549 1544
EMAIL: ADMIN@BEFRIENDERS.ORG
WWW.BEFRIENDERS.ORG

CHILDLINE
2ND FLOOR ROYAL MAIL BUILDING
50 STUDD ST
LONDON
N1 0QW
TEL: 0207 239 1000
FAX: 020 7239 1001
EMAIL: RECEPTION@CHILDLINE.ORG.UK
WWW.CHILDLINE.ORG.UK

CRUSE BEREAVEMENT CARE
CRUSE HOUSE
126 SHEEN RD
RICHMOND-UPON-THAMES
TW9 1UR
TEL: 02089404818
FAX: 020 8940 7638
EMAIL: INFO@CRUSEBEREAVEMENTCARE.ORG.UK

KIDSCAPE CAMPAIGN FOR CHILDREN'S SAFETY
2 GROSVENOR GARDENS
LONDON
SW1W 9TR
TEL: 0207 730 3300
FAX: 020 7730 7081
EMAIL: INFO@KIDSCAPE.ORG.UK
WWW.KIDSCAPE.ORG.UK

MENTAL HEALTH FOUNDATION
20–21 CORNWALL TERRACE
LONDON
NW1 4QL
TEL: 0207 535 7400
FAX: 020 7535 7474
EMAIL: MHF@MENTALHEALTH.ORG.UK
WWW.MENTALHEALTH.ORG

MIND
GRANTA HOUSE
15–19 BROADWAY
STRATFORD
LONDON
E15 4BQ
TEL: 020 8519 2122
FAX: 020 8522 1725
EMAIL: CONTACT@MIND.ORG.UK
WWW.MIND.ORG.UK

ROYAL COLLEGE OF PSYCHIATRISTS
17 BELGRAVE SQUARE
LONDON
SW1X 8PG
TEL: 0207 235 2351
FAX: 020 7235 1935
EMAIL: RCPSYCH@RCPSYCH.AC.UKJ
WWW.RCPSYCH.AC.UK

THE SAMARITANS
10 THE GROVE
SLOUGH
SL1 1QP
TEL: 01753 532713
FAX: 01753 819004
EMAIL: ADMIN@SAMARITANS.ORG.UK
WWW.SAMARITANS.ORG.UK

TRUST FOR THE STUDY OF ADOLESCENCE
23 NEW RD
BRIGHTON
BN1 1WZ
TEL: 01273 693 311
FAX: 01273 679 907
EMAIL: INFO@TSA.UK.COM
WWW.TAS.UK.COM

WINSTONS'S WISH
GLOUCESTER ROYAL HOSPITAL
GREAT WESTERN RD
GLOUCESTER
GL1 3NN
TEL: 01452 394377
FAX: 01452 395656
EMAIL: INFO@WINSTONSWISH.ORG.UK
WWW.WINSTONSWISH.ORG.UK

WORLD HEALTH ORGANIZATION
20 AVENUE APPIA
1211 GENEVA 27
SWITZERLAND
TEL: 00 41 22 791 2111
FAX: 00 41 22 791 3111
EMAIL: REGISTRY@WHO.CH
WWW.WHO.CH

YOUNG MINDS
102–108 CLERKENWELL RD
LONDON
EC1M 5SA
TEL: 020 73336 8445
FAX: 020 73336 8446
EMAIL: ENQUIORES@YOUNGMINDS.ORG.UK
WWW.YOUNGMINDS.ORG.UK

Books that deal with the issue of suicide

After Suicide, John Hewett, Westminister Press, 1980

After Suicide: A Ray of Hope, Eleanora "Betsy" Ross, Lynn Publications, Iowa City, IA, 1986

Andrew, You Died Too Soon, Corrine Chilstrom, Augsburg Fortress, 1993

Breaking The Silence, Mariette Hartley, Signet/Penguin Books, 1990

Dead Reckoning, David C. Treadway, HarperCollins Publishers, 1997

Don't Take My Grief Away From Me, Doug Manning, In-Sight Books, 1979

Forgive & Forget: Healing The Hurts We Don't Deserve, Lewis B. Smedes, Pocket Books, 1984

Healing After The Suicide of a Loved One, Ann Smolin & John Guinan, Simon & Schuster, 1993

Helping Children Cope With Grief, Alan Wolfelt, Accelerated Development, Inc., 1983

How To Go On Living When Someone You Love Dies, Therese A. Rando, Lexington Books, 1988

How To Survive The Loss of A Love, Colgrove, Bloomfield, McWilliams, Prelude Press, 1991

Living Through Personal Crisis, Ann Kaiser Sterns, Ballantine Books, 1985

Mourning After Suicide, Lois Bloom, The Pilgrim Press, 1987

My Son, My Son, Iris Bolton, Bolton Press, 1325 Belmore Way ME, Atlanta, GA 30338, 1983

Night Falls Fast: Understanding Suicide, Kay Redfield Jamison, Knopf, 1999

No Time To Say Goodbye, Carla Fine, Doubleday, 1997

Roses In December, Marilyn Willett Heavilin, Thomas Nelson, 1993

Seven Choices, Elizabeth Harper Neeld, Ph.D., Delta, 1990

Stronger Than Death, Sue Chance, Avon Books, 1992

Suicide: Prevention, Intervention, Postvention, Earl Grollman, Beacon Press, 1988

Suicide: Survivors, Adina Wrobleski, Afterwords, 1994

Survivors of Suicide, Rita Robinson, Newcastle Publishing Co., 1989

The Bereaved Parent, Harriet Sarnoff Schiff, Penguin Books, 1977

The Courage To Grieve, Judy Tatelbaum, Harper & Row, 1980

The Grief Recovery Handbook, James & Friedman, HarperCollins, 1998

The Suicide Of My Son, Trudy Carlson, Benline Press, 1995

Transcending Loss, Ashely Davis Prend, Berkley Books, 1997

Understanding, Coping, and Growing Through Grief, Collection of Authors, HOPE FOR BEREAVED, 4500 Onandaga Blvd., Syracuse, NY 13219, 1995

Understanding Grief, Dr. Alan D. Wolfelt, Accelerated Development Inc., 1992

Why Suicide?, Eric Marcus, HarperCollins, 1996

CRIMINALITY

AWARENESS

The following information is included to raise the social awareness and understanding of ministers in relation to the contemporary issue of criminality.

Why criminal are imprisoned if convicted. Firstly as a punishment, the obvious and basic punishment of prison is one's loss of liberty or freedom which is considered a fundamental human liberty. The period of incarceration will depend upon the seriousness of the crime or offence. A second reason given for prison sentences is as a deterrent to other would-be offenders. Often this can act against the interests of the offender as in certain cases some offenders are used to make an example of, because of their role in society such as a Minister, bank manager or a policeman. Thirdly there is the practical need to protect the general public from certain forms of criminality, especially violent and sexual crimes.

Working with people in prison can be frustrating with few immediate positive results. I have purposely chosen to state this because if you are interested in prison work because you are hoping to see numerous immediate life-changing conversions you are likely to be soon disappointed. Prison ministry is about showing God's love to those in great need.

It requires much effort, perseverance, and lots of prayer. Whilst men and women do make commitments while they are in prison many more hear about Gods love for the first time.

Prison ministry is about sowing the seeds In England and Wales there are nearly 140 prison establishments. Young Offender Institutions house juveniles aged 15–17yrs and young offenders 18–21yrs. Adult prisons house those 21+.

Each establishment has a security rating, which is from "A" most secure to "D" open prison. Rules regarding visiting and searching vary depending on the security status of the prison. Generally you can expect to have your bags searched and to have a rub down body search. You are not allowed to take mobile phones into prisons.

Inmates are classified as either "Remand," "Convicted" or "Sentenced." Remand prisoners are those who have not admitted the offence and have not been found guilty at a trial. Convicted inmates are those who have admitted the offence or have been found guilty at trial and are waiting to go back to court to receive their sentence. Sentenced inmates are those who have been sentenced by the court to a period of imprisonment. The status of the inmate will effect the number of visits they are allowed and remand inmates are allowed to wear their own clothes.

Each establishment has a Governing Governor who heads a team of Governors who have responsibility for different aspects of the prisons functions.

All prisons have a chaplaincy department. The senior chaplain is Anglican and they are responsible for the spiritual welfare of the inmates and prison staff. Some prisons also have an assistant chaplain. The senior chaplain heads a multi-faith team of staff although most team members are employed in the community and engage in prison work on a part-time basis. The easiest and most appropriate way to get involved in prison ministry is through the prison chaplain.

Assessment

The following are some of the most up-to-date statistics in relation to crime. (Please see appendix . Statistics change so rapidly, it would be advisable to refer to the Home Office and other related world wide web sites listed below.

Addressing

The following is a list of practical suggestions that may enable churches and organizations to minister effectively to those trapped in a cycle of crime.

- Church seeking to minister to the criminal in prison should appoint a person to take lead responsibility for prison work. This person needs to be someone who is spiritually mature and able to co-ordinate and support those involved in the prison work.
- Ideally the prison team should include a male and females of different ethnic and social backgrounds all who have a keen desire to work with prisoners. Prison rules stipulate that volunteers must be at least 18 years old. It is easier to be involved if you do not have a criminal record.
- All volunteers wishing to visit a prison have to be security cleared. Minor offences and offences committed several years previously may not prevent you from being allowed in the prison but it is best to declare these prior to the security check. Each prison will make an individual assessment of the security risk to the prison.
- The information you will be required to provide is as follows;
    Full name (including maiden name when applicable)
    Date of Birth
    Place of Birth
    Current Address
- Not everyone interested in prison work will want or even be able to have direct contact with inmates within the establishment. Letter writing and prayer support are two valuable and essential aspects of the prison ministry team. In letter writing it is of course wise to use the church address.
- The person co-ordinating the prison team should make contact with the prison chaplain at each of the prisons within your churches locality. It is advisable to make contact by letter expressing the interest your church has in supporting the work of the chaplaincy team. You may wish to follow this up with a telephone call.

- The response you receive will vary greatly from prison to prison. If the opportunity to get involved does not develop immediately don't give up but encourage your church to keep praying for your prison and the chaplaincy teams. The chaplain may ask to meet with you to discuss how your church can get involved. Opportunities will range from letter writing, visiting, running Alpha groups, taking Sunday services, meeting inmates on release, providing transport for families who genuinely have problems visiting the list is endless.

- One area that is currently developing in the secular field especially with the 18–21-year-olds is mentoring. This is when a young person is linked to an individual who becomes their 'mentor'. A mentor is someone who offers support, advice, friendship and a good role model. Christian volunteers would make ideal mentors.

- For some churches the potential risks associated with working with offenders will unfortunately be a major barrier to them being involved in prison ministry. Whilst we need to be wise when working with offenders it is important to remember that when engaging with offenders at least you are aware that they have an offending history and can be alert to the issues. Very often men and women will come into our church and we are totally unaware of their background yet we feel more able to accept them because they do not carry the 'offender label'. The lesson to learn is that issues about offending such as church security, personal belongings, work with children and other vulnerable people need to be addressed whether or not we are engaging with known offenders.

- You may not be aware of the full criminal history of the inmates you work with. Some inmates may choose to share information with you, others may not. It is essential that you check that your church has a child protection policy and that it is being implemented. Guidance on child protection policies and issues can be obtained from the Churches; PCCA Christian Child Care, (Address under affirmation).

- When the prisoner is released into the community you may wish to make your work with them more formal by writing a contract with them so that they are aware of what is expected of them when attending your church this is essential when working with sex offenders. For example there may be some activities it would be inappropriate for them to be involved in such as work with children.

- It would be wise for initial contact on release not to involve visits to homes but to make contact at a neutral meeting place or at the church. When writing letters always use your church address.

- All prisoners under 21 years of age and all over 21's serving 12 months or more are supervised by the probation service on their release into the

- community. On the day that they are released they will be required to report to their probation officer. If you are working with an offender who is being supervised by probation contact your local Probation Office to let them know about the support you are offering their client. It is important that the offender complies with their period of licence as non compliance can result in them returning to custody.

- Reintegration into the community can be difficult especially if someone has served a lengthy sentence. Your support and concern is essential at this time however there will be some issues that you are unable to deal with.

    Offenders can face many problems on their release such as;
    Money
    Accommodation
    Relationships
    Drugs/alcohol
    Unemployment

- Don't expect to be able to solve all the issues yourself. Make yourself aware of the agencies offering specialist advice in your locality. Your local Probation Office is a good source of information and advice. Encourage the offender to use the services available. For some offenders the problems and temptation to re-offend are too great and a return to custody becomes inevitable. Learn to be patient. Don't expect immediate transformations and above all keep praying for them.

AFFIRMATION

The following is a list of churches, organizations or individuals who are ministering to those trapped in a cycle of crime. They will, we believe, be able to offer practical and professional advice to assist you in your efforts to minister. (Please see Appendix B.)

CHILD PROTECTION ADVISORY SERVICE

PCCA CHRISTIAN CHILD CARE,
PO BOX 133
SWANLEY
KENT
BR8 7UQ
TEL: 01322 667207
HELPLINE: 01322 660011

THE PRISON FELLOWSHIP (SCOTLAND)
CONTACT: THE PRISON FELLOWSHIP
ADDRESS PO BOX 366
101 ELLESMERE STREET
GLASGOW
G22 5QS

TEL: 0141 3328870

THE PRISON FELLOWSHIP (ENGAND AND WALES)
CONTACT: PRISON FELLOWSHIP
PO BOX 945
MALDON
CM9 4 EW
TEL: 016121 843232

THE PRISON FELLOWSHIP (NORTHERN IRELAND)
CONTACT: ROBIN SCOTT
ADDRESS: PRISON FELLOWSHIP
39 UNIVERSITY STREET
BELFAST

BT7 1FY
TEL: 01232 243691

ALPHA IN PRISONS RESOURCE
HOLY TRINITY BROMPTON
BROMPTON
BROMPTON ROAD
LONDON
SW7 1JA
TEL: 020 7581 8255

CRIME CONCERN
BEAVER HOUSE
147–150 VICTORIA RD
SWINDON
SN1 3UY
TEL: 01793 863500
FAX: 01793 514654

HOWARD LEAGUE FOR PENAL REFORM
708 HOLLOWAY RD
LONDON
N19 3NL
TEL: 0207 249 7373

JOSEPH ROWNTREE FOUNDATION
THE HOMESTEAD
40 WATER END
YORK
YO3 6LP
TEL: 01904 629241
FAX: 01904 620072
EMAIL: INFO@JRF.ORG.UK
WWW.JFT.ORG.UK

JUSTICE
59 CARTER LANE
LONDON
EC4V 5AQ
TEL: 0207 329 5100
FAX: 0207 329 5055

LEGAL ACTION GROUP
242 PENTONVILLE RD
LONDON
N1 9UN
TEL: 0207 833 2931
FAX: 0207 837 6094
EMAIL: LAG@LAG.ORG.UK
WWW.LAG.ORG.UK

NATIONAL ASSOCIATION FOR THE CARE AND RESETTLEMENT OF OFFENDER (NACRO)
169 CLAPHAM RD
LONDON
SW9 0PU
TEL: 0207 582 6500
FAX: 0207 735 4666
EMAIL: COMMUNICATIONS@NACRO.ORG.UK
WWW.NACRO.ORG.UK

NATIONAL YOUTH AGENCY
17–23 ALBION ST
LEICESTER
LE1 6GD
TEL: 0116 285 3700
FAX: 0116 285 3777
EMAIL: NYA@NYA.ORG.UK
WWW.NYA.ORG.UK

PRISON REFORM TRUST
THE OLD TRADING HOUSE
2ND FLOOR
15 NORTHBURGH ST
LONDON
EC1V 0JR
TEL: 0207 251 5070
FAX: 0207 251 5076

WORLD WIDE WEB SITES THAT WILL BE HELP:

METROPOLITAN POLICE SERVICE
WWW.MET.POLICE.UK

WOMEN IN PRISON
WWW.WOMENINPRISON.ORG.UK

THE HOME OFFICE
WWW.HOMEOFFICE.GOV.UK

PRISON SERVICE
WWW.HMPRISONSERVICE.GOV.UK

THE POLICE FEDERATION OF ENGLAND AND WALES
WWW.POLFED.ORG.UK

CRIMESTOPPERS
WWW.CRIMESTOPPERS-UK.ORG

Books that deal with the issue of criminality

An excellent source that offers guidance to churches seeking to involved in prison ministry has been produced by Alpha Publications entitled *Caring for Ex-Offenders*. (Address under affirmation)

ALPHA PUBLICATIONS
ALPHA IN PRISONS RESOURCE
HOLY TRINITY BROMPTON
BROMPTON
BROMPTON ROAD
LONDON
SW7 1JA
TEL: 020 7581 8255

SHORT INTRODUCTION TO FUNDRAISING

BIBLICAL PERSPECTIVE

Fundraising sometimes is met with the objection "God will provide all our needs"; of course that is true and He can use the ungodly to release finances for the work of the Kingdom (See Exo12: 36, Prov １８: 22 & Isa 61: 6).

Unethical

It is unethical to change the Church's vision to get available funds, just as it is unethical to use raised funds for purposes other than what they have been given for.

Getting Started

A funding application should include a business plan. A business plan is a document, which explains;

1. Why the project is required.
2. How the project will operate.
3. How it will be managed.
4. How the users will benefit.
5. How the project will be evaluated.
6. What the project will cost and how it will be funded.
7. Why you believe you should set up and run the existing or proposed project.

A good business plan is likely to include;

1. A one-page summary.
2. The Church's/organization's aims and objectives and how the project fits into these.
3. A description of the proposed or existing project.
4. An analysis of the need, with figures of potential or existing service users.
5. A survey of similar or related services or projects provided by other organizations in your locality.
6. The projects aims and objectives.
7. A work plan for year one which should include objectives, methods of achievement, and a target to be achieved within a set timetable.

8. Details of how you will monitor your achievements.
9. A project management structure.
10. A budget and cash flow forecast for the first year which can be separate form the Church's budget.
11. Staff requirements, including the skills of key people involved in the project.

Consider carefully the language you use, churches according to political rhetoric are "Faith Communities"; refer to yourself as one. When it comes to issues of equality and discrimination, the service you aim to provide should be open to every individual. If you say you are open to "every group" then when you say "no" to the "local pagan group" wanting to use your service, they can accuse you of discrimination. Use popular words like "inclusion," "empowerment" or "Volunteers."

Read carefully the Funder's stipulations and write your application appropriately, don't just send the same package to a thousand Funders.

Where to Start

Government, Charitable Trusts, Local Trusts, CVS & Charity Commission

Government Grants

DEPARTMENT OF THE ENVIRONMENT, TRANSPORT AND THE REGIONS (DETR) TEL: 020 7890 4333
HOMELESS ACTION PROGRAMME (HAP) TEL: 020 7890 3823
SINGLE REGNERATION BUDGET (SRB) TEL: 020 7890 3828
ENGLISH PARTNERSHIPS TEL: 020 7976 7070
EUROPEAN UNION PROGRAMMES SEE THEIR WEB SITE WWW.EUROPA.EU.INT

Charitable Trusts

CD-ROM TRUST GUIDE AND A GUIDE TO MAJOR TRUSTS (VOLS 1, 2 & 3)
BOTH PUBLISHED BY THE DIRECTORY OF SOCIAL CHANGE
2 STEPHENSON WAY
LONDON
NW1 2DP
TEL: 020 7209 5151
EMAIL: INFO@D-S-C.DEMON.CO.UK

THE DIRECTORY OF GRANT MAKING TRUSTS
PUBLISHED BY CHARITIES AID FOUNDATION
KINGS HILL
WEST MALLING
KENT
ME19 4TA
TEL: 01732 520000
EMAIL: CAFPUBS@CAF.CHARITYNET.ORG

THE HENDERSON TOP 2000 CHARITIES
PUBLISHED BY HEMMINGTON SCOTT CITY INNOVATION CENTRE
26-31 WHISKIN STREET
LONDON
EC1R OBP
TEL: 020 7278 7769

RATHER THAN BUY THE ABOVE YOU COULD REQUEST THEM FOR YOUR LOCAL LIBRARY.

Local Trusts
The best way to find these is to contact local solicitors and ask them if they represent any local trust and to whom you should address your application.

Community Volunteer Service (CVS)
Most towns have a CVS who can point you in the right direction to find funders.

Charity Commissioner
Look on the Charity Commissioner's Web Site www.charity-commission.gov.uk go to the "Register" and you will find every charity in the UK listed. This is perhaps the quickest way of finding a charity suited to your requirements.

THE INSTITUTE OF CHARITY FUNDRAISING MANAGERS
CAN OFFER GOOD ADVICE AND SUPPORT IN YOUR FUNDRAISING EFFORTS
TEL: 020 7627 3436
WWW.ICFM.ORG.UK

Acknowledgment

Praise the Lord for His Provision
Also write and thank funders for their donations

JOE HAYES 2001

APPENDIX A

ADVICE ON STATISTICS

Statistical Sources

The statistics contained with in these notes are taken from *Social Trends* and *Annual Abstract of Statistics*. Both are Publications of the Governments Statistical Service.

Statistical Support

"Statistical information is vital for pointing us to patterns and trends, in society which we could not otherwise discern. Statistics can raise questions, alter us to 'surprise factors', give us a glimpse of the weight of a problem, indicate how much is changing, what is continuous in population trends, in mortality and birth-rates, in voting behaviour, consumption patterns, economic indicators. They can give numerical summaries of complex information."

Startling Statistics

Whether it be women's pay, men's health, homophobic attacks and even racially motivated assaults, statistics are used to shock us in to the belief that there is a problem.

It would be foolish to accept statistician's conclusions as "Gospel Truth." It is important to recognize that all statistics are collected, compiled and presented with certain preconceived questions and at times preconceived conclusions in mind. Even the most "comprehensive" figures and the most "official" sources of statistical information should be treated with caution, their conclusions should be considered at best as "approximations of the truth".

Twisted Statistics

Statistical percentages, graphs, and averages can so easily be presented in a fashion that will support the argument of those presenting the statistical evidence. What perhaps is most important about the information that is being presented via statistics is the information that is being left out!

Stigmatising Statistics

Who is compiling the statistics? This is perhaps the most important point to observe in relation to social statistics. Because the compiling of social statistics is not an objective or value free activity we must ask which organisation or individual has compiled this information. More often than not they are using this information to support their argument and undermine and stigmatise their opponent.

To further reinforce the importance of the need for caution in our use of social statistics, take time to read the following article from the *New Statesman and Society* May 1990.

Numbers Crunched

After the poverty figures fiasco, Malcolm Wicks calls for a non-partisan national statistical service;

> Statistics are one of the first casualties of political warfare. The truth about unemployment, health care, or social conditions has often been camouflaged by concealment, dubious interpretation, delay or the introduction of new methods.

Last week saw two examples. Inflation fast becoming the key political indicator again is not, the government tells us, as simple as it seems. Rather than the inflation rate itself, which climbed to 9.4 per cent last month, the government now emphasises another measure, the underlying inflation rate. This excludes housing costs, mortgages and rents, and the poll tax. By this measure inflation was just 6.3 per cent.

Last week also saw a new controversy about poverty, and its measurement. These statistics get increasingly complex, and the people who understand them correspondingly fewer. As the key data for the eighties now turn out to be simply wrong, owing to an unfortunate government statistician putting data in the wrong column, confusion is added to complexity.

Over ten years, there has been growing inequality between rich and poor. But, to the amazement of the critics, ministers could point to data that showed the poor doing comparatively well. These data record increases in real income, after housing costs, for the period 1981–85. They look at what has happened to percentages of the population ranked by income. The result was that, while the total population had income increases of 4.8 per cent, the poorest did almost twice as well, at 8.4 per cent. This seemed to support the much-heralded "trickle-down" theory, which holds that the poor benefit from rising living standards and that overall economic performance is crucial, not government anti-poverty measures.

Now, thanks to the vigilance of the House of Commons select committee on social services, a major error has been found. The committee had been unhappy about the Department of Social Security's decision to change the way in which poverty was measured, as the department preferred to assess the fortunes of the poorest against average income, rather than, as previously, in relation to supplementary benefit rates. The select committee asked the Institute of Fiscal Studies to undertake some analyses, based on the original method. While doing this work the Institute discovered the error.

The corrected data shows that the lowest 10 per cent in fact had a real increase, after housing costs, of just 2.6 per cent, not 8.4 per cent. As the committee's report notes: "Far from this group experiencing the largest percentage increase in living standards, they have now been found to have had an increase over the period 1981–85 of only half the average increase experienced by the total population." (The new average increase was 5.4 per cent.)

The match between the poverty lobby and the DSS, seemingly over, is now into extra time. It could serve to re-open the debate about poverty and raises crucial questions about the role of the state. As Frank Field, the committee's chairman, said: "There is no hidden hand to protect the poorest in our community unless voters and government decide to do so."

Now another debate should open, about the integrity of official statistics. The mistake now unearthed was a genuine one, but the debate about poverty has been dogged in recent years by controversy over measurement. The select committee itself has had a running battle with the DSS on this question, and much of its report contains polite requests to the government to present proper data.

All too often in recent years, official statistics have been called into question by the opposition and other groups. When government presents new measures and new methodologies the results seem to be to scale down the size of the social problem under scrutiny. Should not official information of this kind be the property of the whole democracy, and not just the plaything of the executive?

Years ago, the argument was accepted that public broadcasting was too important to be run by the government itself. Similarly, should not our ways of measuring key developments be placed in the hands of a public body similar to the BBC, and charged with reporting to the nation? Such a body would measure and monitor, examine and publish. Of course government, like any large organization, needs its own statistics. But its administrative political requirements are not always the same as those of democracy as a whole.

APPENDIX B

DISCLAIMER

The organisations affirmed within this manual have been included because it is believed that they have experience and expertise of working in the community and with people facing different social issues.

They should not be regarded as being the only organizations working in this area of social concern, nor should they be considered to have exhaustive knowledge.

The Author does not necessarily accept the ideologies, opinions and values of all the organisations listed, but considers that even where differences of opinion exist such bodies may well be extremely helpful in appropriate situations.

It is therefore up to Christian ministers and leaders to decide whose assistance to solicit in light of the circumstances with which they are dealing.

APPENDIX C

Postmodernism

The ideological shift from "Modernism" to "Postmodernism" in comparison to the biblical perspective.

Appendix C (Part 1)

Subject	Modernism	Post-modernism	Biblical View
Human Nature	Humans are purely physical machines. They exist in a material world. Nothing exists beyond what our senses perceive.	Humans are simply cogs in a social machine. They are primarily social beings.	Humans are the only beings on the earth created in the image of God. They are both spiritual and material.
Free Will or Personal Autonomy	Humans have full autonomy over their lives and thus are free to choose whatever directions they wish.	Humans only have imagined autonomy as they are purely the produce of their social and cultural environment.	Humans were created to be dependant upon God, the desire for autonomy from God is the core of sin. Free will has been diminished by the fall, however they still remain responsible for the directions they choose.
Reason	People in their autonomy should be rationalistic optimists who need only depend on the data of their senses and reason.	There is no such thing as unbiased reason or senses. People are affected by their social and cultural surroundings.	Reason is necessary but insufficient for understanding reality. Reason can disclose truth and reality however faith and revelation are required.
Human Progress	Humankind is progressing via science and reason, to a wonderful future.	"Progress" is a word used by the west or European culture to justify it's domination of other cultures.	Humankind is not progressing toward a glorious future. However where reason and science relieve suffering, that is good.

Appendix C (Part 2)

Subject	Modernism	Post-modernism	Biblical View
Knowledge	Teachers should be authoritative communicators of unbiased knowledge.	Educators are biased facilitators and co-constructors of knowledge	Knowledge is profitable, but can distort the truth Rom 1:18ff The Teacher and student roles are similar to the modernist viewpoint. Prov 22:15
Culture	Culture can be a barrier to learning when diverse cultures come together, so therefore one unified language must be adopted to communicate and study the different cultures.	All cultures are of equal value and importance, each with their own reality. Unity can only result in exploitation and domination of students from minority cultures.	Scriptural principles enable us to judge the right and wrongs of all cultures. Can adjust our cultural values to love and win the lost to Jesus 1Cor 9:19–23, Matt 6:43–47
Values	Teachers can communicate values. However, education should be value free and simply pass on the facts.	Teacher should help students create or construct their own values that are personal and useful within their cultural context. There are no universal values. Teachers cannot be free of personal values and so can be free to promote their values and social agendas as long as they are not fundamentalist. Important values that should be communicated to students include diversity, tolerance, freedom, creativity, emotional expressiveness.	The Spiritual and moral commandments form the basis of all values.
Self Image/Esteem	Teachers help students to enhance their self-esteem and thus have mastery their own object knowledge and thus apply that learning to progress society.	Self-esteem within a student is created by social conditioning. Educators are there to help them to discover and attain their chosen goals	All people are made in the image of God and have sinned. Yet they remain of such value to God that he sent His son to die for them. Self-esteem needs to be Christ based.

TABLES ADOPTED AND ALTERED, FROM THE © *DEATH OF TRUTH* BY DENNIS MCCALLUM, PUBLISHED BY BETHANY HOUSE PUBLISHERS.

EXAMPLE OF A FAMILY CENTRE

Wigan ICCC, Family Centre

Aims and Objectives

Our aim is: To reach the hurting and needy people of Wigan so that we can input into their lives – physically, mentally, socially and spiritually – to bring them to a realization that they can become part of God's family.

Our objectives are: Identify the direct needs of the local community and build our services around those needs. Identify the people who directly need our services and find ways of reaching these people. Look at the Family as a whole and not just the Family member with the need.

Make the set up and structure of the Family Care Centre thus that the clients and users feel that this is their centre and that they have a voice and rights within it.

Link with professional bodies and faith groups to make this the best possible service. To bring our clients/users into the main body of the church so that they can become part of God's family where they can be cared for long term.

The Project's Structure

Initially a study was carried out into the social needs in Wigan. This was done:
A) So that we could identify the areas most in need.
B) To enable us to see the major problems specific to Wigan so that we could target actual problems.
C) To gain the information we needed to build the framework of services offered.

The study was done by collecting statistics from the local Health Authority, talking to professional bodies within Wigan and by talking to key workers within the areas needed. The outcome of this study was then taken into consideration when planning our services.

We continue to judge the areas of need by talking to the general public, keeping up to date with the current Health Authority reports etc., and by feedback and involvement with our clients. A large scale survey of the town of Wigan is planned which will be invaluable to our future planning.

Our services are ongoing and the need for new services is under constant review. Services are added as and when they are needed. All the services we offer strive to fill one or more of the needs unique to this area.

The most important part of this project, we believe, is the fact that all the people we meet within the centre need to know the love of God. If we can help them to meet their need now, we can show them some of God's love.

Our services include:

PREGNANCY CRISIS CENTRE: A drop-in centre for confidential counselling, free pregnancy testing, information and post abortion counselling. All our volunteers have a basic counselling qualification specific to the pregnancy crisis situation.

PARENT AND TODDLERS GROUP: This is a weekly session where parents can meet and socialize whilst their babies and toddlers play in a safe environment. Visiting speakers include such things as First Aid, Safety in the Home, Health and Beauty and Parenting Skills.

PLAY GROUP: A three times a week session for the pre-school child. We are registered with the Social Services Department and staffed to their guidelines. This is a place where the younger child can learn through play in a safe and secure environment.

FAMILY LEARNING COURSE: A college course run by the Wigan and Leigh college. It is aimed at parents of younger children who are interested in learning how to help in their child's education or for people who may have missed out on, or struggled with, some of their formal education. It is held alongside the play group and free childcare is available.

MARRIAGE MINISTRIES: A recognized course is available at the centre where people can gain more insight into their marriage and improve it. We also can provide a service where people can obtain help with direct problems in their marriage.

DIVORCE CARE: A recognized course which runs for eight weeks each term where people can work through different issues of their separation or divorce thus helping them come to terms with it. Personal counselling is available and can work alongside the children of divorce with a special programme for them.

OLDER PEOPLE: We have a Luncheon Club and a Day Care Centre for the over 55's. This is aimed at the people who need friendship, companionship, stimulation and a new outlook on life, all in a safe environment with friendly and dedicated staff.

SUPPORT GROUP: We have facilities for support groups to hold their own meetings aimed at people with specific needs i.e. Cancer Support Groups. These groups use our facilities, have our support and can readily access any of our support network if and when it is needed.

HELP LINE: During office hours our telephone line is manned by a counsellor who will deal with any initial problems and will then arrange one to one counselling as required.

COUNSELLING: We can provide counselling in a wide range of issues within the Family Care Centre, but we can refer people to outside agencies as and when this is needed, or when it is in the best interests of the client.

BEREAVEMENT SUPPORT: We hold a weekly Support Group for people who have been bereaved. One to one counselling is available if necessary.

PEOPLE WITH ADDICTION: We are currently training a team of people to work alongside clients with addictive problems using a recognized programme and liasing with outside agencies

LOCAL INVOLVEMENT: We have a direct involvement with other local churches in the Wigan area, our services are inter-denominational and are open to all. Staff in our Family Centre come from a wide background and a variety of walks of life. We have representatives of most of the areas of Wigan. We are linked into other professional bodies for advice, networking, organization, resources and some initial finance. We have an equal opportunities policy throughout our entire centre, which welcomes anyone regardless of colour, race, religion, gender or age. Members of our team are actively involved with the running of community advice/support agencies outside of our centre.

Management Structure

MANAGER: The senior Pastor of our church is the overall manager of the Wigan Family Care Centre. He is directly responsible to the trustees, as he is with all other works in the church.

COORDINATOR: Our Family Care Centre Coordinator was appointed by the Trustees and is directly answerable to the Senior Pastor and the Trustees. The Coordinator acts as a liaison between the Team Leaders and the Senior Pastor. The Coordinator has direct responsibility for the day-to-day running of the centre and the financing.

TEAM LEADERS: All departments within the Family Centre have Team Leaders who are responsible for their deputies and their team as well as their clients. Each Team Leader attends a bimonthly leadership meeting where they receive instruction, support and care from the overall pastoral staff of the church. Each Team Leader is expected to nurture and care for the staff and clients under their care. They should also pick up, and act upon, any problems or complaints which may arises.

STAFF AND CLIENTS: We recognize that our clients are the reason we exist and so therefore value their comments and ideas. We actively encourage our clients to become involved in their own care. We have a built in complaints procedure for all departments within the Family Centre whereby the clients and the staff have a written procedure to follow. This will allow them access to every level of leadership including our manager.

Skills and Training

Management Skills and Training

MANAGEMENT: The Manager and the Trustees are all experienced in Pastoral care, they have worked for a long time in supervisory roles within the church and in secular employment. They can also draw on their experience as Business men, Administrators, Supervisors and Pastors.

COORDINATOR: Our Coordinator can draw on her Nursing experience, qualifications in Community Care, Communications skills, Basic Counselling qualification and Childcare Management experience.

TEAM LEADERS: All our Team Leaders have attended, and are still attending, the church's leadership meetings which aims to improve their managerial skills and communication skills. Most of our Leaders have had training specific to their work. They bring to the centre skills which include – Counselling, Childcare Experience, College Lecturers, Teachers, Professional Qualifications and outside training in their area of work. Some of the Team Leaders are drawn from the community and either bring qualifications with them or are trained 'in-house'. The age range of our Team Leaders spreads right across the adult life up to retiring age.

Staff and Training

Our Family Centre Coordinator is salaried. Most of our other staff are volunteer workers.

STAFF TRAINING: Our staff are trained in the areas of work they are involved in. Some of this training is 'in-house' and others are either from recognized qualifications or trained by external agencies.

Divorce Care – The staff training for Divorce Care staff was carried out by the English representative of Divorce Care International. Further staff will be trained by our own people and this service can easily be replicated elsewhere.

Play group – We are required by the Social Services to provide two qualified children's workers at all times within our Play group. These qualifications have to be recognized and 'in-house' training cannot be provided. Our assistants, however, can gain the experience needed to work with the children at our play group. We have in the past provided placements for college students who need experience to gain their qualifications.

Parents and Toddlers – The leader of this group is an experienced Mother and a registered Child Minder. She also attends the Leadership Training within the church setting. Her team consists of experienced mums who come from various walks of life and so can help the clients in any aspect they may require.

Marriage Ministries – The couple who run our Marriage Ministries have been trained by, and are now trainers for, Marriage Ministries International. They are also members of the National Executive Board and so can help set up other groups around the country.

Family learning – Our family learning tutor is a qualified teacher. She is employed by the Wigan and Leigh College as part of their college in the community project.

Bereavement Support – Our team of workers have all suffered a bereavement themselves and two of the staff have had specific Bereavement counselling training.

Pregnancy Crisis Centre – Our team of counsellors are all trained 'in-house' by our qualified an recognized training officer for the 'Care for life' organization for counsellors. Although our training is done 'in-house', Care for Life award the certificates and accredit the training.

Luncheon Club Day Care – Our Manager for the Elderly is experienced in the care of the older person. Training is carried out initially for our staff by the Coordinator who holds a Nursing qualification and by a qualified Paramedic medic. Further training is offered through agencies like the Social Services Department and Age Concern.

Addiction Support – Our team have all completed a 13-week training course by a qualified instructor before being able to take clients through this recognized programme. We are working alongside the local community Drug Team for services like detoxification etc. We are aware that our expertise in this work is restricted in some areas.

Policy Documents

Equal Opportunities Policy

The Wigan Family Care Centre operates a policy whereby we strive to treat all people as equal. This is regardless of creed, colour, race, religion, sexuality, gender or age. This philosophy will be maintained throughout the centre and will be an important part of all training and induction programmes for all staff. All staff and clients will be advised of this philosophy and any digression from such policy will be dealt with in an appropriate manner.

There will be no distinction made within the workforce between paid and unpaid staff. All staff, regardless of length of service, position within the centre or hours worked, will be given an equal voice within the centre to contribute their ideas and opinions on the services provided. All clients will be treated as equal, regardless of length of involvement in the centre.

Clients and staff alike will be treat as individuals and the centre will strive, as much as possible, to meet their individual needs.

Volunteer Involvement Policy

Each service will be managed by a team leader who is directly responsible to the Coordinator. All volunteers will be vetted and will be required to attend an induction training day prior to working in the chosen service.

The Wigan Family Care Centre values the commitment given by its volunteer staff. The standard of service we provide is dependent on those volunteers and their time, skills and attitude. Therefore these skills and attitudes have to be of the highest standard to ensure quality of care.

Standards:

Leadership – The manager shall provide effective leadership at all times.

Adequacy – The centre will abide by the legal or self imposed staff/client ratios.

Selection – The needs of the clients will at all times remain paramount. All staff will be chosen for their attitudes, commitment and experience.

Competence – Volunteers should be competent for the task assigned to them. This is the responsibility of the team leader.

Clarity of task – All volunteer should be given a clear explanation of the task they are require to carry out.

Teamwork – We expect the team of volunteers to maintain co-operation and communication at all times. Grievances should be taken to the team leader or coordinator at the end of the session.

Support – Volunteers will be offered help and support to enable them to do their job effectively. They should have opportunity to meet together to discuss the work.

Development – Volunteers should be able to develop their skills and experiences through practical instruction, observation, training, counselling and support.

Individuality – Volunteers should recognize that each client is an individual and their wishes and requirements should be respected at all times.

Dignity – The dignity and self respect of the clients should be safeguarded at all times.

Privacy – Each client should be allowed privacy when it is needed as long as it is safe to do so.

Confidentiality – Personal information about the client or their families should be protected and respected. If the client's health or well-being is at risk pass the confidence on only to the team leader and/or coordinator.

Normality – The centre will strive to provide care for the individual which will show no stigma or separation for that client.

Participation – Clients will be encouraged to participate in the planning of the centre and their wishes will be noted in an open manner.

Relationships – All clients should be helped to feel part of the whole group and the volunteers will need to foster good relationship with the clients.

Development – Clients should be able to gain new experiences and skills.

Independence – Clients should be helped and encouraged to retain as much independence as possible.

Protection – The centre will aim to protect its clients and volunteers from all unnecessary risks. We endeavour to identify possible problems to the health and well-being of our clients and to act upon them.

Behaviour – All Volunteers should have an understanding of how to deal with antisocial and violent behaviour.

Physical – Restraint must only be used when necessary for someone's protection and only to the degree needed to overcome the immediate situation.

Managing risks – Protection from risk should be balanced with maintaining independence. In the case of an adult, try sharing concerns with the client about the risky situation they are presenting and reach an informed agreement.

User Involvement Policy

Wigan Family Care Centre will aim to:

- **Value and respect the opinions of the users at all times.**
- **Create within the centre such an atmosphere, that the users can express opinions and feelings freely and without worry.**
- **Provide our users with a recognized complaints procedure which will be dealt with professionally at all times.**
- **Ensure that any review of services is done with the wishes and views of the users in mind.**
- **Use a variety of ways to collect users views.**
- **When using questionnaires, the things asked will be user friendly and appropriate to the service offered.**
- **Share with the users any results obtained from such reviews.**
- **Encourage and provide the means to ensure users of Care Services are actively involved in the planning of their activities.**
- **User involvement should be at all levels and recognized by staff and clients alike.**

An Introduction to Play Group

Welcome

Welcome to our play group. Please take time to read the following information, we hope it will answer some of your questions about the care your child will receive while he or she is with us.

The Play Group

Wigan Family Care Centre on behalf of the International Christian Community Centre offers this Play Group as part of their service to the community of Wigan.

We are registered with the local authority and conform to the stringent requirements laid down by the Social Services Department for sessional care to the under eights. The Social Services department visit us once a year to inspect our premises, equipment and procedures.

Staff
We run on a ratio of one adult to eight children and are registered to take twenty-four per session. Two of our staff are qualified to run the Play group and the others are experienced in child care. All our staff have had the required background checks as stipulated by the Social Services Department.

Admission Policy
We operate a waiting list as needed. When a place becomes available the next child on the list, regardless of their colour, race or religion will be offered a place. We welcome applications from children with disabilities and special educational needs.

The only Criteria for admittance are:

1. The child is over the age of two and a half.
2. The child is toilet trained.

Equal Opportunies Policy
As with all our services, we operate an equal opportunities policy throughout the Family Centre which shows no discrimination regardless of colour, creed, religion, sexuality, gender or age.

Behavorial Policy
While we understand that children of this age group are only beginning to learn the art of social behaviour, we cannot allow behaviour likely to cause widespread disruption or injury. We operate a strict **NO SMACKING** policy, but steps to prevent unwelcome behaviour are taken when needed. The strongest form of restraint we find we need is a "time out" period – where the child involved sits away from the activities for a short period of time, 'till the situation is diffused.

Accident Policy
If your child sustains a minor injury whilst in our care we will deal with it in a sympathetic manner. We will inform you of the accident on your return at the end of the session and you will be asked to sign our accident book.

If your child sustains a more serious accident which, in the opinion of the first aider, requires medical attention we will try to contact you immediately. If you were not available then the health of your child would require us to take them to hospital ourselves, whilst another member of staff keeps trying to contact you. Please keep your contact numbers up to date.

Illness
The Social Services Department require us to exclude any child from the Play Group whilst they have a communicable disease. This would include diarrhoea, vomiting, chicken pox, measles, mumps, meningitis, hepatitis, impetigo or a temperature of 101(°f)/38(°c) or over.

If your child becomes ill whilst at Play Group you would be contacted and asked to collect your child. We would, of course, continue to care for your child while we waited for you.

Collection Procedure

Your child can be dropped off at Play Group anytime after the start of the session.

Your child must be collected prompt at midday. Please inform us of anyone different who is allowed to collect your child in your absence. This information needs to be recorded on your child's registration form. It would be helpful for us to meet this person before they pick up your child. If a difficulty arises after the start of the session please ring our office and talk to the Coordinator or Play Group leader direct.

The law requires us not to release a child to an unknown person without consent from the parent.

Snack Time

Your child will receive a snack mid-session. No child is forced to partake of these snacks which are chosen to reflect a wide range of cultural and ethnic tastes. If you have any food you do not wish your child to eat or your child is allergic to any food please state this in the area provided on your application form. We would always abide by your wishes.

Accidental Soiling

While we expect our children to be toilet trained on admission to us we recognize the fact that at this stage children can have frequent accidents.

This is not a problem. If your child has an accident while with us we will discreetly and sensitively deal with your child and provide clean, dry clothing. All we ask is for you to wash and return our clothes.

Sessional Times

Our Play Group opens at the hours listed below during term times.

MONDAY	9.15 'till Midday
WEDNESDAY	9.15 'till Midday
FRIDAY	9.15 'till Midday

Payment is required only for the sessions actually attended.

Complaints Procedure

We are required to give you the information you would need to register any complaints about the care your child receives. Although we would ask that you first approach the staff with any problem, we have listed below the stages you can make.

1. Linda Rossington – Playgroup Leader
2. Gwen Derbyshire – Family Centre Coordinator.
3. Mr Tony Payne – Operations Director – International Christian Community Centre

4. Inspection Unit – Social Services Department – Wigan

Finally

We hope your child enjoys the time he or she spends here at the centre. We will at all times endeavour to cater for the social, educational, emotional, spiritual and physical well being of your child. Please feel free to approach us with any problems or concerns you may have as we welcome constructive criticism.

We recognize the fact that you, as a parent, should be involved in your child's education and so we will keep you in touch with what topics your child will be looking at and talking about in Play Group. We would like to invite you to continue discussing these topics with your child at home. By working together we can prepare your child for the start of school life.

DAY CARE CENTRE FOR THE ELDERLY

Vision Statement

We aim to create a comfortable Christian environment whereby we can minister to the whole person. Physically, Mentally, Socially and Spiritually.

Statement of Principles

We will provide a safe environment for the physical and emotional well being of the client.

We will provide a high standard of care and activities, giving stimulation to meet both the clients' physical and mental needs. We will take into account the level of disability and social and cultural needs of the individual client. We will seek to be a support to the clients in their personal and family relationships, as well as forging new relationships within the group.

We will seek to retain our clients independence and safeguard their privacy whilst giving them the support and care the need to maintain a safe environment for them and the other users. We will liaise with the clients, their carers and relatives as needed to enable us to provide the best possible service for their needs.

We will endeavour to maintain confidentiality. If we need to contact doctors or relatives we will, if possible, obtain permission from the client first. We will seek to provide training information and opportunities to our clients and staff to enable them to gain new knowledge so that they may reach their personal developmental goals.

We will maintain a cordial working relationship with other organizations and agencies working with the elderly of Wigan. We will foster good relations with the International Christian Community Centre, particularly within the Family Care Centre. We will provide equal opportunities for both our clients and staff regardless of their race, religion, gender, age or creed.

STATEMENT OF PURPOSE

Admission Remit

All our clients must broadly fit our admissions remit.

A. Each client should be as mobile as needed to be able to use the transport provided. (With wheelchair access.)

B. Each client must be able to see to their own personal care without help. (Disabled toilets are available.)

C. Each client should have a reasonable grasp of their own faculties.

D. If a client's health changes and brings them out of the remit, then we regret we will have to withdraw their placement. All possible help will be given in finding them alternative placement within a centre more suited to their needs.

Operational Policy

Each client will be assessed prior to the offer of a placement. This is to ensure they fit our admission remit as stated above. If no place is available on application their name will be placed on our waiting list.

When a placement becomes available then an assessment will be made and if the client fits the remit a place will be offered.

Any client can accept or refuse a place without giving a reason

If a client is refused a placement at our Day Care Centre we will provide a reasonable explanation for our decision. The cost of each session is stated in our Leaflets and may alter as needs arise. The client will always be given ample warning of any changes.

Transport is arranged through the centre and if a client needs to use it, or is cancelling the use of it, we will need two weeks notice. If for any reason we need to cancel our service for one session we will endeavour to inform the clients at the earliest possible time. For this reason it is essential that we keep contact numbers up to date.

We will only cancel a session under extreme circumstances

If you do not require your placement for a short time please let us know by ringing the centre on 01942 322222.

We run a strict No Smoking Policy here at the centre. We do recognize, however, the clients right to a freedom of choice, we would therefore ask you to step outside the building whilst smoking.

Complaints Procedure

In the event of a client wishing to make a complaint about our service please use the following procedure.

Complain verbally to:

Mrs Eunice Bromley
Day Care Centre Manager

Verbally or in writing to:
Mrs Gwen Derbyshire
Coordinator
Wigan Family Care Centre
Pottery Road
Wigan
WN3 5AB

In writing to:

Mr Tony Payne
Operations Director
International Christian Community Centre
Pottery Road
Wigan
WN3 5AB

International Christian Community Centre

Counselling Agreement

It is agreed that the counsellor will listen to and consider all the information given by the client and will not divulge that information outside of the International Christian Community Centre's counselling service and supervisional relationships, or to any other person in any circumstances unless:

1. Require to do so in the course of a police investigation.
2. Require to answer questions in court having been told to give the court evidence.
3. In any case where failure to give information would lead to the conviction of the counsellor.
4. Where the client communicates a serious intention to break the law.
5. If the client is believed to be intending to cause serious physical harm to him/herself or to others.
6. If information given raises a pastoral matter within the church setting.

The client would be notified where possible of the intention to break a confidence.

CONFIDENTIALITY STATEMENT

- In every counselling situation we seek to protect the trust and integrity of the counselee and protect their anonymity with the other members of the service or with anyone outside the service.

- However, it is essential that all our counsellors receive some element of supervision from more qualified or experienced counsellors. This is necessary in order to provide the best help and guidance to the counselee and to maintain a degree of accountability. The counsellor may discuss personal details of the case without naming the counsellee, whilst undergoing supervision.

- It is agreed that where necessary, the counsellor shall work with other parties, and with the clients agreement the counsellor may contact such other parties for the purpose of promoting the client's welfare. For example, medical practitioners, legal advisors, social workers, church leaders and other responsible agencies or individuals. The client will notify the counsellor of any changes to the agreed list.

- The client agrees to give reasonable prior notice of all appointments which they cannot keep.

- The counsellor or the client are both able to terminate this agreement giving reasonable notice. Such a termination will not affect the counsellor's agreement to confidentiality contained in this agreement.

- The International Christian Community Centre Counselling service and counsellors shall not be held liable to the client for the death or injury of the client or any loss or damage to the client's property whether due to the negligence or the failure of the counsellor to perform his/her obligations under this agreement or under the general law.

Signed: Counsellor(s) _____

Signed: Client(s) _____

Date _____

NOTA BENE: IF THE CLIENT IS A CHILD UNDER THE AGE OF EIGHTEEN THEN, WHERE APPROPRIATE, THE PERMISSION OF THE PARENTS OR GUARDIAN SHOULD BE OBTAINED.

© THIS PAGE DOCUMENT IS COPYRIGHT TO WIGAN FAMILY CARE CENTRE AN INITIATIVE OF THE INTERNATIONAL CHRISTIAN COMMUNITY CENTRE, POTTERY ROAD, WIGAN. WN3 5AB, REGISTERED CHARITY 255886